Social selling is no longer optional for salespeople today. Getting attention on platforms that buyers now use and being able to initiate conversations is the difference between winning and losing. Tim Hughes has written a great book that provides the skills you need to win in today's hyper connected and highly competitive world.
Graham Hawkins, CEO and Founder, SalesTribe

Social selling is still misunderstood. It isn't about how to sell through messaging all your LinkedIn connections; it is about earning influence. Tim Hughes is an authority on the topic and this book is the ultimate guide to building or refining your social selling strategies to increase your influence and sales. Get your stationery ready to highlight key points and make notes.
Jo Saunders, LinkedIn Demystifier, strategist, trainer and author of
Connectfluence

Social Selling is the definitive blueprint required to implement a world-class strategy that will drive increased revenue based upon practical application. There are a lot of books that talk about social selling, but they fall short. Tim Hughes shares a mix of proven processes, tools, and personal anecdotes that show how his success can become yours, that you can immediately add to your sales arsenal to supercharge your business!
Roderick Jefferson, Senior Vice President, Enablement, bestselling author,
global keynote speaker

This is not a business book, it is a definitive and vital guide to social selling, a must-read and must-have for every business owner, entrepreneur, marketer and sales professional! Tim has compiled a comprehensive step-by-step resource and playbook which will positively transform your relationship building, increase your bottom line and see phenomenal return on your investment.
Jaz Greer, CEO, Make A Difference

Digital dominance, or owning your verticals' narrative on digital, is critical in social media strategy. Tim Hughes gives you the digital dominance secrets you need to implement a winning game plan. Every marketer needs to read this book!

Terri Nakamura, designer, writer and social media consultant and author of *Blogging on Instagram*

A network gives you reach... but a community gives you power. It's time to stop making excuses and start bringing in personal social skills to the digital world. Tim Hughes understands this critical issue, and this book give you the tools to make it happen.

Ted Rubin, speaker, author, strategic adviser... provocateur

Digital has thrown a spanner into the works of traditional B2B marketing. With this book, Tim Hughes provides light in the darkness for today's digital marketing. Highly recommended.

Joel Harrison, Editor-in-Chief, *B2B Marketing*

This book is a must-read for sellers wanting to hone their craft in buyer engagement. If you want to get ahead of the competition knowledge is powerful and the skill of social selling will give you the step-up necessary.

Janice B Gordon, Customer Growth Expert, Scale Your Sales

Tim Hughes has taken his already powerful, revolutionary book on social selling to the next level. Social selling is no longer a fad, but a core tenant of modern selling. Tim has seen this evolution and his book is for those who want to stay ahead of the game.

Jim Keenan, CEO of A Sales Growth Company and author of *Gap Selling*

Tim Hughes' first book is one of my go-to books when thinking about the concept of social selling and on developing 'social organizations'. The world changed and the way that people buy continues to evolve. It provides actionable advice to sales and marketing teams on how to embrace social and Tim's thinking is always ahead of the game.

Samantha Andrews, Global Marketing Director, GPA Global

People are the key to digital transformation. As digital technologies proliferate and humans begin to share work with AI and robots, it is the people who excel at being human who will thrive. In this book, Tim Hughes explains

that executives that invest to enable people to network and build relationships virtually will have the necessary foundation for winning today and in the future.
Lenwood M Ross, Founder and CEO, Accelery

This book walks you through the reality of the post-pandemic world, defines what a digital organization must be and outlines the detailed steps of making that a reality within your organization. It is a must-read for anyone leading or executing within a business of any size today.
Robert M Caruso, EngageDigitalInc.com @fondalo

The world of sales has changed. You can no longer rely on cold calls and spam emails to make your number. Tim Hughes has created a practical methodology that teaches sellers how to engage like a real human on digital and win.
Andy Paul, Author and Creator of *Sell Without Selling Out*

This update is a practical guide for every sales professional who wants digital success in a world that becomes more digital every day. If you want to boost your sales success online this book is a must!
Leigh Ashton, Founder and CEO, The Sales Consultancy

A real gem of a book that gets you started on your social selling journey, providing all your key enablers to build a culture of social selling, and making this daunting subject easy to understand. A simple read that demystifies social selling so you can get involved.
Chris Learmonth, Managing Director, BMW & Mini Park Lane

I bought the first edition of *Social Selling* in 2018, and immediately applied some of the very actionable advice in the book, refining my entire digital networking and marketing strategy. I can't recommend the new edition strongly enough.
Michael O'Connor, Founder of the Service Professionals Network

The problem with sales books today is pre-Covid thinking. In this second edition Hughes has really taken the time to update the book with modern case studies and chapters that make it relevant and a must for sales people in the post-Covid world.
Ian Moyse, cloud industry leader and influencer

Social Selling

*Techniques to influence buyers
and changemakers*

Timothy Hughes

KoganPage

First published in Great Britain and the United States in 2016 by Kogan Page Limited
Second edition 2022

2nd Floor, 45 Gee Street
London
EC1V 3RS
United Kingdom
www.koganpage.com

8 W 38th Street, Suite 902
New York, NY 10018
USA

4737/23 Ansari Road
Daryaganj
New Delhi 110002
India

ISBNs
Hardback   9781398607385
Paperback   9781398607323
Ebook   9781398607378

British Library Cataloguing-in-Publication Data

A CIP record for this book is available from the British Library.

Library of Congress Control Number

2022043413

Typeset by Hong Kong FIVE Workshop
Print production managed by Jellyfish
Printed and bound by CPI Group (UK) Ltd, Croydon CR0 4YY
Kogan Page books are printed on paper from sustainable forests.

CONTENTS

FOREWORD

I was recently asked this question:

> In the many years you have been immersed in social media and social
> commerce, what has been the biggest change?

My answer came easily. Business has taken the 'social' out of social media.

In the early days of the social web, businesses were determined to join and master this new 'social conversation'. And they did so, by engaging in real dialogue with people. I remember having direct conversations with real people from the biggest brands. Some of these early pioneers became better known and more beloved than the brands themselves!

They're all gone now. Over time, big business wanted to scale the work and cut costs by turning conversations into automated reactions and human engagement into efficient, algorithmic replies. Soon, all those conversations, and brand relationships, were gone.

Happily, this is turning around again. Companies are seeing that there is real value in connection and caring. There always has been. There always will be. The human touch in social media – on the brink of extinction – is making a comeback.

I'm not saying there is never a place for technology or automation. I'm saying that we have gone too far and used technology to erect annoying barriers between our teams and our customers, instead of using these wonderful tools to tear those barriers down.

I've written extensively about how 'the most human company wins' and gratefully Tim Hughes has not lost sight of this truth. He's built a blueprint for you in these pages that re-centres the sales function on relationships and using social media in a way that amplifies the most human qualities that already made you great. He's put technology in its proper place.

The most human company wins. This book shows you how.

Mark Schaefer
Consultant, college educator, and author of *Marketing Rebellion*

PREFACE

Welcome to the second edition of *Social Selling: Techniques to influence buyers and changemakers*. Welcome if you are a new reader or have purchased this book having read the first edition.

So, why a second edition?

Since I wrote the book back in 2015, to be published in 2016, a lot has happened. The first edition was myself and Matt emptying our heads of everything we knew about social selling into one place. But I have to be honest, the subject was new, we had little practical experience. That said, the book has outsold my and the publishers' wildest dreams and still sells.

What has changed is that my business partner Adam Gray and I started DLA Ignite on 17 September 2016, and here we are with an extensive list of clients and a lot of practical experience. What I have done is poured that practical experience into this book. I have also invited practitioners, people who do this day in and day out, to contribute. I have asked customers to contribute quotes, sales teams across the world who do social selling and do it all the time.

That's why it's key for you to walk away with the notion that social selling isn't new. Companies and salespeople are already doing this. They are getting competitive advantage, and if you're not doing it, you are behind. But that's why you are reading the book, on a search for knowledge. The experience of running DLA Ignite over the years has made me realize that there comes a point in a company's growth where marketing isn't working and something has to happen. This book is the catalyst to that change.

This second edition of the book aims to be far more practical than the first. It is written as a workbook and is a practical guide, not to my journey or a LinkedIn training book, but to how you and your business can use social media to sell. More critically, I want you to understand that every keystroke your sales team make can be measured against revenue and earnings before interest, taxes, depreciation, and amortization (EBITDA).

What I'm going to walk you through is not about playing on social, it's about how your business can strategically sell on social media and win. Better still, how you can digitally dominate your vertical or market sector.

Many a salesperson shared with me that they carried the first version of this book with them wherever they went, and referred to it during their day-to-day sales activity. I hope you do with this version too.

ACKNOWLEDGEMENTS

When I wrote the first version of this book back in 2015, I only had one objective. My father's dementia had set in and I wanted to sit with him and show him what his son had achieved. I still have the photo of my father, the book and myself. To sell that one book was enough.

I'm lucky that my father is still alive, but his dementia is such that he doesn't know what he had for his last meal.

To my parents, you have always been my inspiration. Thank you.

I also need to thank my partner, Julie Harris. She has been my support through starting and scaling up DLA Ignite. She has been my anchor though this, she has also been my counsel through writing three books, somebody to turn to through this. She has been incredible and I thank her for this.

I also need to thank the team here at DLA Ignite, my business partner, Adam Gray, as well as the team that have contributed, both in terms of their time and their innovation and inspiration.

Changing the world isn't easy – there are so many vested interest that don't want change, but when you know you are right it is so much easier to stand against a narrative, no matter how strong. My favourite quote is this one by Mahatma Gandhi:

First they ignore you, then they laugh at you, then they fight you, then you win.

This has been my journey. When I first wrote this book we were seen as niche. It will never catch on, people said. Then Adam Gray and I started DLA Ignite and we got our first customer, then our second, then our third, etc. More and more companies looked up and realized there was another way and realized better results could be achieved for less spend. I want to thank all those customers that put their trust in us in the early days and those that trust us even today.

Finally, I want to thank past and present associates and partners of DLA Ignite. We thank you for your contribution. Adam and I love how the team still want to drive the business of our clients forward. Thank you all, you are a daily inspiration.

I want to thank all of the contributors to this book:

Catherine Coale
Eric Doyle
Jon Ferrara

Chris Fleming

Adam Gray

Danielle Guzman

Brentney Hutchinson

Christian Jumelet

Chris Mason

Priscilla McKinney

Steve Rafferty

Mark Schaefer

Robert Tearle

Bill Trim

Michaela Underdahl

Anita Veszeli

David Watts

In the preface, I set the objective that I wanted to make this far more practical than the first edition and I hope that you the reader will find it insightful and will have plenty to think about and action in your day-to-day work.

Introduction

The selling revolution

Twenty years ago, in the pre-internet age, if we wanted to know about a product as a buyer we would ring the company up and hopefully a brochure would appear in the post three days later, provided by a salesperson. If, as a seller, we wanted a person at a company to know about our products, we would call them up and interrupt the potential buyer and tell (broadcast) to the person at the end of the phone about our product. Cold calling and cold email are both 'interruption marketing' – we call a person up, interrupt the person and tell them, often called a sales pitch, about what we do.

The other way to tell people what our product did was to advertise, again, interrupting people and broadcasting what we did. Advertising like this has been around since the 1930s and in the pre-internet age it was how the public were able to get information about brands. It's how brands such as Unilever told us about its washing powers and toothpaste and Nestlé and Rowntree told us about their chocolate. As consumers, we would go to a shop and ask for the brand, because we trusted the brand.

Back in the 1930s, when advertising and interrupt and broadcast marketing were invented, we lived in a different world. There was no internet, no mobile, and the only way we got to hear about new things was through the press, the radio or the television. 'You'll wonder where the yellow went when you brush your teeth with Pepsodent' was a TV advertising slogan for toothpaste, in use in the USA and UK from the late 1940s to 1960s. When people saw these messages and they went into a shop they would reach for these brands as they knew and trusted them. Many brands grew rich on advertising. They knew that the more they spent on advertising, the more the business would sell. You measured a correlation between the spend on advertising and the amount of product you sold.

Fast forward to the current time and we now have access to mobile, the internet and social media. This has given us so many new choices. A friend of mine said to me recently, 'I love advertising, as I find out about a product and then go onto the internet and buy it from a competitor, at a cheaper price.' And that is the problem for brands today and any company that is using interruption and broadcast – we are all empowered to go online and research products and services. If I tell you the iPhone is the best mobile phone in the world, you can go online and research Android phones and give me 10 reasons why iPhone are not the best cell.

Broadcast marketing is still prevalent today. Sometimes called push marketing, it is where a company will tell you about their products and services, the features, the team, the founders, the methodology. It is always about 'you'. Companies do this time after time, hoping that at some point the customer will say, 'That's the product for me.' Or salespeople just keep ringing and ringing you, pestering you to buy. As we used to joke about one of my salesperson colleagues, his customers would strike a deal with him – they would buy as long as he left them alone.

The internet changes everything

Last weekend, I was sitting in a café with my partner and we decided to go to Iceland for a short break. Each of us took a different responsibility. My partner checked on the flights and I looked up the Airbnbs. The process was easy, and while we didn't make a decision on when we would go, the companies didn't know we were searching and there was no salesperson involved.

Now if we want to buy something, we go straight onto the internet, usually through our mobiles. The world of buying has been disrupted twice in the last five years and continues to be disrupted, as we will cover in this chapter. First came the internet. Now I can go online and get any information on your products and services. You will have brochures online, YouTube videos, price lists, and as a buyer I also know your competition is just one click away.

I'm aware of one seller who works for a mid-market accounting software supplier, average deal size £150,000 ($195,000), who took a call from a prospective client that went like this:

Prospect: Hi! I've read your brochures, watched the videos on YouTube, I just need to know how much the accountancy software is and how do I buy?

Salesperson: Don't you want a demo?

Prospect: No, there is no need – I've watched the demos on YouTube.

Now that person isn't the best negotiator in the world, but it proves that in the business-to-business (B2B) space, contracts worth a significant amount of money are being done online. Or at least 80 or 90 per cent of it is being done online.

The second level of disruption to the buyer process is mobile. Now, as buyers we are able to search, research and buy products and services not just at our desks at work or at home, but on the way to work on the train, sitting in bed, sitting in the park. Personally, I cannot remember a Christmas where I haven't purchased all the presents I was going to give online. No need for me to walk around shops. Or if I did go to the shop, it was to a 'showroom'. Go and see the product was the right one, only to buy it online later on. If you think this will never happen to your business because you're too big, too successful or simply you have to much brand recognition in the market-place, think again. A few years ago, I was told by a shoe retailer that they were not afraid of the internet as everybody will have to try shoes on. Now I buy five pairs, get them delivered to my house, try them on, buy a pair and send the other four back. As CapGemini Consulting (2017) pointed out, you are very clearly 'not safe' no matter how much your business appears to be a safe and secure 'institution'. Since 2000, 525 per cent of the Fortune 500 companies have either gone bankrupt, been acquired or ceased to exist

In their bestselling book *In Search of Excellence* (2004), Waterman and Peters talk about what makes a great business. All of those companies mentioned in the book no longer exist or no longer exist in that form. All of the processes that made a good company that Waterman and Peters told people to emulate actually put the 'best practice' companies out of business. No company or vertical won't be impacted by digital in some shape or form.

IT GETS WORSE

Our ability to get information and the power that gives us means we have become more and more intolerant of people pushing information (broadcast marketing and push marketing) about their products or services on us. In the past we would have tolerated a salesperson calling us up and telling us about their products. We all have an inbuilt curiosity and it was, after all the only way we found out about new things. Now, nobody gets up in the morning and says, 'I need to talk to a salesperson today.' In fact, salespeople (and marketers) interrupting us has become an annoyance. We have all had a salesperson 'pitch' at us, using manipulative techniques to try and get us to say 'yes' and buy something we never wanted. We are all bored of cold callers. In fact, I've given up answering the phone to anybody's number that isn't in my phone's address book. People hate to have emails sent to them cold where a salesperson just pitches. The same with social media. Everybody hates a pitch.

It's worth pointing out that social selling is *not* selling on social. Spamming on social is just spamming on social. What social selling is, we will come to shortly.

Sales and marketing in their current form are broken

THERE'S NO SILVER BULLET

We often forget (or choose to forget) that there is no such thing as a silver bullet, a panacea that can cure all ills. We're not saying that technology isn't important as an enabler of change, because it is. Technology is a vital platform or launch pad for success, but often organizations embrace technology as if it, of itself, is the solution. As if it is the technology that will catapult the organization from laggard to early adopter, as if it will compensate for many of the organizational shortcomings with which they are battling. But it won't. 'A fool with a tool is still a fool,' as Grady Booch once said, and never is it truer than if they believe that the shiny new tech tool the business is hoping to use will do anything other than speed the inevitable decline.

As we discussed above, the way we sold in the past was through interruption and broadcast. The modern world is such as we are able to filter out marketing messages using either technology or our own abilities so we don't have to listen to 'corporate noise' or 'corporate propaganda'. Every business is going to market with the same message, 'Buy my product because we are great.' If you do ever hear anybody saying 'Our product isn't the best, it's a little expensive and our customer service is frankly appalling' then let me know.

ADVERTISING

At a recent training event, I asked the audience of 10 how many people watch the advertisements on television. Only one person put their hand up. Everybody else admitted that they avoid adverts as much as they can. Technology provides the ability to fast-forward through television adverts. At a recent conference, at the start of my presentation, I got everybody to stand up and then said, 'Sit down, if you can remember the last three adverts you saw.' Nobody sat down. At another conference, people were so not interested in a company's brochures that they were putting them down the toilet, and the company had to put up signs asking people to stop doing this.

Just a few recent examples of changes in advertising practice are:

- Hootsuite estimate that 38.8 per cent of Americans use ad blockers, which means that the reach of advertising is getting less and less (Hootsuite, 2022).

- At the 2018 World Cup Adidas, for example, didn't use advertising because they know people in the niche they are targeting are big users of ad blockers (DigiDay, 2018). In fact, they switched their advertising to social media and influencer marketing.

- Procter & Gamble recently reduced their ad spend and there was no impact on revenue (Forbes, 2021). When they cut $200 million in digital ad spend, they increased their reach 10 per cent (AdWeek, 2018).

- Chase Manhattan began limiting their display ads to pre-approved websites to avoid proximity to content like fake news and offensive videos (*New York Times*, 2017). The results were the same.

- Uber was paying an agency $10 for each app install. They reduced this spend by 80 per cent and it made no difference. Why? Because of the fraud in the system (UKTN, 2020).

- Research shows that people don't like being interrupted by advertising. In 2015 Nielsen's extensive research showed that, with the exception of personal recommendation, pretty much all forms of media were only trusted 50 per cent of the time.

- As reported by DigiDay (2017), ads are lumped in the the same bucket as fake news – online advertising was regarded as a disruptive experience by 83 per cent of the 2,500 people polled and, perhaps more telling, 63 per cent of people positively 'distrust advertising'.

- Research by eMarketer from 2021 shows that only 16 per cent of people on social media thought ads were extremely impactful.

So, let's talk about how you measure advertising. Number of impressions is often used as a measure, but what is an impression? How does Facebook measure an ad impression? Ads are counted at 'greater than zero pixels and greater than zero seconds' (Fou, 2021). This measure is so small that anybody will be shown as an impression. It does make you wonder what Facebook is hiding by running measures like this.

EMAIL MARKETING

The introduction of the EU General Data Protection Regulation (GDPR) has pretty much killed email marketing. Email marketing was simple – you fired as many emails at people you could. In fact marketing automation provided companies with a 'Gatling gun' where brands could fire at will. GDPR means that as a business you are now accountable and responsible for all the data you hold on somebody. We have also seen similar legislation implemented in the US, for example the California Consumer Privacy Act (CCPA), a state-wide data privacy law that regulates how businesses all over the world are allowed to handle the personal information of California residents.

Many companies, like DLA Ignite, have deleted any email lists as it's simpler than risk the GDPR 4 per cent of turnover penalties. Examples of fines for data breaches are:

- Facebook was fined £500,000 by the UK Information Commissioner's Office in the wake of the Cambridge Analytica scandal, after allowing third party developers to access user information without sufficient consent.
- Dixons Carphone was also fined £500,000 for a massive data breach. Holding email data is high stakes for any corporate, which is why so many companies have stopped email marketing.

The other issue for email marketers is there is an argument that nobody actually reads the emails, which is why there is such a massive industry that uses 'manipulative' techniques to get you to open the emails in the first place.

One of the pieces of research to emerge from the Covid-19 pandemic was from HubSpot (2020). This was not research asking a person's opinion, this was based on data pulled from their own 121,000 customers. To quote this article from The Drum (2020): 'Thank you, Covid-19, we just broke the record for poor performance'. According to HubSpot, the response rate to emails fell to a record low of 2.1 per cent in April 2020. Said differently, 98 per cent of our efforts to reach new prospects failed. In the webinar from HubSpot (2020) Yamini Rangan, CEO, says 'We are inundated with email, especially busy executives, and we are overwhelmed. So how do you cut through this? That is where the key is.' Kipp Bodnar, the HubSpot CMO, says in the webinar, 'HubSpot is sending less email' and 'We have doubled down in our investments in content. And what I will tell everybody. The more educational the content the better it is.' This is all from a company that sells email marketing tools and has a vested interest to talk this market up.

According to DMA, more than 347.3 billion emails will be sent each day in 2022 – nearly 50 billion more per day than in 2019. That's a staggering increase. But that also means that your email is, well, just another email, vying for attention. A person's inbox is the nosiest place you can put your message and it's so easy for people to ignore it, delete it and do what I do, which is create a rule that all future emails from you will bypass my inbox and go straight into the wastepaper basket.

CORPORATE MARKETING

Similar to advertising, most corporate marketing has just become noise that people ignore. 'We are great', 'We are number one', 'We are market leader' are all comments that marketers use to market their products and services. So much so, we don't believe any of it and we just filter it out. The problem with this 'corporate propaganda' is that the 'Buy my product because we are great' message just merges into a sea of sameness. Take a moment out of this book and have a look at your competitors – are they saying the same thing as you? Yes, I know you are very excited about what you do because it pays your mortgage and puts food on the table, but I have to be honest, I'm not interested. Why? Because I have my own products to sell. In the field of social selling this is a key concept that we have to overcome – more on this later.

By the way, if you find anybody that markets by saying, 'We are actually number two in the market, our product is overpriced and the customer service diabolical', please let me know.

WEBSITES

Which brings us onto the corporate website. Ten years ago, a corporate website was a priority. I'm not saying that websites are not required, but today for the buyer it's a 1:1 draw. Buyers will check a company's website to see if the company exists – like somebody might check a pulse. If you have a website, you exist; if you don't have a website, you don't exist. But more than that, buyers don't really get much from a website. Why? Because most websites are the same. In research of 10,000 websites, it was found they all look the same (TNW, 2020).

I worked with a marketing agency in the last six years and I noticed they had used the same WordPress template for each website they had built for their clients. While the business words were different, the structure in terms of the list of services, details of the management team, were all the same. I've also worked with businesses where the owners of the business were 'technical'. The website was therefore written in a form that the average person couldn't understand. I met with the sales leader and he asked me, 'So what do we do?' I had to admit, I had read the website and just couldn't understand it. The sales leader responded, and said, 'Yes, this is one of the challenges we have. How do I challenge the CEO when he understands totally what we do?' The issue always is to be heard above the noise of everything else. Many companies even try and push their clients away by having spammy pop-up boxes and asking you to subscribe to email lists, etc.

COLD CALLING

While writing this chapter, my mobile rang. I didn't recognize the number of the person calling me, the number wasn't in the address book of my phone. I assumed it was a cold call and so I ignored it. While I run my own business and it could be a person asking to buy something, I always let cold calls go through to voice mail. Why? Because I hate being cold called. The caller will have a script where the answer will be yes, and so the only way you can get rid of them is to be rude. I always let cold calls go through to voice mail because I know if it's important that the person will either call back or leave a voice mail. The call that came through as I was writing this chapter was from a company offering a free water cooler. I then just blocked the number on my phone.

This attitude and process is being replicated across the world as people have had enough of cold calls. I found it interesting that Merrill Lynch have banned cold calling and have moved all their people to social selling (WSJ, 2021). Now I would totally get a company outside of financial services making this decision, but this is a conservative financial services company. While some companies will make decisions based on gut or they think something is a good idea, Merrill Lynch made this decision based on data. There are probably many of you reading this thinking, but surely cold calling has a better return on investment than social selling? Not according to Merrill Lynch. In the article the bank says about their cold calling agents, 'They will also be encouraged to contact prospects over LinkedIn, which has a higher hit rate than cold calling.'

SEARCH ENGINE OPTIMIZATION

Simon Kemp (2021b) has been tracking the world's search behaviours, and comments, 'It was interesting, the other week I was part of an invited panel to discuss search. The thing that concerned me about the whole thing was the assumption that search = Google. If you read this research, this is just not the case and for 16–24 age group it certainly isn't the case.'

Search has changed so much since Google was started in 1998, and let's not forget that Google was late to the party, there was Yahoo, AskJeeves, etc., but you are not here for a history lesson – you want to know about the future. Let's look at social search: 57.6 per cent of the world's population, that's 4.55 billion people, are active social media users and they spend 2 hours and 27 minutes each day on social media. That's a lot of people spending a lot of time on social. For context, that adds up to more than 37 days per year, or 15 per cent of our waking lives.

This is where things start to get interesting. Did you know that 'Social networks are now the second-top channel for online brand research after search engines, and amongst internet users aged 16 to 24, they're already the top channel' (Kemp, 2021a)? This means that Google is not the first place people go to search, it's social media. 'Overall, more than 7 in 10 internet users between the ages of 16 and 64 say that they use some kind of social media platform to research brands and products'. This means that if you want to be found as a brand, while Google is important, the place you need to be putting the vast majority of your search budget is into social media.

One of the great things about Google is that it's one platform and easy to work out what the algorithm wants so you can tune content to be found. With social, each platform is different, so you will need to understand the different rules. For example, Twitter is an open platform and search works based on word in Tweets, rather like on Google, where it indexes words within an article. However, on LinkedIn search works based on centricity to you and your network.

Try an experiment. Search on LinkedIn for a specific term, and ask a colleague to do the same. You will get different answers. That's because it's based on your network, and your colleague's network will be different. One of the best ways to be found on LinkedIn is to have a wide and varied network, but we will come to that. You also have to have the key words on your profile, and we will cover that as well.

Buyers are looking for personality, not brands

There is an old saying in sales that 'people buy people'. Never has this been more so than today. As I've mentioned already, brands go to market with a message all about themselves. They say, 'Buy my product because it is great.' Every company says it. Buyers just see this as a sea of sameness.

GESTALT THINKING

FIGURE 0.1   Gestalt thinking

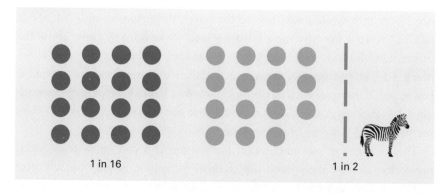

As humans we get impacted by Gestalt thinking, which is a school of psychology that emerged in the early twentieth century in Austria and Germany. This is where the brain forms patterns. In Figure 0.1 you can see a set of 16 circles, and the brain forms a pattern. This is what our brain does with a company's websites and people's position on social media; as everybody looks the same, the brain does not make any differentiation. Whereas, the moment we make ourselves look different on social we stand out. It has also changed our win rate from 1 in 16 to 1 in 2 as the buyer's brain can see we are different from all of our other competitors that all look and sound the same.

Even on social media, people are making themselves look the same as everybody else. If you take the summary title on LinkedIn, which is the most visible thing about you on the internet, there will be often millions of people with the same title. You can do the search yourself. This is not differentiating yourself – this is making yourself look like everybody else.

WHY BRANDS HAVE BECOME A COMMODITY

As I mentioned above, brands used to be the thing that drove marketing. Cadbury, Unilever, Nestlé all have products and brands that our parents probably purchased. I recall my mum using Persil washing powder, and the brand assumption would be that I would use it for life as well. In fact, once I left home, I used different brands. The brand I use now is sold off the back of its sustainability credentials, not that it washes 'whiter than white'.

I totally understand that some brands like Nike, Adidas, Levi may be seen by some people as having magical qualities, but that isn't the case for the vast majority of brands. If you are a guttering company in west London, how do you stand out? Well, you can do what all guttering companies do and say, 'We are the best guttering company in west London, so buy from us.' Or you can use your only unique feature as a company – your people.

THE *TOP GEAR* CAR SHOW

In the UK a television car show was started in one of the provincial BBC studios and it was called *Top Gear*. When it first started it used presenters that we all knew and loved. But the focus was on the cars, and that was what people remembered. Then the show changed; it became about the personality of the presenters and the experience. You remember the show about the team driving through the Namibian desert; you won't remember the cars.

But when it comes to cars, the world has changed. Now if you want to sell a car you go to 'Supercar Blondie'. Alexandra Mary 'Alex' Hirschi, known online as Supercar Blondie, is an Australian social media celebrity, presenter and vlogger based in Dubai, United Arab Emirates. According to her website she has 70 million followers on social media, Facebook, Instagram, YouTube, TikTok, Snapchat and Twitter.

So now, as a brand, if you want to sell something you use people to do it. While Nike has a great following, if they want to sell tennis shoes they talk to Serena Williams as she has a bigger following; for basketball shoes they turn to LeBron James and for football (soccer) boots they turn to Cristiano Ronaldo. The saying that 'people buy people' is just as true today as it has always been.

Ignorance (information and knowledge scarcity)

For many years, marketing departments had the knowledge. Their customers were largely ignorant of what their products did, whether they were well regarded, reliable and well-supported and whether the competitors were better or worse. In fact, for many years the buyer had trouble even finding out who the main players in an industry or sector were. How many times have you heard the phrase 'We are our industry's best keep secret'?

Not anymore. Buyers are now knowledgeable. Buyers sometimes know more about the product or service than the seller. Certainly, they are equipped with more information than they ever have been and this very clearly has changed the landscape in which sales and marketing operate. No longer is the role of the marketing department to weave mellifluous prose about their products that extols their virtues. Now, it would seem, the buyer has facts and comparisons, they have the hard data and they have it at their fingertips. So, what do they want? Above all else what they want is help.

In the enterprise B2B world where my customers are, people are looking for 'experts'. Experts that can help and guide the buyer. They want the seller to empathize with them and understand their issues and drivers, they want the seller to solve their problems and to create solutions. They don't want the seller to talk 'platitudes' or to talk about themselves. They want the seller to befriend them and genuinely help them. They want advice, (wherever possible) impartiality and honesty, and they want to be empowered to the point that they can be sure in their own minds that they are making the right decision.

You know that this is true. Whilst you may fight against it, this is how you behave. You don't believe company literature and wade through loads of marketing speak, even if you yourself are a marketer. What you want is someone you can trust to give you their 'expert' help and guidance.

The revolution in B2B buying

Every year Gartner undertake research of the B2B buying process across the world. It looks at different buying habits and patterns. In 2017, CEB, now owned by Gartner, found that most B2B buyers were 57 per cent of the way through the buying process by the time they contacted a salesperson. This is a fundamental change from the days when I started selling, where the only way to find out about my products and services was to ring me up and talk to me.

Gartner (2022) breaks down the time the modern buying process as follows:

- meeting with potential suppliers
- researching independently offline
- meeting with buyer groups
- researching independently online

The time buyers have to meet suppliers is now only 17 per cent of the buyer group's time. Whether a business is on a shortlist of three or five, the time does not increase. The time a salesperson has for face-to-face 'selling' has drastically reduced. This time has been reduced even further by the Covid-19 pandemic, as more and more people carry on working from home and buyers must use Zoom or Microsoft Teams to make calls.

I was talking with one CEO and he said one of his sales team has admitted, 'I cannot sell unless I am in the same room, talking face-to-face.' It would seem that the salesperson's opportunity to do this is getting less and less, and the need to recruit people with these skills gets less and less.

Information asymmetry

Economists talk about information asymmetry. The way to visualize this is to think of a set of scales or a children's seesaw in a playground with the buyer at one end and the seller at the other. Obviously, we would want there to be balance, but, like a child's seesaw, one side will have dominance over the other.

FIGURE 0.2   Information asymmetry

Previously in sales, the salesperson had more knowledge and therefore the balance of power was with them. If you turn up at a second-hand car showroom without doing any research beforehand, the salesperson will have the upper hand. The key phrase is 'doing research beforehand' and today we all do research. If I tell you the iPhone is the best mobile phone in the world, you can go onto the internet and social media and search and you can come back with 10 reasons why an Android phone is better.

The balance of power in any sale today is with the buyer, who can go online and research a business, watch the YouTube videos and probably get pricing. All without the selling organization knowing. Social selling addresses the balance of power.

Sales taking back control

Over the last five years, traditional marketing has had a perfect storm of failure: cold calling, email marketing, advertising – for all of these traditional ways of marketing, the results have got less and less. We know that our buyers are on social media and Covid-19 has seen a shift from social media being a destination, that is a place we go, to being a place where we are. It's a place where we actually hang out.

The growth of social media

In October 2021 there were 7.89 billion people in the world, of which 5.29 billion (67.1 per cent), had a mobile phone, 4.88 billion (61.8 per cent) had access to the internet, and 4.55 billion (57.6 per cent) were *active* users of social media (Kemp, 2021b). Over the last year the number of people on social media has grown by nearly 10 per cent, that's 409 million, or 13 new users of social media every second. Social media usage by 60 per cent of the population is on track for mid-2022. One other figure to pick out is that the average person spends 2 hours 27 minutes per day on social media. You can no longer say that your customers are not on social media. Your buyers are on social media and it's your job now as sellers to find them and sell to them. That's why you are here reading this book.

Just a quick piece of advice – people hate being sold to, regardless of the platform, and if you think social selling is about selling on social then you are not going to get very far.

A NEW WAY OF ENGAGING WITH THE MARKET – BILL TRIM

I am the sales director of an IT professional services firm, and two years ago my marketing manager and I realized that the traditional methods of starting new conversations and generating new leads were starting to diminish in success. Whilst they still have a place, we realized we needed to find new ways of engaging early in the buying cycle. In the new, better informed and self-researching buyer world, we needed to ensure we would be viewed as trusted subject matter experts and to influence the thought process towards the most appropriate solution, therefore earning the right to have a place on any shortlist.

At that time, I was introduced to one of the authors of this book. It opened my mind to a whole new way of engaging with the market – creating and seeking out communities of interest online and using social media (mainly LinkedIn) to raise the profile of my sales and marketing team (and later to include my technical team). I pledged they would build new skills that would set them apart to become a modern sales team.

At the time it was known as social selling. However, I have come to associate that term with the kind of unsolicited junk messages I get in my LinkedIn mailbox. So I steered away from calling it social selling and rebranded the programme the 'Digital Organization'. I set about enabling the wider company to have the confidence to put themselves out there as they would have done when networking at industry events and keynote speaking to get their expert opinion heard.

More by luck than judgement, when lockdown took hold because of the Covid-19 pandemic, my whole team was already able to exist and communicate in the online world. Coupled with the new video conference culture, it became far easier to translate online conversations into face-to-face (albeit still online). This resulted in one of the best quarters we had achieved in the past 10 years and thankfully kept us very busy during the waves of the pandemic.

I am now an advocate of this new way of working where a modern sales team bridges the gap between sales and traditional marketing to self-generate their own 'leads'. They are best placed to build a relationship and take the conversation through the buying cycle to a successful outcome.

The digital organization

What is a digital organization?

While this book is about sales and more particularly using social media to help with sales, I want to digress and talk about the digital organization.

In the past we have called this the social organization, shortened to social org, but that didn't resonate with the market. Social is a word that is often used to mean non-for-profit or wellness, so, like Bill Trim in the case study above, we settled on 'digital organization', and for the rest of the book that's the term we use.

Should social media still belong to marketing?

We have already talked about how the world of sales and marketing has changed. Twenty years ago, we knew that if we spent $20,000 on advertising we would get \$50,000 in sales, or whatever the ratio was. Now we are spending \$30,000 on advertising and getting \$40,000 in return. At some point we will spend \$40,000 on advertising and get \$40,000 in return and then we will spend \$40,000 on advertising and get \$30,000 in return. At what point as a management team do we cut across and look at alternatives?

We know that social media, the internet and the mobile phone have changed buyers' behaviour, but we are prisoner to a number of decisions that were made when the internet became part of 'business as usual' for a company. The thing was, back then, nobody knew what the internet or social media would become. The internet meant that a business needed a website and social media meant something else. In many cases, businesses still do not know what social media really means. As they both seemed to mean something about marketing, the responsibility for websites and social media was given to marketing.

Since then, nobody has questioned that.

Social media as a business tactic

In most organizations we talk to, social media is seen as a tactic rather than a strategy. In this book we suggest that social media needs to be a strategy. It needs to be led by your board. Who has responsibility for this will be discussed later. I'm hoping that with this second edition more people will come to realize that social media isn't just about posting cat photos and photos of your lunch – it's a strategic platform on which business is done. It is a way for you to be more efficient as a business, to strip out cost and provide a better customer experience. Doing more for less is something that all board members need to review and understand, which is why your board must understand social media.

'We are already doing social'

In talking with senior leaders, I hear that 'We are already doing social.' That is probably the case. Social will be part of digital, which will be part of marketing. Or social is part of the recruitment process within the human resources department or part of customer service, where people can post complaints.

Social is all over the business, but in each case it's tactical and siloed, as shown in Figure 0.3.

FIGURE 0.3   Tactical and siloed social media

'We are all over social'

Many businesses we talk to tell us, 'We are all over social.' Just by looking at their company's social media profiles, the social media profiles of their employees, the engagement taking place on social media, it is clear they are not. We are often told that being 'all over social' means posting bi-weekly on social media by marketing and then an email is sent around, asking the employees to like that post.

In 2022, the average person on LinkedIn has 930 connections, and those connections will be made up of ex-colleagues and recruitment consultants. None of these people are the ones most businesses are trying to influence or sell to. This means that the content that is posted bi-weekly by marketing is not being seen by the people that you are trying to influence. Activity like this is a cost to your business and certainly isn't a profit.

In a high-performance business today, the board will know exactly how much revenue is generated from social media. A modern business can in effect connect and understand how every keystroke of a salesperson on their keyboard can be connected to profit or EBITDA.

Social media needs to be strategic

Social media has changed the world – it's changed society and it's changed business. From the Arab Spring, to the elections of US Presidents, to the

FIGURE 0.4   Social media needs to be strategic

Brexit vote, all of this has been attributed to the use of social media. Of course, social media is omnipresent in our lives, and while some people may not be big users of it, many are using it and are influenced by it in some shape or form, good or bad.

But we are not here to debate the good or bad impact of social media on society – this is a business book and we want to understand how to use social media to market and sell our products or services. Social media has grown so much that it touches all parts of our lives, not just in sociality but in business too, across all parts of the business, as shown in Figure 0.4.

We see social as the glue that holds companies together. In every department where conversations happen (or ideas and concepts are to be communicated) social has a role to play for both the person and the company. As a business we run our company on Slack, and the team prefer it to email as it's a shorter form. We have all got used to sending messages through text or using a messenger app, where the short form communication is faster and preferred. This creates an efficiency at work, as shown in Figure 0.5.

There has also been a shift in the culture of employees. When I first started work, 'knowledge was power', and what you knew meant you kept your job. Over the last 10 years there has been a shift to sharing. Now you are seen as a good citizen at work if you share your knowledge and help people. A 2012 article by McKinsey suggested that 'By using social technologies, companies can raise the productivity of knowledge workers by 20 to 25 per cent.' I certainly worked on a project where we implemented an internal social network, often called enterprise social network, and saw massive time

FIGURE 0.5   Social creates efficiency at work

savings. I recall one meeting where we set up two hours to brainstorm a subject, but because we had collaborated online for the week before that meeting, we got the work done in one hour.

Now, of course, people still had to spend time in advance of that meeting, but it was far less than the hour saved, and with social media it was at a time that was convenient to them.

Definition of a digital organization

Our definition of a digital organization is one that uses digital, that is social media, throughout the business to support that company. There is a strategy set at board level, there is governance at board level and there are measures. Digital provides a business with leading indicators that can be used to find out how the business is performing. Currently, for a business to make investment decisions about whether to invest in people or resources, they will look to customer relationship management (CRM) which is, or should, be a central repository of how the business is doing and will do in the future. Digital will provide more measures, way before anything hits the CRM, which will show if salespeople, marketing, etc., are contributing in the way we want.

What high-level measures should we expect?

These are the high-level measures that our customers expect:

- visibility and recognition in the marketplace
- achieving trusted advisor status to their clients and prospects
- measurable pipeline, revenue and new logos growth
- access to the best talent and skills and therefore becoming employer of choice in your chosen markets and topic areas
- employee engagement and shared sense of purpose

Let's break them down in more detail.

VISIBILITY AND RECOGNITION IN THE MARKETPLACE

This is the area that used to be covered by traditional PR, where you want people to be aware of the business and the brand. Being front of mind for your prospects and customers is critical and this all can be done now with digital with better, measurable results and where you are in control.

Often we talk to businesses about digital dominance. This is where you as a business control the message and share of voice across all of the digital channels. Just take a look at your competition. If they are not present on social or are just posting brochures and brochureware, you have an opportunity to totally wipe them out from a digital prospective. While this sounds very 'marketing' just think about the opportunity for sales. If you own the digital channels, we know our prospects and clients are on digital, every time they go onto these channels, they will see you being insightful, educational and entertaining. Then you will always be front of mind. When a client or a prospect has a business issue that you can solve then you will be the obvious choice.

It is very common for clients to tell us that a prospective client, walked towards them and asked whether they could help. It is at this point that you use your sales skills to close that business. You will find that in many cases 'close' is too harsh a term – it will be more like empowering people to buy. One of our clients had exactly this situation and they closed a $2.5 million deal, no competition.

ACHIEVING TRUSTED ADVISOR STATUS TO THEIR CLIENTS AND PROSPECTS

Many clients we talk to in professional services, high-tech and financial services want to be invited in by prospects as this enables the selling organization to engage early in the sales cycle, to set the agenda and control the sale. As we talked about above, by being omnipresent on social media and by offering a platform of help, insight by a group of authentic employees will mean business will see you and recognize your expertise. This will often mean that, in addition to the salespeople, you will activate the technical people to talk on social. Salespeople still have a stigma attached to them that they want to sell you something. There is an old joke, 'How can you tell if a salesperson is lying?' The response to that is, 'Their lips are moving.' I'm a salesperson myself and that is harsh, and by writing this book I hope to start a revolution where salespeople regain the moral high ground. And in fact, salespeople don't need to be manipulative if they follow the advice in this book.

By activating your technical people on social, you are able to get those technical people to connect to and have relationships with other technical people. This is where you start the process of knowing, liking and trusting people. Technical to technical people. Then when it comes to making a decision, who is the prospect going to buy from? The people they know, like and trust of course, so your business is the obvious choice.

This is how your business becomes the trusted adviser.

It's worth saying at this point that this all works regardless of whether you are a large or small business and we haven't found a vertical this does not work in, B2B or business to consumer (B2C), if you are a big company trying to stop smaller competition or if you are a small business selling against larger competition. You can control the market.

MEASURABLE PIPELINE, REVENUE AND NEW LOGOS GROWTH

This is something we all want in business – new sales, more logos, existing clients renewing. All is possible with social. We will cover this in the rest of the book, so let's move on.

ACCESS TO THE BEST TALENT AND SKILLS AND THEREFORE BECOMING EMPLOYER OF CHOICE IN YOUR CHOSEN MARKETS AND TOPIC AREAS

In the section on human resources below I explain in more detail about how social media can be used for finding and accessing the best talent and how it can be used for retaining that talent as well. Critical for any business is finding top performers that will stay. Social can do that, in fact we have seen businesses become the employer of choice in their market and vertical.

EMPLOYEE ENGAGEMENT AND SHARED SENSE OF PURPOSE

In the post-Covid era, as an employer being able to offer a culture where all generations feel safe is critical. Social media is able to do this, partly because we live our lives in social outside of work, so we want to have the same look and feel to live our lives inside work.

How departments can be transformed by social media and digital

DIGITAL SALES

If you are looking to drive a transformation for digital across the business then sales is an obvious place to start. You can run a pilot to see if it works, as you can easily measure the results. It's interesting to know that, when using our methodology, we've had a number of clients complain to us they have too much pipeline – a great problem to have. But transforming sales is just a random act of social. It will create great benefits for your business, but there are so many more benefits to have than just more pipeline and winning more deals.

DIGITAL HUMAN RESOURCES

There are many ways that digital and social media can transform how a business can work. One of those is attracting and retaining staff. Yes, many businesses are probably using LinkedIn or Twitter to put out job ads. I'm talking about using social media as a strategic platform that will actually remove the effort and cost of that.

We have a client in Canada that has stripped out the cost of recruitment advertising and recruitment consultants, purely by being social, on social. I should point out that they have done this in a market where they couldn't get enough candidates. A brave move, but it paid off.

Choosing your social media platform for recruitment may be different from the platforms you sell and market on. For example, if you see a recruitment post on LinkedIn you may share it, you may like it, but unless you have done work on your network, the people you want to see it probably won't see it. But if you are using Facebook, people act differently; they will take a job detail and physically send it to somebody they think this will help.

Research from Careerarc in 2021 shows that the Covid-19 pandemic will have a massive impact on the movement of staff. Sixty-one per cent of full-time employees want new jobs this year, and the Great Resignation shows that they're taking action and abandoning companies in droves in search of better opportunities. Social human resources could make an impact on your business.

DIGITAL PROCUREMENT

If you talk to people in procurement and supply chain, 'social media' is dismissed, mainly because people don't understand what it means to be 'social'. But also because social media is seen as the domain of sales and the battle lines between 'sales' and 'procurement' have been drawn for tens of years.

If you talk to somebody in procurement and say, 'Let's see if social can help you', most of them will say, 'As soon as I put my head above the parapet I will be inundated with salespeople pitching at me.' How about if we changed all that around? There is already a movement on LinkedIn called #socialprocurement which you can check out with that hashtag. You will also see buyers posting with the hashtag #Iambuying. These buyers are also using keywords in their profiles to attract the sellers they are looking for. These procurement teams are posting on LinkedIn posts and articles about what they want to buy. It is then down to the salespeople to log onto LinkedIn and find these buyers.

In my conversations with the buyers doing this, they tell me that they do get approaches from salespeople who pitch to them out of hope and desperation but this is reducing. Selling to people who won't buy is one of the problems of legacy sales methods such as cold calling and email. With social selling, you get efficiency savings by qualifying out people you cannot sell to. More on that later.

Social pulls the people you want towards you

In a recent conversation I had with a procurement professional they said social procurement is about 'pulling people (the people you want) towards you'. Just think about the lost opportunities there are in procurement. We live in a global marketplace where suppliers are just a click away, and those suppliers may be cheaper and higher quality than your current supplier. I totally get there are the time-wasters, but with a few clicks we can qualify new suppliers in as we can make a few clicks and qualify suppliers out.

By being active on social media, you can get to know suppliers better and they can get to know you better. You can be very specific about your needs and requirements. People have talked about innovation in procurement for 20 years and we are seeing a step change take place, because of social media. Social allows us to move away from our current supplier echo chamber and gives us diversity of thinking. We can engage with and have conversations with suppliers from all over the world. The more you know about the suppliers and the more they know about you, your requirements and culture, the better it is for everybody.

Let's start a movement

If you are reading this and are in procurement or know people in procurement, please pass on the word. Get them to start with a pilot, something low value and low risk, and experiment with buying on social media. This isn't a revolution that starts with the chief purchasing officer, it starts with the category manager.

DIGITAL MARKETING

If you are in marketing, as you read this you will start to sense that marketing is changing. In a digital organization, PR, search engine optimization (SEO), old school advertising, old school email marketing will change.

We all know that change can be scary, but there is no reason to be scared by digital marketing. This is your opportunity as a marketer to be in control of this change and lead the charge. There was a time when marketing was the cool, sexy department, but it's currently seen by some as the 'colouring in' department. Now is the time to take marketing front and centre of the business.

I'm not saying that all the old ways have to be thrown away. The business needs to start with a pilot in sales to give the quick wins. But if you have read the book so far, I hope you understand that many of the areas that you are spending budget on can be switched. Our clients usually go through a process of switching budget. I will go into more detail of this through the book.

I could go on discussing department after department, in fact there is a complete book on this. Instead, let's move onto how you as a business start thinking strategically about social media.

How to create a digital strategy for your organization

My company and our partners work with many organizations to help them creating a digital strategy. This is about getting the board of directors, also referred to as the C-suite due to their usual job titles (chief executive officer, chief finance officer, etc.), to buy into the strategy. It is with their sponsorship that more budget will be made available and the efficiencies can be realized. I talk later on in the book about getting different executives involved in this process.

STRATEGY STRUCTURE

It's important not to try to impose something – you need to run a collaborative workshop where the leadership team is empowered to come up with the strategy they want. It is at such times that I recommend you use external consultants as they can share their expertise and offer support and guidance. At the end of the day this is about all of the leadership team buying into (and executing) a strategy.

WHAT SHOULD A STRATEGY SESSION LOOK LIKE?

Introductory session

To get the board used to the concepts I would suggest a 60-minute introductory session (40 minutes presentation and 20 minutes for questions), where you can walk board members through the link between social media and revenue and profit. Subject areas could include:

- how social media has changed the world, supported by the relevant research
- how social media has changed customers' behaviour
- how the future of their business will be impacted

We recommend that you use stories and case studies of people that are doing this already. It is critical to make the connection between using social and the future profitability of the business. This should be delivered (and recorded) the week before the workshop. At this point, your leadership team may well be cynical about the use of social media for business and it's critical that this is high-level, business related, tells a story and is crammed full of case studies.

Questionnaire

Following the introductory session, send out a questionnaire to get an understanding of the 'as is' position. This should feature no more than 20 questions. The results for that questionnaire can feed into the workshop.

Workshop

The workshop will discuss:

- What is your 'to be' position?
- How crucial is social going to be?
- What are the challenges to implementing? People, process and technology.

- What are the blocks to success?
- What will you call this initiative? The initiative mission statement?
- Pledges.

An example of a mission statement for this project could be:

> A digital organization sees social media as the platform for closing the distance between clients, prospects, remote employees and potential recruits.

Following the workshop, issue a report so that people have a written document of what they agreed.

As to how many people should attend this? There should be a restriction on numbers of people attending. At a minimum it should be the C-suite team, plus their 'number ones' – their trusted advisers, the people they turn to for advice on matters.

Measures of a digital organization

As discussed above, there are five measures of a digital organization:

- visibility and recognition in the marketplace
- achieving trusted advisor status to their clients and prospects
- measurable pipeline, revenue and new logos growth
- access to the best talent and skills and therefore becoming employer of choice in your chosen markets and topic areas
- employee engagement and shared sense of purpose

With digital now a strategy in your organization, your board and leadership team should be able to measure and report on the digital activities of the business. You should also have many leading indicators that provide the business with more data and insight, before you use a CRM database to inform your business if it's on the right course.

Summary

In this section we have gone through the need for a business to take digital seriously, not as a set of tools or systems replacements but to make sure that the board have a digital vision that is executed and measured. Digital gives the business a different operating model, one that is attuned with the market and data, rather than the guesswork of a CRM. Digital and social media has to come out of marketing and be driven by the board for it to have the revenue and EBITDA expectations that the company both wants and deserves.

ADVICE FROM A DIGITAL TRANSFORMATION PRACTITIONER – ADAM GRAY
We are where we are

Humans are social animals. Anyone who has taken even a passing interest in anthropology will have seen pictures of cavemen clustered around a fire sharing food and being, well, social. Since then, the environment has changed, and there are forums, bars, weddings, nightclubs, sporting events and countless other environments where we can share time with each other and share experiences together, but the basic mechanics of being social haven't changed. We meet, we discuss. We debate, we agree/disagree. We laugh. We cry. We share the full gamut of human emotions. We talk about ourselves. We listen to others talk about themselves. We share knowledge. We learn. This is the very essence of being human.

The advent of the world of social media hasn't created a new behaviour; on the contrary, it has simply aggregated existing behaviours into larger and larger groups. At the time of writing this, Facebook is just shy of three billion users (that's nearly 40 per cent of the people on the earth) with many other social sites racking up a billion or more subscribers. This isn't a worrying phenomenon; this is simply people being social. Larger and larger gatherings of people getting to know each other, forging friendships, businesses, clubs, romances. All freed of the constraints of having to go to the same room at the same time and the room only being able to hold 20, 500, 25,000 people. Social media is humanity at scale.

One interesting thing about this is that it permeates so many areas of our lives, whether we acknowledge it or not. Our elderly parents use it to keep in touch with their grandchildren. Our children use it to keep in touch with each other. We use it to decide whether the hotel we are about to book is a safe choice and whether the book we are about to buy is well-written. There is no escaping it... but, outside of 'social interactions' like maintaining friendships and starting romances, does social media really serve a purpose?

Now, at this point you might be thinking to yourself, 'But I'm not really a social media kind of person so I expect my clients aren't either.' That would be a rather dangerous conclusion to draw. It may be the case that you don't use

Facebook or Instagram, it may also be true that you don't read (and believe) Amazon reviews of the things you're going to buy. You probably do, however, watch occasional YouTube or Vimeo video, and you might well read Trustpilot or Trip Advisor reviews. But this isn't about you, this is about *them*. This is about the other 4.88 billion people.

It doesn't matter about someone's political persuasion, whether they're an Obama or a Trump supporter. Both presidential wins were, in part, credited to their understanding and use of social media. With Brexit, whether someone voted to leave or stay, they were influenced by how the debate played out on social media. Whether a person believes Covid will be the end of mankind or is a hoax – once again, social media is helping to shape their opinions. Social media is everywhere and everyone is susceptible to its effects.

According to Simon Kemp (2021b), between July 2020 and July 2021 the number of social media users increased by 520 million, which shows that the migration towards these platforms is not only continuing, it is accelerating. You may be a rarity, an anomaly, you may be totally immune to the effects of social media and you may make all of your decisions on data which is verifiable and peer reviewed. The rest of the population, though, is not so sensible in its decision-making process. They are influenceable by what they see and what they read on these channels and the challenge that we all need to acknowledge is that in a business environment our prospects are making their decisions based (in part) on what they discover when surfing social media. If they aren't able to find us there and jump to the conclusions that we want, they might well end up choosing a competitor. And being bankrupt but right is not a good position for any of us to be in.

For some years now we have known that the buyer is more empowered than they have ever been. The famous CEB (2017) research suggests that the buyer was 57 per cent of the way through the buying journey before the seller even know they existed. In the intervening years it is likely that this will have moved well past 75 per cent by now. Therefore, by the time the seller is aware of the buyer, the decision is all but made. This same research also showed that the trend was an increasing complexity of purchase process, because the number of people involved was increasing. Where once it was one or two, now it's typically more than 10 and can be many times that in some cases. What this means is that each of these people who is being asked to share some of the risk of the decision will do their own independent research on the seller and will share their thoughts and feelings with the wider team.

It means that the seller needs to make sure that not only do they have the technical capability and a suitability of product/service but that they look like the sort of business I would like to work with. Any seller who doesn't think this is important should just consider the importance of the 'social element' of the relationship. A client/prospect I've been out to dinner with is much more likely to 'like' me and therefore will find it more difficult to say 'no' to me when I ask a favour, or for the business.

The great news for every business is that despite the fact that all of this seems pretty obvious, most businesses don't think this way and leave themselves open to attack from their competitors. If I look at the people within your business and they look like nice, interesting, friendly, kind people and I look at the people who work for your competitor and they look dull and boring (or, worse still, invisible) that gives you a huge advantage. It gives you the opportunity to be approachable, helpful, people I would actually *like* to talk to. Now, given that most of the people within your prospect account are not technical experts they will have no idea whether your 'thing' that you do or make is technically better or worse than your competitors so simply having a better product isn't going to be enough when these people are asked for an opinion. For this reason you should be giving them something they can be confident about. 'I don't know if your product is better but you seem like a really good company' is a very compelling purchase driver if everyone seems to be saying it.

And *this* is the battlefield where you should be fighting because most organizations have absolutely no idea about how to be social, how to look attractive, how to open conversations and develop dialogue in a way that genuinely builds trust and relationships with the prospects. So, *this* is the quick win for your business. You look better... you are better.

However, social media is not just a method for developing conversations to sell more. This book could be retitled *Social Influence: Techniques to transform every element of your business* because the techniques discussed are equally relevant whether you are in sales, marketing, HR, procurement, consulting, customer care... any role within a business where you need to have conversations (externally or internally) can be better facilitated by considering the 'social' element to it. The framework is always the same. If you look attractive, credible, interesting and kind people are more likely to listen to you (and believe you) when you speak whether you are saying 'Buy our product', 'Come and join our company', 'Invest in our shares', or 'Become a supplier.' And these conversations are key drivers for success whatever the size of your business.

To not embrace social media, particularly now, is a very dangerous tactic. If social media can influence global elections and belief systems, it can certainly influence the decision to purchase your product/service. The irony is that people already have the skills that they need to be good at this, but what they often don't have is a framework, guidance and empowerment to be able to do this successfully. Because all of this is very natural and, with the right support, comes easily, often organizations say 'We know this, we know what we need to do,' but for some reason they simply don't actually 'do it'. And this is their downfall. There is a window of opportunity to do this, and be good at it, before your competitors start to learn, so grasp that opportunity with both hands.

And if you think you are above this idea of being social as you still view it as a stream of people sharing photos of their lunch, you are very mistaken. To ignore social media is to ignore the very essence of humanity.

THE MARKETER'S VIEWPOINT – CATHERINE COALE

90 per cent of everything B2B marketing creates is dull

Fact-based, features-driven, same-old, same-old marketing and content. Yawn.

Paul Cash, Rooster Punk (2018)

This pretty much summed up our world in 2018. I was leading a marketing team at Telstra Purple whose predominant role in life was to deliver leads to the sales team. For four years we'd been pretty good at it. Month after month we'd generate the leads, and the 'qualifiers' who also worked in my team would warm the leads up until the prospect was ready to meet one of our account managers. Happy days...

There is so much wrong with the last paragraph that it's easy to see now why things went into decline. We were 'behind the screen' marketers. Writing whitepapers, email and advertising them to lists we had purchased. We were watching interactions on Google analytics and processing responses. Yes responses... not people.

Throughout 2018 things went into a steady decline. Even our reliable campaigns started to under-perform. We were having to work five times as hard to achieve the same results. We spread our message over different channels, increased volumes and sends – nothing resonated. People stopped listening.

We'd lost sight of what mattered... the humans

In 2018 I made a decision to change everything we were doing. I wrote my first statement to that effect in our marketing strategy stating that 'We will evolve from a product-led strategy, to an experience-led strategy.' That was the polite version anyway.

We put people at the heart of that strategy and focused on what they needed personally to be successful. We stopped doing any marketing that was transactional or didn't create an experience that mattered or that we could share with them. It was ground-breaking.

We went on to grow four communities centred around the advancement of the people in them, and created the Social Organization, focused on using social media to close gaps between us and our clients.

We learnt a lot about growing peer support communities that people trusted

To give you an illustration of this, our ClubCISO (the CISO being the chief information security officer who was our target contact) community was formed around 2014 but in 2018 we gave members WhatsApp as an experiment. Soon, the members were swapping 1,000+ messages a month, 24 hours a day, 7 days a week. What started out as a community famous for its once-a-year in-person live vote of 50 London-centric CISOs arguably became the biggest pool of real world, peer to peer, vendor free advice available almost 24/7 with ridiculously enviable response times. There was, literally, always someone there to help you out.

So who are the most important voices for brands today?

From the moment we are born, we start to figure out who we like and who we trust. A new-born baby will often complain when picked up by a friend because they don't smell right or feel right. We develop both conscious and unconscious choices about who we trust as we grow up and engage with in adult life; making friends, getting jobs, voting, reading the news, buying products.

What I've found fascinating over the last few years is watching how changes in society and widespread use of the internet have impacted buyers. And when I say buyers, it sounds fancy. I really mean people. People making everyday choices about where they spend their time and money.

Brands today are people. We trust our fellow humans, and so helping our own people to be heard and to listen well, was central to my idea. I believe that social media has fundamentally changed not just how we chat but how we consume information and how that information helps shape our decision-making process. It's become perfectly normal to read a review on Trip Advisor or Amazon from someone we've never met and let that advice shape our decision. Or to read a review on Glassdoor and perhaps trust this information more than the brand messages on our potential employer's website.

The Social Organization initiative was one of the most progressive pieces of work I'd ever led

In April 2020 I launched an extraordinary programme at Telstra Purple to deeply explore social media as a place for closing distance between our clients, our remote employees and our future recruits.

FIGURE 0.6   Using social media to close the distance

> A social organisation sees social media as a place for closing the distance between clients, remote employees, and potential future recruits.
>
> Catherine Coale
> Telstra Purple

Let me be clear, this was *Not* employee advocacy. We took a more maverick approach. Participants had total autonomy over what they wrote. There was no formal approval process for content – just their own team's support to review their blogs *if* they wanted it. We actively encouraged everyone to write original content in their own voice. We had no appetite to create an army of corporate voices who'd been through PR training.

Dan Pink is well known for evangelising the science proving autonomy, mastery and purpose as the three drivers for modern day motivation (RSA, 2010). This was where we were setting the bar, and Telstra Purple were generous in their programme to provide professional training and coaching support to employees who were interested in becoming more visible on social media through blogging. We worked with them to develop their writing skills, to trust their own personal style and find like-minded people in their network to spark their creativity.

FIGURE 0.7   Modern-day motivational drivers

Dan Pink

3 factors that lead to better performance and personal satisfaction

- Autonomy
- Mastery
- Purpose

How did we decide whose voice is most important when building trust for our brand? We were fortunate to have access to some brilliant research from the Edelman Trust (2020). They publish a Trust Barometer, which asks 'If you heard information about a company from each person, how credible would that information be?' This barometer lists the most trusted sources by rank.

FIGURE 0.8   Edelman Trust Barometer, 2019 and 2019

Edelman Trust Barometer – 2019

Percentage who rate each source as very and extremely credible

| 65% | 53% | 47% | 44% |
| Company technical expert | Regular employee | CEO | Board of directors |

Company voices

Edelman Trust Barometer – 2020

Percentage who rate each source as very and extremely credible

| 68% | 54% | 47% | 44% |
| Company technical expert | Regular employee | CEO | Board of directors |

Company voices

Who mattered most?

Company technical experts ranked top in both 2019 and 2020. In 2019, regular employees were the highest climbers in the Trust chart. In both 2019 and 2020, both roles were more trusted than the CEO or the board. The message was loud and clear – activate your employee voices if you want people to trust your brand. When you book a holiday, you check out your destination on Trip Advisor. When you buy something on Amazon, you'll steer clear of the products with poor reviews. And when your mate suggests something good to watch on TV, you know where I'm going with this. We trust the voice of our peers – often more than the voice of the brands we're buying from. So ask yourself – do they matter more to your B2B brand now?

The way you activate employee voices really matters

Our programme focused heavily on LinkedIn. I conducted my own study of 10 people, writing 288 articles and posts over five months, and published the results in an article titled 'LinkedIn is more social than ever and here's the staggering proof' (2021). We discovered that when people connect with an individual from a company on a platform like LinkedIn it's the person they want to hear about, not the business (sorry).

Be original if you want to strike up a good conversation

FIGURE 0.9   Sharing others' thinking vs sharing own thinking

Examples

When a lot of people start writing on LinkedIn for the first time, they often begin by sharing other people's articles. But as our team started to write more regularly, they noticed a pattern so we explored this in our study to see what the data showed us. People who wrote their own original thoughts, rather than sharing company content or third party content, got twice as many likes and almost four times as many comments.

What this told us is that we should be confident in who we are and what we have to say. It is *our* original thinking that people connect with and start conversations around more than anything else… more than the latest HBR report, Gartner statistic or your company's latest bulletin.

That doesn't belong on here, it belongs on Facebook

When we sat around the table at the beginning, talking about what we'd really like to achieve in then Social Organization, visibility was up high on the list. We wanted people to know what we did. One of the things I kept hearing was that LinkedIn was a business networking platform and whilst we came ready to share business content what we discovered was a revelation. Human stories about ourselves were magnitudes more popular than stories about our work. And it didn't matter who was doing the writing… people in sales roles, marketing or technical experts – the outcome was always the same.

Traditional B2B marketing was broken

Forget product-centric messages. Forget gated content on social platforms. Stop broadcasting branded messages in the hope that some of it will stick. The data from our pilot told us that hardly anyone was listening anymore.

Field salespeople must build up their digital presence

This was an interesting one. If we listened to Edelman then we knew that the salesperson's voice couldn't be the solo arrowhead of our businesses anymore. Edelman were telling us that the company technical expert was a vital role in building trust for our brand. And that we needed more 'regular employees' voices to be heard.

Increasing consumerization of B2B buying

We were also very tuned to Gartner predictions that the sales role was about to go through one of the most fundamental shifts of the last few decades. Gartner talk about changing buyer preferences. In a Gartner webinar (2021), they tell us that B2B buyers prefer to engage through digital and self-service channels. This was fact, not opinion. They cite an increasing consumerization of B2B buying, with a third of buyers being fine not meeting with a salesperson at all throughout the sales process. And if you look at millennials, that's even higher – almost 50 per cent don't need to meet with a sales rep anymore. They want to do things online. Maria Boulden, VP of Sales at Gartner,

FIGURE 0.10   Human stories are more popular

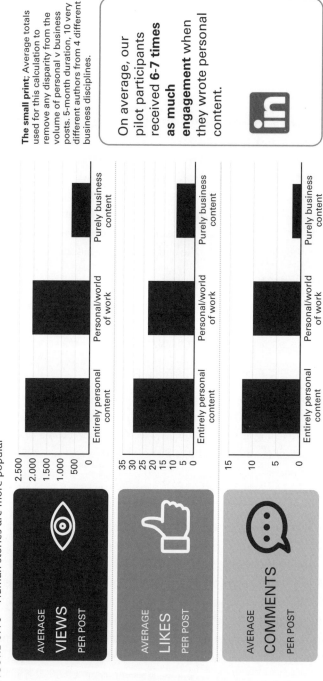

AVERAGE
VIEWS
PER POST

AVERAGE
LIKES
PER POST

AVERAGE
COMMENTS
PER POST

VIEWS chart:
2,500
2,000
1,500
1,000
500
0

Entirely personal content | Personal/world of work | Purely business content

LIKES chart:
35
30
25
20
15
10
5
0

Entirely personal content | Personal/world of work | Purely business content

COMMENTS chart:
15
10
5
0

Entirely personal content | Personal/world of work | Purely business content

The small print: Average totals used for this calculation to remove any disparity from the volume of personal v business posts. 5-month duration, 10 very different authors from 4 different business disciplines.

On average, our pilot participants received **6-7 times as much engagement** when they wrote personal content.

believed the best thing that organizations can do is help people to evolve – to support the people who are willing to make the shift.

The Social Organization programme offered a new way of doing things, including using LinkedIn to build direct connections deeper within every account they wanted to be talking to, both in the client organization and across our own. We'd never been able to create such interconnectivity before. We were talking 20, 50, 100 contacts in some client organizations. And this unrivalled connectivity gave us new ways to understand their business and how we could really serve them. Forget measuring supposed clicks and views to assess intent to buy, we were having conversations with real people about real needs. New business salespeople said they'd never felt more in control of their pipeline and account managers called it the 'drumbeat of large account selling'. We'd found a new way of doing things.

And did we deliver tangible results?

So often you read things like this, and the talk remains theoretical. You want to know the hard truth, don't you? Did it work?

It was astounding. Let's start with the impact on marketing. Our tiny pilot team racked up 470,000 impressions of Telstra Purple content, and 8,060 interactions in five months. Every single one of those interactions was attributable and actionable.

Our existing community of security professionals experienced a 295 per cent increase in membership enquiries in 12 months. Its showcase annual event sold out in 24 hours. The year before we'd worked for weeks, messaging on multiple channels, and struggled to fill it.

FIGURE 0.11   Results of the pilot

The last year at **ClubCISO** has been phenomenal, with a huge rise in membership numbers and engagement. A three-fold increase in membership applications! It is humbling to see this group grow not just in terms of numbers but also in terms of how much support the CISOs offer one another, how much they share their insights and experiences.

Thank you to my fellow board members and to **Catherine Coale** and her team for the incredible work they do.

We created a brand-new boutique community called Data Journeys. We hired a fabulous community manager who embodied the values of the Social Organization and within the first 12 months over 330 people had interacted with the community's content, 79 came along to the meet-up events in person, 40 per cent came along twice or more. We had zero reputation or network in this space when we began. And there was no advertising, direct mail or email strategy for building this community. Almost everything was created in the beginning by connecting, blogging, sharing and then building on this attention, goodwill and reciprocity.

Now let's talk about sales

This was a ridiculously fast way to be connected on a personal level with targeted audiences. It offered an almost instant way for people and organizations to get to know us, like us and trust us. What's more, every interaction was attributable and actionable and when done well, started from a place of goodwill. Our small pilot team went from zero to 115 new business calls and meetings within 10 months, with a conversion rate to opportunity of 25 per cent. This outstripped all other means of securing new business meetings.

And the technical team? Well, they accidentally sold a small piece of consultancy work from one of their early blog posts written during the initial training phase. It was never the intention for them to directly sell but a client read the article and asked if we could do the same for them.

During the Agile Retrospective sessions, they cited the opportunity to be more visible as an organization to the UK tech circle as personally important to them. And they said, 'The programme reset my understanding of LinkedIn and how to use it. We learnt a lot about our team-mates through their blogging, and now understand that this must be the same for our wider colleagues and clients as we become more visible.'

We were definitely ahead of our time and of course there were challenges

People have mixed and strong views about 'social'. Hear them. Some people saw the words 'Social Organization' and it stirred up some polarizing views around Facebook and privacy etc. that they brought into the training with them. This got some sessions off on the wrong foot and we had to take some lessons from that.

There have been times I've reflected since and wondered whether we would have been better branding the programme the 'Digital Organization'. After all, what we were asking people to do is exactly what they'd do at a conference, on client site or at a client hospitality event – but instead we were asking them to bring that same warmth and relationship building online. The platform was almost irrelevant. It was about becoming a digital organization and being able to translate our company's experience in the digital world.

Be cognisant of people's starting points

If your sales team has been used to receiving gift-wrapped new business appointments from the marketing team then they may need more understanding of why they suddenly need to start doing some of this work themselves. But if they're cold calling from lists then they'll likely bite your arm off for a chance to do things differently. Take time to really understand your starting point. Don't pretend this is marketing. It's a transformation programme.

It's also important to note that this is not a marketing initiative that someone can fit in around their day job. It changes people's roles and the skills they need. It moves workloads around the business and challenges traditional hierarchies. If you try to ignore this, you will fail.

10 of my personal observations from running our Social Organization programme

1   If you're doing structured employee advocacy today, consider reviewing your scope. Edicts to share company content without putting your people in the narrative are just another form of broadcast marketing. They are not well received on social platforms. Attempting to create a single brand voice is also a mistake.

2   LinkedIn is a very social platform, just like all the others. The way we use social media in our private world has significantly impacted our behaviour at work. Original and personal content is preferred.

3   You wouldn't walk into a face-to-face event, shake hands with someone new, then launch into your pitch – so don't do it on LinkedIn. It's a definite no-no. (And let's face it, some people are doing it before they've even shaken hands.)

4   Networking on LinkedIn is much more democratic than the events network, where typically only the most senior decision makers are wined and dined. We all know there are many more influencing voices in a buying process now and engaging digitally allows a much more balanced range of voices to be heard.

5   The thing people find hardest when they start blogging is sharing something about themselves in their stories so that people could get to know them

like they would do over a coffee or a beer. Yet we also discovered that human stories about ourselves were magnitudes more popular than stories about our work.

6   This is the fastest way to get a conversation going with someone new. It's insane. As a marketer by original trade, I have been hired many times over to help organizations find ways to start conversations with new people. This is by far the fastest way to connect with new people and get to know them. It's also one of the nicest ways. if you do it well.

7   You can solve your perceived collateral gap with employee advocates. In my experience, salespeople often like brochures. That magic piece of collateral is perceived to be the missing link in the sales process. At the start of our programme, senior account managers told me that our business had a collateral gap that was holding them back. Three months later this problem had vanished. The articles and posts that our employees were writing had more than filled this hole.

8   Being entirely genuine will attract the right people. We encouraged the people we coached to be themselves. In the B2B technology world, sometimes your only differentiator is *you*. People that like you are more likely to buy from you. So be yourself and you will naturally build a network of people that connect well with you.

9   Our industry has a ton of marketing automation and often still no decent leads. Everyone wants to buy tools. We live in a subscription society. We have tools that can give us so much insight and intelligence about who's clicked what and when, but how real is this data? Our people would pick up the phone to follow up and the recipient of the call wouldn't know what we were talking about, or they'd get halted by the gate keeper. For the first time in a long time, we were face to face (online and in person) having conversations with real people (no gatekeeper) who worked in companies we could help and they were open and welcoming. It was a great feeling.

10   Intellectual acceptance of a concept is not enough to create lasting change. I should not get excited because people say they're going to do something. I should get excited when they consistently take action.

Change is always hard but, as Maria Boulden of Gartner says, if you have a willingness to build the skills then this is an opportunity to define a new mode of operation. Some people go their whole careers never getting to do anything like this.

Social selling

The idea of social selling always sounds appealing. All you have to do to sell on social media is log in, find opportunities and close deals. Easy, right? The problem is that social selling isn't selling on social. Well not in the traditional sense. The mistake people make is that they take what they have been doing for the last 30 years and apply it to social media. Sorry, but it won't work. I guess that is why you are here.

Moreover, the question 'Why should you do social selling?' seems like it has an obvious answer. In reality though, the standard answer of 'It's a new, good way to find leads' is misleading. As we shall go on to explain, the reality is that social selling has become the only way that B2B selling can be done at all. In fact, social selling is now selling.

What is social selling?

Think about this: what if I suggested that I pick you up tomorrow and drive you to a place where all your prospective clients and customers hang out? Would you be interested? Of course, you would. All you have to do is walk up to the people and have conversations. You can stay as long as you want, and the longer you stay, the more conversations you have.

Now think about what it means to be social in that environment. You walk up to a person and ask them questions such as 'How are you?', 'Did you travel far?', 'So what brings you here?' It would be the start of a conversation. At some point one of you would say, 'So what do you do?' At no point would you walk up to somebody you didn't know and pitch. It would be seen as rude. People would call security and you would be thrown out and certainly not invited again.

That's the difference – social media requires you to be social, and traditional sales and marketing require you to interrupt and pitch.

Traditional interrupt selling or marketing

Sales has traditionally worked by having the salesperson 'interrupt' a C-suite executive – those people with the most important positions in a company. In this book, when we talk about selling or marketing at the highest level in an organization, we use the term 'C-level'.

The salesperson would traditionally have to fight through the gatekeeper (personal assistant, secretary or voice mail) to eventually have a conversation with a C-level executive. From there the salesperson would pitch, sorry, sell an idea into the business. In order for the deal to work, that idea would promise to solve some problem that was causing pain to the business. The idea would then be nurtured into strategy, and from there into implementation. Sales was a partnership, that partnership being formed at the top level of the organization.

The problem with the classical sales approach is that the salesperson naturally brings bias into the organization. Although salespeople selling complex solutions will act in a way that's like a consultant, their agenda is to sell what they want to sell – perhaps more properly put as 'in a position to sell' – and that solution might not be exactly what the business needs.

This has been a historic fault in how businesses buy throughout the whole history of commerce – this method of allowing the C-level exec to be 'sold at' by an external agent will always bring in bias. Businesses accepted this bias and attendant inefficiency because it used to be too difficult to approach the problem in a different way. Having the C-level exec constantly interrupted by salespeople was a good enough way for the business to get its needs met.

However, businesses, like all complex organisms, will tend to find more optimal solutions to problems, and so now businesses are actively evolving to change the way they run the buying process so that this external bias is removed. Businesses are now finding they achieve better results by asking employees to use social networks to research solutions to problems in a way that removes bias. By going out into the social networks and using the 'hive mind', 'network effect', 'connected economy', and so on, businesses can design solutions for themselves that are as good as those designed by external salespeople, but don't have the problem of bias. The upshot of this is that the salesperson is being squeezed out of the buying process – or rather being pushed further down the process until such time as they have to be included. That's clearly not ideal for the salesperson, although it does produce better results for the business.

In the last 10 years there has been a perfect storm of change in sales and marketing – the internet, mobile, social media, the Covid-19 Pandemic all have been contributing factors to the way we buy. If the way people buy has changed, then surely the way we sell has to change? This book explains the basics of being social, as being social and having conversations are the key to new ways of selling and to your business being successful today.

Social selling is a different way of buying

Social selling is a reaction to this change in buyer behaviour. It proposes a way of getting the salesperson back into the buying process so that they can once again control and influence the buying decisions of the business. This is a very important fact to appreciate. Social selling isn't an opportunity that has come about because social media creates a different way to sell. Social selling is a *reaction* that has come about because social media creates *a different way to buy.*

It is worth talking at this point about the names of different types of selling. I see social selling, digital selling, remote selling, virtual selling and modern selling as, basically, the same thing. I read a book recently that tried to cling on to the old ways by saying that virtual selling is cold calling, emailing, etc., but done virtually. Sorry, this just isn't the case.

Social selling is by definition:

> using your presence and behaviour on social media to build influence, make connections, grow relationships and trust, which leads to conversation and commercial interaction.

Traditional selling has stopped being effective

What sales organizations have started to feel as this change in buyer behaviour takes hold is that traditional methods of selling have stopped being as effective as they once were. A common symptom is that C-level execs are much harder to reach on the phone than before. This is not a result of society (and hence C-level execs) becoming ruder, it's because the C-level execs would rather listen to information coming up through their business from social networks as opposed to information coming in sideways from salespeople, because ultimately they get a better, less biased/more efficient, result.

Today, the mechanism by which this process works is straightforward. C-level execs generally don't engage on social networks, because typically they are in their mid-40s (at least) and mostly don't 'get the point' of social networks. We often hear C-level executives say that social media is for kids or for posting photos of your lunch. They don't see how it can also make a transformational impact on their business. This book aims to break the 'glass ceiling' of this traditional notion that salespeople are wasting time on social media. In fact, we will explain how social media is a revenue-generation engine for your business. A digital organization should be able to connect every keystroke of a salesperson to revenue. This book is also about showing you how you and your business can use social selling to transform your business to drive revenue through social media.

Changemakers

Nowadays, the C-level executive is likely to turn to people in their organization who do get the point of social networks and task them with using their social networking skills and experience to 'ideate' solutions to the business's complex problems. Even if there is no formal top-down decision to use this tactic, a certain type of person lower down in the organization is increasingly taking the initiative to ideate in this way. We call these individuals lower down in the organization 'changemakers', and they are so important to social selling that we have developed the 'Changemaker Method' as a way of framing our social selling methodology. This methodology describes the path a business must take to transform from one where the market is engaged through classic sales techniques, to one where the market is engaged through social sales techniques. The Microsoft Azure sales team actively look for changemakers, as they will be the best people to have conversations with and build relationships with, but they will also take Microsoft's influence and content and share that with prospect accounts.

WHERE DO CHANGEMAKERS COME FROM?

It is likely that you were a changemaker before you reached the senior position you hold in your own business. A changemaker will either find or be given a problem to fix. For example, they might be asked, 'Can you find out why our phone system keeps cutting people off mid-call?' You, as a salesperson of (in this example) hosted telephony systems need to find this person and get them to buy your product in order to fix this problem. Let's look at the process the changemaker uses to solve this problem. Again, we want to look at buyer behaviour, not the behaviour of the salesperson.

CHANGEMAKERS IN ACTION

Today we have a situation where changemakers have left an education system that was – mostly accidentally – designed along the principles of a connected economy. Throughout their schooling, people who are today in their 20s and 30s learnt to create ad hoc teams, to connect with people through social media as well as face-to-face, to bring out the best in themselves and manage out weak spots in teams. They've learnt, essentially, that to do something good, they need to work with groups of people that don't necessarily have affiliations to the classical reporting structure. This is hugely different to how C-level execs in their 40s and older learnt how to operate within business.

IDEATION

Today's changemaker solves the problem of 'customer calls keep getting cut off' by going out to their social network and asking, 'Hey, has anyone got any idea what I should do about the phone system at work? It keeps cutting people off!' From there, the network effect kicks in – the information about how to fix the customer's problem comes from within the network. This process is called 'ideation'. It is how the vision of a solution to a problem gets developed.

Online, networks have become part of everyday living. Why? Networks and their scale allow us to get answers quicker. A friend of mine asked a question on Facebook as to what was the best car to buy. She shared a shortlist of three and asked where should she buy it from? She ended up buying it online, not from her local dealer. A friend of mine uses a type of foundation as it was recommended on Mumsnet, a network for parents.

The changemaker takes their vision of the solution to the C-level execs for approval. The C-level execs approve the strategy, and provide funds to back it up. The changemaker then needs to implement, which is very easy for them because they can just outsource it to an expert in implementation. Again, that implementation expert will often be selected by asking for referrals on the social network. And that's the scary part for traditional salespeople, because they are almost totally uninvolved in that buying process. They certainly do not get to have a major influence within it. If they're very lucky, they'll work for the selected vendor and get to take the order.

This book will change this. I want you as a salesperson to be able to take change of this digital buying process, so that you will become the obvious and best choice to the buyer.

CHANGEMAKER PERSONA

So, what is the persona of a changemaker? What is it that makes them tick? How do you spot one?

Changemakers will have authority. They may not have it by position, for example by being a vice president (VP), but they do have it, as VPs often turn to them when a decision is needed. We discuss later in the book the need for influence in the digital economy, which is the way that changemakers have authority online. It could be argued that changemakers are, in the digital world, the new decision makers. Most C-suite executives don't understand the connected economy, but have probably read an article somewhere that says they need to do something about it. They therefore turn to their trusted changemakers for guidance.

Research for Google found that the C-suite have final authority on 64 per cent of decisions. But non C-suite can influence 81 per cent of purchase decisions (Tuomisto-Inch, 2014). How can that be? It may be that the C-suite have signed off an overall project budget, but the components of that project are passed/delegated down the organization to 'people in the know'. For example, there might be an overall customer experience transformation project, but the individual software components that make that up are purchased lower down the organization. In addition, in the new world of software as a service (SaaS)/cloud, software can be switched off as quickly as it's switched on, and there can be very short implementation timeframes, so there may not be a need for traditional IT involvement. Based on Google's same research, of the 'people in the know', 48 per cent of them are 18–34 years old and 24 per cent are 35–44. This is placing B2B enterprise decisions in the hands of 'changemakers'.

It is worth saying that, while decision making is taking place lower down in the organization, project sign-off is still taking place at a high level. This means that the modern salesperson needs to build relationships and have conversations across the enterprise. One of our clients, a supply chain software company, say there are 100 stakeholders/decision makers in any of their sales. The job of the salesperson is to have built relationships with these people and had conversations, so that when the committee meeting is called for the buying decision, the vote is for your solution.

WHERE ARE CHANGEMAKERS GOING?

Essentially, tomorrow's C-level execs have emerged from education and gone into commercial life having a very good understanding of how to use a network to ideate solutions to complex problems. Importantly, this ideation happens without bias, and, as we said before, bias is a block to efficiency. Now we're in a situation where the C-level exec doesn't have to be interrupted by salespeople anymore, because he can just pass problems down to changemakers who very keenly go out and find a solution to the business's problem on social media.

Social selling is all about getting the salesperson back into that process. The theory of 'how' this is done is extremely easy. The changemaker is using their social network to ideate and design the solution, and they do this by creating an ad hoc team of advisors that 'spitball' the problem and come up with an answer. All the salesperson has to do is get themselves invited into that ad hoc team created by the changemaker. Or they need to have the influence and social media skills that enable them join changemaker conversations. In turn, all that involves is getting the salesperson to a point where they can be discovered and listened to.

In this book we discuss the need for community. Community is often talked about in the realms of some sort of hippy idealism. But community can be used in driving leads and revenue, and killing the competition. Sorry if you are looking for a fluffy view of the world, but this is a book about how salespeople can use social to crush their numbers. Hack the buying process.

Becoming a digital organization is going to take change – if you are a changemaker then get in touch using the hashtag #changemakers and let us know what you are doing.

Buckle up

This book has some pretty radical ideas and methods, but sales organizations have been the same for the last 50 years. They no longer meet the needs of a modern digital organization. We provide a method that organizations can implement so rather than being an analogue organization that carries out random acts of social, an organization disrupts itself so that it meets the needs of a team of social sellers. This journey won't be easy and we have a number of new concepts to grapple with, so buckle up for the ride.

Hacking the buying process

This book has been designed to be a manual. It outlines the changes that have taken place in society due to the connected economy and provides practical help to salespeople, sales leaders and marketers on how this connected economy works. It explains the changes organizations now need to embrace if they are to stay relevant. With buyers spending more and more time in salespeople avoidance mode, what can you do to leverage this exciting new buying process to your advantage?

This isn't new, it's tried and tested

Some people see social selling as new and think that it's somehow not been tried and tested. I did my first social selling roll-out in 2014, which became the backbone of the first edition of this book. I then set up DLA Ignite, where the global team have implemented social selling in thousands of companies in different countries with different society structures and across different business verticals. While this book focuses on B2B, we have done work in B2C too. In many places you will find that B2C is very similar to B2B, especially when it's a considered purchase, like a car or a carpet.

THE CEO'S VIEW OF THE DIGITAL ORGANIZATION –
CHRIS FLEMMING
The Cyberhawk journey

In 2020 we decided to adapt our marketing strategy because it was no longer possible to visit our customers in their offices or at conferences due to Covid-19. I still believe that nothing is better than face-to-face meetings, but given we are in the middle of a global pandemic there probably isn't a less risky time since the dawn of the internet to give social selling a try, and for us, it has worked. It has also been fun, and that's important to me and our employees. Why can't we have fun at work and enjoy it?

I had been a LinkedIn advocate prior to fully engaging, using it frequently but not routinely. We decided to employ a firm of outside consultants as we felt that the knowledge needed to come externally. The firm we employed gave us an easy-to-follow plan that allowed us to maximize our efforts and interactions over the ensuing months, which has led to conversations with prospects that have led to quotes that have led to jobs that have led to increased revenue and a shorter sales cycle and less stress for me and the business. Stress is caused when we are unable to predict the future. Getting more leads into the hopper sooner means more visibility and thus a greater ability to predict the sales pipeline, and thus fewer butterflies for me.

My take on social selling is the ability to tell the story of what you do through the human lens. The more your stories or posts talk about the human behind the machine and less about the product, the more likely customers are to connect with you on a human level. The quicker potential buyers connect with the real you, the less time you have to spend building rapport or proving you are trustworthy, and the quicker you can help them by providing your service or solution. It's a bit like having a warm introduction from a friend who can vouch for you. You can skip half of the spaces on the snakes and ladders board game and start halfway around the board.

By the way, you can't just say 'I'm trustworthy'; you have to show up regularly in their life or news feed and present the real you and let them decide. It's a bit like seeing your friendly next-door neighbour who happens to be an estate agent. You never talk about houses when you meet on the street but if he consistently shows up in your life, is interesting, stops to say 'Hi' and seems to know what he or she is doing, why wouldn't you give him the first opportunity to sell your house? You are just being given the opportunity to enter the room by building a credible online presence.

To be successful at most things requires consistency. I wish we didn't have to do things regularly but, just like exercise, if you really want to see results you have to be consistent and form a habit. I post six days a week on LinkedIn, and it's the first thing I do in the morning before brushing my teeth. Sometimes I do it the night before, but if I don't do it I feel like something is missing as my brain has now formed a habit and wants me to continue. When someone in my network requires the services we offer, I'm going to be the first person they think of. They won't have to rack their brains to remember – they know that I will be walking past their window six days a week and all they have to do is give me a wave.

Since embarking on our social selling programme at Cyberhawk, we have had a couple of viral posts in the hundreds of thousands of views. We can't seem to work out why one receives more engagement than others but, statistically, one ingredient produces dividends every time – making a post personal. Have the confidence to make a personal post that shows you being normal, having fun with your kids or dogs, or celebrating somebody else. This is where the real juice comes from. It is best saved for the weekends when technically the LinkedIn Police who like to scream 'This isn't Facebook' will cut you some slack.

The work dynamic has undergone rapid change over the last 18 months, making people reassess their jobs and their futures. People are quitting companies in their droves. As we have doubled the size of our business in the last twelve months, we have hired an additional 60–70 people to grow the business. One of the ways we have attracted talent is by having a bigger social media presence than any of our competitors. People will do their research, and if you have a dozen people from within the organization posting relevant positive content it will have an impact. It can't come from the official corporate account because nobody would believe it. The words need to come from the individuals themselves. Part of the solution is to empower everybody to speak and encourage them to post. It's very rare that we have had to ask someone to take something down, but of course it has happened!

If you are running a business in 2022, you are actually running two companies. One is the obvious one, that's the one on your business card, but the other one you are running is your own little social media company. If you are not aware of this, you will slide further and further behind in the digital maze.

CEOs need to get comfortable with telling their story and getting in front of the camera so to speak. My kids can bang out engaging content on TikTok in a matter of minutes and they are the buyers of the future. You don't need to be creative, but you do need to be authentic and willing to stand up and lead personally. Look at Elon Musk and what percentage of his order book is filled compared to other car manufactures. Sure, he has a great product, but he shows up authentically, is trustworthy, and people buy into that.

So, be you, show up regularly, and try not to brag. If you want to demonstrate how fantastic you or your company are, recognize the team and their achievements.

References

AdWeek (2018) When Procter & Gamble cut $200 million in digital ad spend, it increased its reach 10 per cent. www.adweek.com/brand-marketing/when-procter-gamble-cut-200-million-in-digital-ad-spend-its-marketing-became-10-more-effective (archived at https://perma.cc/9D89-QHK3)

Capgemini Consulting (2017) *When Digital Disruption Strikes: How can incumbents respond?* www.capgemini.com/consulting/wp-content/uploads/sites/30/2017/07/digital_disruption_1.pdf (archived at https://perma.cc/8URM-FUWL)

Careerarc (2021) *2021 Future of Recruiting Study.* https://explore.careerarc.com/future-of-recruiting (archived at https://perma.cc/DFB3-EQPJ)

Cash, P (2018) B2B marketing is screwed. www.linkedin.com/pulse/b2b-marketing-screwed-paul-cash-/ (archived at https://perma.cc/NXT8-56JH)

CEB (2017) *All Roads Lead to Digital: The new B2B buying journey.* www.cebglobal.com/content/dam/cebglobal/us/EN/best-practices-decision-support/marketing-communications/pdfs/mlc-infographic-b2b-digital-journey.pdf (archived at https://perma.cc/3DKH-9UR4)

Coale, C (2021) LinkedIn is more social than ever and here's the staggering proof. www.linkedin.com/pulse/linkedin-more-social-than-ever-heres-proof-catherine-coale (archived at https://perma.cc/9EEW-M3GM)

DataReportal (2021b) Top 10 digital trends in July 2021, YouTube. https://youtu.be/YfnNSwYHGtA (archived at https://perma.cc/4YUZ-B56Q)

DigiDay (2017) The global state of consumer trust in advertising in 5 charts. https://digiday.com/media/global-state-consumer-trust-advertising-5-charts/ (archived at https://perma.cc/J6J6-UNUJ)

DigiDay (2018) Adidas tests new media strategy with World Cup campaign. https://digiday.com/media/adidas-tests-new-media-strategy-world-cup-campaign (archived at https://perma.cc/6K5N-JPT9)

DMA (2019) *Marketer Email Tracker 2019.* https://dma.org.uk/uploads/misc/marketers-email-tracker-2019.pdf (archived at https://perma.cc/2J46-TF36)

Edelman (2020) 2022 Edelman Trust Barometer. www.edelman.com/trust/2020-trust-barometer (archived at https://perma.cc/CV9D-NGZC)

eMarketer (2021) What most affects US social media users' decision to engage with ads or sponsored content on social media platforms? https://www.insiderintelligence.com/chart/250084/what-most-affects-us-social-media-users-decision-engage-with-ads-sponsored-content-on-social-media-platforms-of-respondents-june-2021 (archived at https://perma.cc/YPC9-EWFA)

Forbes (2021) When big brands stopped spending on digital ads, nothing happened. Why? www.forbes.com/sites/augustinefou/2021/01/02/when-big-brands-stopped-spending-on-digital-ads-nothing-happened-why (archived at https://perma.cc/EYN7-U8LL)

Fou, A (2021) Ads are counted at 'greater than zero pixels and greater than zero seconds'. Forbes. www.forbes.com/sites/augustinefou/2021/02/22/the-devil-is-the-details-of-ad-measurement/?sh=5b07f3702343 (archived at https://perma.cc/7NKN-LSE2)

Gartner (2021) Panel discussion: 2021 post pandemic scenario planning for sales leaders. www.gartner.com/en/webinars/3995469/panel-discussion-2021-postpandemic-scenario-planning-for-sales-l (archived at https://perma.cc/5XZ2-XQU7)

Gartner (2022) New B2B buying journey and its implication for sales. www.gartner.co.uk/en/sales/insights/b2b-buying-journey (archived at https://perma.cc/LJ2L-NP4S)

Hootsuite (2022) The global state of digital 2022. www.hootsuite.com/resources/digital-trends (archived at https://perma.cc/BG5V-L3QH)

HubSpot (2020) Data trends and insights from an unprecedented year. https://offers.hubspot.com/adapt-2020-retrospective (archived at https://perma.cc/72QL-B8U2)

Kemp, S (2021a) Future trends 2022: The evolution of search, Datareportal. https://datareportal.com/reports/future-trends-2022-evolving-search-behaviours (archived at https://perma.cc/568L-ETKN)

Kemp, S (2021b) Digital 2021: October global statshot report, Datareportal. https://datareportal.com/reports/digital-2021-october-global-statshot (archived at https://perma.cc/AZ4K-EUGQ)

McKinsey (2012) https://www.mckinsey.com/industries/technology-media-and-telecommunications/our-insights/the-social-economy (archived at https://perma.cc/SW78-4L27)

McKinsey (2012) The social economy. www.mckinsey.com/industries/technology-media-and-telecommunications/our-insights/the-social-economy (archived at https://perma.cc/SW78-4L27)

New York Times (2017) Chase had ads on 400,000 sites. Then on just 5,000. Same results. www.nytimes.com/2017/03/29/business/chase-ads-youtube-fake-news-offensive-videos.html (archived at https://perma.cc/6KJR-J76R)

Nielsen (2015) *Global Trust in Advertising*. www.nielsen.com/wp-content/uploads/sites/3/2019/04/global-trust-in-advertising-report-sept-2015-1.pdf (archived at https://perma.cc/8CWW-8GE8)

RSA (2010) RSA Animate: Drive: The surprising truth about what motivates us, YouTube. www.youtube.com/watch?v=u6XAPnuFjJc (archived at https://perma.cc/3U4J-JU7A)

The Drum (2020) Email marketing isn't working what's a B2B marketer to do? www.thedrum.com/opinion/2020/09/30/email-marketing-isn-t-working-what-s-b2b-marketer-do (archived at https://perma.cc/K9SZ-CRKF)

TNW (2020) Researchers analyzed 10,000 websites – and yes, they all look the same. https://thenextweb.com/news/researchers-analyzed-10000-websites-and-yes-they-all-look-the-same (archived at https://perma.cc/Y8PR-Z2JR)

Tuomisto-Inch, H (2014) Digital tipping points for 2015. https://fdocuments.net/document/digital-tipping-points-for-2015.html?page=1 (archived at https://perma.cc/JT9A-3U2Y)

UKTN (2020) Fraudulent players are costing app marketeers billions. www.uktech.news/news/fraudulent-players-are-costing-app-marketeers-billions-20200209 (archived at https://perma.cc/9XEJ-A7TA)

Waterman, RH and Peters, T (2004) *In Search of Excellence*. Collins

WSJ (2021) Bank of America's Merrill Lynch to ban trainee brokers from making cold calls. www.wsj.com/articles/bank-of-americas-merrill-lynch-to-ban-trainee-brokers-from-making-cold-calls-11621850400 (archived at https://perma.cc/DUL2-ZJ9V)

01

Community and tribalism

Before we jump in and talk about social media and how it can be used to help you create leads, revenue and gain competitive advantage, let's go back in time and discuss community.

Way back in time (it was recorded in 1086 in the Doomsday Book) humans formed into groups and tribes. The objective was survival, living on hunting, fishing and farming. When a crop failed, people realized it was better to work together as a team than as individuals. As time went on, people were required to work in jobs that were not related to hunting and gathering, for example smelting metal for weapons or for horseshoes, made by a blacksmith and fitted to the horse by a farrier.

Even before the introduction of money, people would have bartered their wares. The ploughman wanted shoes for his horses and the farrier wanted food for his family. The society was based on a common purpose. In a village community, everybody knew their role and worked for the common good. Society expected you to support each other for the survival of the tribe.

In the Nordic countries there is the Law of Jante. The Nordic counties can be pretty harsh places, and people found that if you did things for yourself, if you stood out, if you didn't work for the common good, in such a harsh place nature would hit back. The ten Laws of Jante were defined the ten rules of Jante Law by the Danish-Norwegian author Aksel Sandemose in his satirical novel *A Fugitive Crosses His Tracks* (*En flyktning krysser sitt spor*, 1933), but the Laws actually go back further than that and are now part of the DNA of Nordic people.

It wasn't just about fulfilling your role; you might also help out other people. During the harvest, people would work together to make sure the crops were harvested in time. People would also unselfishly make introductions for the common good. Contrary to the view of Darwin that the world is 'dog-eat-dog', many scientists now believe the human ability to collaborate is what has made us so successful (Keltner, 2012).

Today, people use sites like Tripadvisor, where you leave your views and recommendations about hotels. The rationale is that you are more likely to book something that your friend, or a friend of your friend, has recommended. The theory is that if you trust friend A, then while you have never met their friend, on the basis that friend A is OK, surely their friends are OK too.

In fact, many of us have booked hotels based on the reviews on Tripadvisor, when in fact the reviews were left by total strangers, people we have never met and never will meet. That is because we trust the social platform. People who come to that social platform are just like you and me, therefore we trust it. Research conducted by Ipsos Media and Crowdtap in 2014 showed that the recommendations of strangers on such sites have a powerful influence on behaviour (Knoblauch, 2014).

Recently, a friend of mine was intent on taking a destination vacation with his family. He booked 10 days in a hotel, thinking that was his best option, but after I had raved about Airbnb, thought he would try that instead. A search revealed he could rent a beautiful private house in the same location as the motel he had chosen, for half the price. But there was a catch. He learned that Airbnb landlords are not obliged to rent their property to anyone who can afford it. Instead, they only rent to people they trust.

How does someone who has never met you and lives thousands of miles away come to entrust you, a stranger, with one of their most prized possessions? The answer might be obvious – social media. If you are an Airbnb renter who has never used the service before – and, therefore, has never been rated on the website by a landlord – you are an unknown entity. In order to reduce the risk, the service encourages property owners to do something unusual. They learn how to check you out online via sites like Facebook, LinkedIn, Twitter and company websites. Your public presence, on social media, in particular, helps determine whether or not you represent a high risk, the kind of tenant who might ruin their home. Of course, you need to give your passport details and a credit card, but they can be faked. I cannot fake 10 years of being on Facebook. Or if somebody has only posted three photos on Facebook and it was in the last year, you might assume they are fake.

FIGURE 1.1   Influence on where to stay

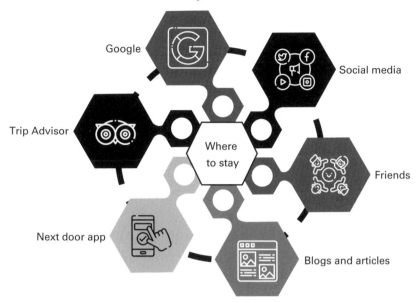

While in the next chapter we discuss how you can create a personal brand, here we discuss how, for the business-to-business (B2B) and business-to-consumer (B2C) salesperson, community is now the de facto place to live, work and sell online.

The mistake many people make about communities or tribes is that it's all about the number of people in that tribe. A modern term for that could be 'followers'. Or people often mistake it as market reach. Community isn't that either. The key is that people share amongst themselves for the common good of that community. There are no egos. In our communities on social media, if there are people I think would benefit from my connecting them with each other, I effect that introduction. For example, a friend of mine was setting up a website to help students find jobs. So I introduced her to students that I knew had found work through LinkedIn, which gave her validation of her ideas and strong case studies. It is highly unlikely I will profit from that enterprise, but I will be pleased to see it thrive and maybe I can help my friend and other people. We call it social karma.

FIGURE 1.2   Social karma

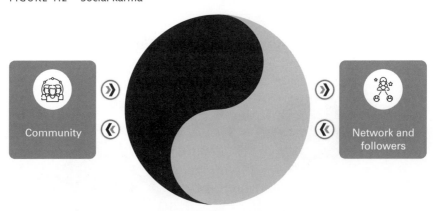

Communities or tribes have always had leaders. If we continue our ancient history analogy, it could be the lord of the manor or the tribal chief. The tribal chief had a role to provide leadership, was ceremonial and provided governance, but in the majority of cases the community lived and thrived by itself.

Dan Newman (@danielnewmanUV) is CEO of Broadsuite Media Group, a *Forbes* contributor and author of five books. He said to me, 'My definition of community is that your tribe will carry your torch for you; if you carry it yourself you are just a person'. Having worked in many corporations, I know that this can be contradictory to common thinking. Yes, I understand that a company has a common purpose as defined by the board of directors and itemized in the annual accounts, but at the shop-floor level people have their own agendas. I've worked in teams that have 'knowledge is power' and 'not invented here' attitudes, where any good idea is immediately stolen and presented as a manager's own. All of this fosters negative feelings. Why would you want to innovate when you don't get the acknowledgement for your efforts and thoughts?

In any company, regardless of size, there are often more demands on you than hours in the day; you therefore have to decide what is today's priority. You also have to obey the rules, whether this is the corporate culture or to meet the needs of shareholders or regulation. This often 'institutionalizes' the way people think. How many times have we heard 'But we have always done it like that', when we asked people why they are following that particular process?

The big jump that people need to make in the move from corporate thinking to working in the networked or connected economy is that you are working in communities or tribes. Not in a corporate structure. Based on the way communities have thrived since history began, you need to be supportive. This isn't some 'hippy' life construct but a need to allow give-and-take in that network. Somebody has to smelt the metal, the blacksmith will make the horses' shoes and the farrier will fit them to the horses. If you are not passing on the baton of help (adding value, as people often call it) then there is no community. People are hungry for real conversations and real relationships. It just has to be authentic, genuine and sincere.

FIGURE 1.3   In a network, pass on the baton

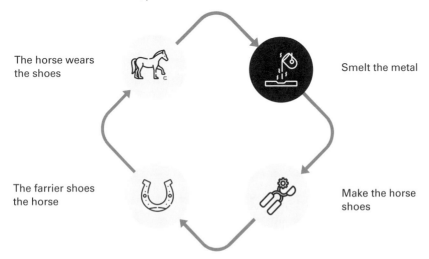

The horse wears the shoes

Smelt the metal

The farrier shoes the horse

Make the horse shoes

If you are reading this, we hope you are one of the vendors and services providers attempting to trigger and engage in online digital conversations within your target market segments. This will increase awareness, reputation, thought leadership, online connections and lead origination.

Remember that you only get out of community what you put in, and if you are taking and not giving in at least equal quantity then you won't grow your follower base or community and you won't get to create the leads and revenue you want. For example, a friend of mine offers Instagram training, and when I come across people who need training in this area, I connect them. When he gets an inbound from me, he tweets a blog we wrote together. This gives me amplification over his network, which is generally a different type of person to my usual follower, and allows for cross-pollination of networks.

Another example is where a contact sent me a LinkedIn message about a LinkedIn group he created for people who train others on LinkedIn. Michael (let's call him that) is going to gain, as he will get advice from some of the best LinkedIn experts like us. But he knows that to gain that knowledge he also needs to share his own. In the world of connected networks your competitor is also your friend. They are often called 'frenemies', and require the building of mutual trust and respect across the connected economy.

The struggle people often have is that when you are working in a network you need to shake off the shackles of corporate thinking. When you get online you will find connection requests and you will be followed by people you don't know. People (whom you have never met and are unlikely to meet) will make decisions about you based on your social profiles. If your LinkedIn profile or Twitter account is stuffed with corporate speak, then people will see you as a corporate suit. Whereas if you are sharing insight, helping, telling people how to solve their business issues, telling people things they don't know, or being entertaining, people will start to know, like and trust you. Where will people go to buy? From people they know, like and trust, of course. More on personal branding and how to set up a social profile can be found in Chapter 2.

But this journey from corporate thinking to social karma is not something that most people will be able to grapple with and come to terms with overnight. It may take time to 'find you voice', after all it's about relaxing, being authentic and sharing your expertise.

This isn't a 'self-help' book, but we do want you to realize that getting online and working in the connected society isn't about pressing a button and automatically being switched over. It takes time to change and adapt your thinking. What we often see with social is that people do a bit and then go back to what they were doing before. This is because social media and social selling requires a methodology. It also requires habit change and mindset change. If, like me, you need to lose weight and get fit, that requires you to go to the gym, not for an hour or for a day, but three times a week for the rest of your life. It also might help if you got an expert in to help you with your diet.

Social is a maturing science. This book does not hold all the answers, as social will change as we find new ways of using it to drive profit and competitive advantage. One way to look at community is based on social proximity. This is a relationship-based approach of assigning opportunities and accounts based on the social connections and engagement of your sales team. In other words, the salesperson most closely connected to and engaged with the buyer through friends and professional networks owns the opportunity. If you are in sales, you can see your territory as your digital community. It's really about understanding who your best-fit customers are, based on the value you can deliver to those customers and the business outcome you can help them achieve.

The importance of owning your community

In the next chapter we will talk about which social networks to be on. Some great research complied by Simon Kemp (follow him on LinkedIn) and paid for by Hootsuite and We Are Social and that uses a number of data sources compiled the definitive report on social media numbers (Kemp, 2021a). You may recall these figures from the Introduction, but they are worth repeating. In October 2021 there were 7.89 billion people in the world, of which 5.29 billion, 67.1 per cent, had a mobile phone; 4.88 billion, 61.8 per cent, had access to the internet; and 4.55 billion, 57.6 per cent, were *active* users of social media.

In terms of social media growth, this is an increase of 409 million people, which is 9.9 per cent growth. People often think in the 'first world' that social media is saturated, and of course, more and more people join. In this research it shows that these people are active for at least 2 hours 27 minutes per day. The suggestion that 'My clients are not on social media' just isn't true anymore. Or, as we know that people buy in buying teams, one person might not be on social but the other nine people in the buying team are active users. If we are to focus on B2B sites, then in the case of LinkedIn we are now in the situation that, if you are not on LinkedIn, then you don't exist. A millennial friend said to me, 'If somebody isn't on social media, then I assume they have something to hide.'

B2B and B2C companies have, to this point, seen the battle to gain market share, competitive advantage and ultimately revenue and profit as an offline task. Companies at a macro (corporate) and micro (employee) level need to wake up and move the fight online. They need to build their own communities to drive their message and share; not in a controlling, corporate way, but using the commonalities of community we discussed earlier, adding value to your community members, being supportive and sharing.

As outlined above, companies need to find and create a community, so they move from carrying their own torch to having a community that carries it for them. They become the 'lord of the manor', with customers, employees and, even better still, a wider network working to their common good.

FIGURE 1.4   The importance of community

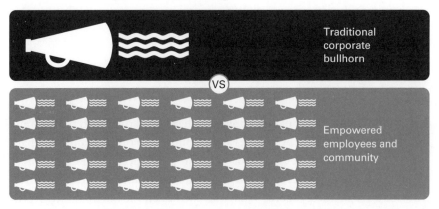

Figure 1.4 shows the traditional corporate 'bullhorn', which often trans-mits nothing more than 'corporate propaganda', versus an empowered workforce, and we suggest the latter will have more reach, more engage-ment and be able to grow a community. A great example of this in the B2C space is gambling companies. Gambling is a highly regulated industry. Businesses can no longer advertise and say 'Come gamble with me and your life will be complete' as they may have in the past. They create communities using humour, asking questions and getting interaction. We know of people who don't gamble, but follow and interact with the gambling sites as it's fun. You might be thinking, why would I want to interact with people who are not customers? As marketers/social salespeople, the opportunity is to use social as a way to get new customers. Those people we know who interact with gambling sites might one day decide to gamble, and who do you think they will turn to? Yes, the company with whom they have the best connec-tion or affinity.

One of the key strengths of social selling is using social techniques to find new prospects to convert to customers. The community will find you con-nections, people that don't even know your product or service exists, and turn them into top-of-the-funnel (ToFu) prospects. Community will also nurture those prospects as they undertake their research in the market at the middle of the funnel (MoFu). Strength of community should also allow prospects to approach you; we would call this 'inbound'.

The chief executive officer (CEO) of one of our clients told me the story that, two weeks after completing our social selling and influence course, a client found one of their salespeople on social media, and walked towards them. Because they didn't look like just another salesperson, they asked if the salesperson could help them. Then using the powers of sales that the salesperson has had for a number of years he converted that into a $2.6 million deal.

A word of warning: it's understandable that you might not believe this, and hope this social media stuff will go away. But just remember that your competitors will be reading this (we hope) and they may be building a network to pull customers and prospects away from you into their network and community. You don't just press a button and create a community. Like the lord of the manor, you need to grow and nurture one.

Battle of the networks

The connected community means that your prospects, customers and competitors are all now online. The Covid-19 pandemic has accelerated this, changing social media from being a place to go, a destination, to a place we now exist. Customers, B2B and B2C, can go online and discuss (good or bad) your brand, products and services. Word-of-mouth marketing has always existed in the offline world, but the connected society has accelerated the speed and distance that good and bad news can travel.

Engaging prospects early and often in the decision cycle is now a prerequisite of modern business, and the battle for attention is fought through subject matter expertise and thought leadership in a non-promotional format. Conversion of that hard-earned attention into prospects and leads is a combination of science and art, one that few understand. Research shows that people come to social media to be social and not to read brochures or brochureware. In fact, if you look at people who are sharing brochures and brochureware they get little or no engagement, which proves nobody likes what they are sharing. But it is worse than that, and we will come to that soon.

Done right, the result provides branding, awareness, thought leadership, reputation, demand generation, lead nurturing and sales. In fact, social media and social selling can be used for proactive prospecting, lead nurturing, right the way through to closing. Of course, now in a world of SaaS there is often a renewal required. Social selling, by building your territory and community, allows your business to land and expand supporting account-based marketing (ABM).

We salespeople have always been 'control freaks'. Twenty years ago I was selling into the healthcare market in the UK. The accounting software company I worked for had no customers in that area. We worked hard on selling the first deal and made sure the implementation went well. That customer (while most customers will always justify a decision) went out of their way to tell people how great we were. This helped us sell the second deal. We then created a healthcare user group, which was an environment for the customers to exchange ideas and best practice. They also fed back into product development. This user group helped to sell the third, fourth and fifth deal, and so on. We became market leaders and then controlled the narrative. A number of competitors looked at what we had created and must have said, 'I want some of that', and we often had them trying to sell into that market. We gave them six months before they lost interest. Why? We would like to say it was our great selling techniques, but it was because of our strength of network. Twenty years on, those organizations are still using the products I sold.

I was in a meeting recently where a salesperson discussed a plan to try to sell a prospect a new system and he said, 'It's really difficult to sell to them, they are very loyal and have a strong community and network.' Move that notion offline: online and through an online community you have the ability to shift markets and take markets from competitors. If you are a small business you can, at very little cost, undertake David and Goliath situations. If you are a major corporation, if you are not proactively creating community, companies will steal your market share. Community is the new competitive advantage.

With my current company, it only took us two years to become global, and don't forget we spend $ zero on advertising, $ zero on email marketing and $ zero on cold calling. Everything we do is with social ; we are after all a social/digital organization. Twenty years ago that would have been unheard of – you would have had to spend $ millions on advertising.

Many people reading this might be in a situation where your competitor has already embarked on a community-building project. This is fine. While you could employ a company that writes books on community, there is an action plan you can deploy right now, which we will cover in the rest of the book.

Community exists online and offline. It can be built with your customers and employees as well as your industry influencers. As you build the community, you need to understand that people trust certain types of message and don't trust others. In low socially mature organizations, it is seen as the norm that the employees are used to push out a corporate message. Organizations like 'employee advocacy' programmes as they can control the message and increase the noise out in the market. The view is that we should

FIGURE 1.5   How people are more impactful than brands

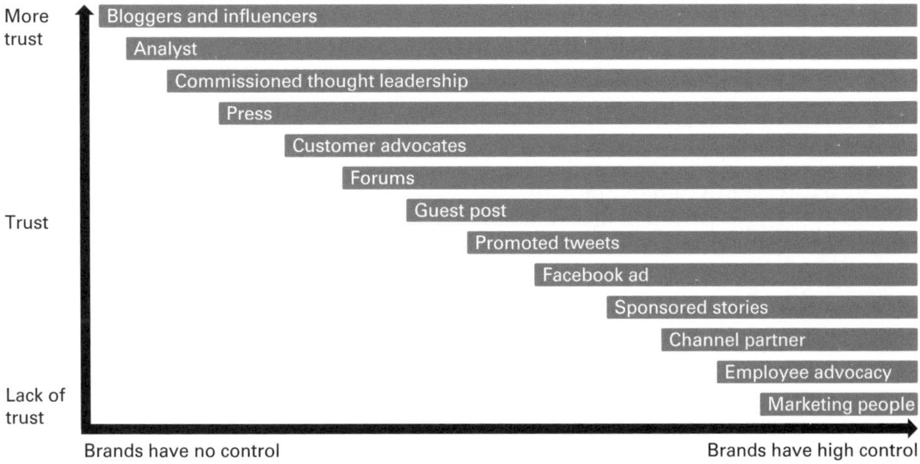

be 'doing' social and if we throw enough mud at the wall some of it will stick. Managers have often proudly shown me reports that demonstrate they have thrown more mud than their competitors. This is all well and good, but prospects and customers will say, 'Of course that employee will say that, they work there and are therefore biased.' Corporations get control, but your prospects and customers won't trust the message – brochures and brochureware are seen as corporate propaganda.

As we move up the axis, organizations will engage in turning customers into references and references into advocates. Customer references are where organizations will say how great you are but do so in the confines of what you want to hear. This enables you to get your message out and we might trust it more than employees, but we all know there is corporate control. For many corporations moving up the curve is scary, as they lose control of the message. Moving to the position where our customers are more than just references, they are advocates, is where we lose control of the message, but the community finds it of a higher value. The fact that there may well be bad mixed with good can actually amplify the good. We are more likely to trust that message. If we trust that message, we will amplify and share it without our communities and tribes. Being open and supportive in your community gains you wider sharing and amplification.

The highest level of maturity is to find influencers to discuss and amplify your message. If you can get other 'lords of the manor' to positively discuss and share items about your brand then you will grow your community as they give you access to their communities. This is very scary for brands, as, while you may gain a high level of trust, you have no control over what those influencers will say.

We often have marketers saying that social has to be 'on brand'. If that means boring and brochures, surely not? We then show examples of employees who have shared content they have created themselves that shows how happy and content they are in their work. It's certainly on brand, but its human and as a buyer that is what I'm looking for. Let's not forget that people are on social to be social. More on that later.

Further on in this chapter we discuss how to work with these 'tribe masters' and not do what I've seen, which is to try to use analogue methods. For example, in the past, brands have used 'vice presidents' because they were, after all, important in approaching influencers. But in the connected economy, the tribe masters have seen these people on social networks with little or no social profile, and have just laughed at their approach, in many cases going onto social networks to do so. These brands must then carry out a brand damage limitation exercise. In Chapter 9 we show an organizational social maturity model, where we discuss how employee and customer advocacy programmes can work as you move up the model.

Not too long ago, DVDs ruled the world. For years, the DVD store Blockbuster seemed unbeatable. At its peak, the company operated 10,000 stores globally, and in 2002 had a market value of US $5 billion. Many of us have seen the David-and-Goliath story of how Netflix swept Blockbuster away and became a must-have for 'teenagers'. Netflix seemed to have come out of nowhere for many of us (maybe living in the UK made it seem so). But it actually started in 1997 and built a distribution model that relied exclusively on mailing DVDs to customers through the low-cost US postal service. It was as convenient as a Blockbuster neighbourhood store but at a fraction of the price – and without the late fees that annoyed Blockbuster customers. In 2007 Netflix started a video streaming service. This was a pretty visionary move for CEO Reed Hastings, as less than 50 per cent of US homes had a broadband connection at that time.

Netflix disrupted the market by creating a new business model that pushed their major competitor into bankruptcy in 2011 and full shutdown by 2014. Netflix have also created a community and tribe, where word-of-mouth recommendations are driving people to the channel and teenagers beg their parents to take subscriptions just so they can watch their favourite shows. Netflix has started to create original content (it has to, as content is king) to drive the next level of growth. It will affect television companies like BBC and ITV, as well as removing the need for postage, disrupting the third-party logistic companies.

Like the offline Coke and Pepsi wars of the past, with marketing and advertising moving online, so do the brands. While many B2C brands have led the way, many still work very much with analogue methods in the digital world. In this online world there need to be new methods and best practice. Companies, large or small, must go online and form and build communities using new strategies and techniques. Social karma requires corporations to think differently, to think about their customer, create a community and advocates, and maybe even work with competitors. For many people this is a scary thought, but help is at hand. After all, talking with customers is scary, or seems to be for some people. However, there is a new type of person for whom this is second nature. In the next section we will talk about this person, the 'changemaker' – somebody for whom community comes naturally. We will discuss where they probably sit in your organization, and how you can employ them to take your fight online.

Building your community

Twenty years ago, many salespeople had a 'little black book' of contacts or a Rolodex of business cards. Often jobs were given as a result of how big your contact group was. Then came the long-gone first social media websites like Ecademy, and Myspace, and then came LinkedIn, and people moved their business card list online. But how many people do you know that use this to create a community? They tend to be 'one-dimensional' groups or lists of people.

Within your organization – and I doubt they will be currently in the boardroom – will be people for whom social is second nature. One of my salespeople admitted to me that his dog has 2,000 followers on Twitter. Martin (not his real name) was a sales guy we always went to as part of a social selling roll-out to try new ideas and techniques. We would go to Martin and say, 'We are thinking of doing this.' He would try it and, if it was a success, other salespeople would talk directly with him, learn from him and often slowly but surely the field adopted our ideas. Social came naturally to Martin; he built his own blog and Twitter handle, he networked, shared, created content and built a community. He was the lord of the manor but also understood how to grow community and get his message out across other communities, thus allowing his own community to grow and thrive.

FIGURE 1.6 The evolution of community

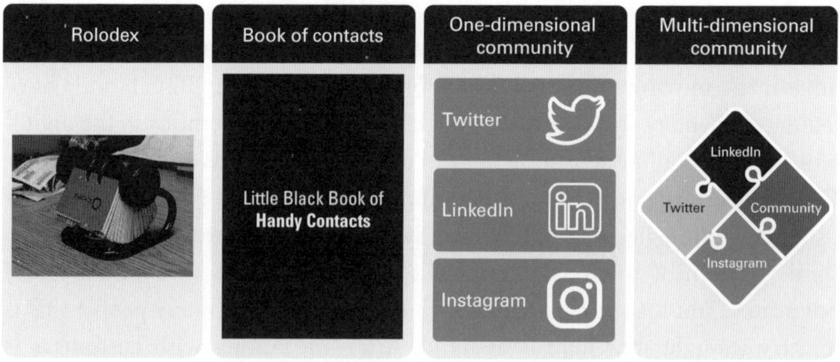
Rolodex
Book of contacts
Little Black Book of
Handy Contacts
One-dimensional
community
Twitter
LinkedIn
Instagram
Multi-dimensional
community
LinkedIn
Twitter
Community
Instagram

A modern selling organization

Revenue operations (RevOps)

In my last corporate sales role I was on the board of the UK part of the business, a role I cherished as it gave me insight into a significantly sized business. Like many businesses we were broken down into silos, not due to any fault of the business, it just happened like that.

I recall, we did a review of the pipeline of the sales development representatives/business development representatives part of the business. This team had separate management, a different leadership structure and reported to a separate profit and loss (P&L). Their job was, first and foremost, to find and generate leads that would then be passed to our salespeople. While their job was to generate leads, they had a separate management structure, different reporting lines, set their own objectives and measures. Can you see where this is going?

The first pipeline and forecast review we did, after we put the phone down in the meeting room, we all sat back and all took a deep breath of air. Their pipeline was empty, a desert, nothing. This was the stuff of firings for that team and it meant no leads for us. When the team presented the pipeline to the European management, it was a completely different situation. They were heroes, they were 'knocking it out of the park.'

How can a business report in two different ways? It took us three months to work out what was going on and how the data in the customer relation-

COMMUNITY AND TRIBALISM 67

ship management system (CRM) was being viewed differently. Happy to have a call with you and I will explain.

This is just one example I have; I'm sure you have more, about how, in business, different silos can be rowing in different directions. Yes, we worked for the same business, but, really, we could have been different companies. Add to this, the massive shift that has taken place in sales due to the internet, social media and mobile and it's clear the old way of organizing sales isn't fit for purpose anymore.

The future is RevOps

RevOps looks at getting all revenue generating parts of a business under one strategy and leadership. This means that marketing, lead generation, business development, sales development representatives, business development representatives, account executives, account managers, account-based marketing, social selling, remote selling, digital selling, customer success, renewal sales is all under one leadership team. One strategy, one leadership team, an overall governance structure and measure.

Why RevOps?

Before the Covid-19 pandemic, it was OK to lose a few deals. What the lockdowns taught us is that both big or small companies have to find all the opportunities they can and have to win all of them. This is not because of greed, this out of economic necessity.

Selling is social and social is strategic

As we explain in previous chapters, social for a business is now strategic. Whereas once it was kept in a box in marketing, now it is for the whole business to embrace. The mistake that most companies make in low socially mature organizations is to think that employee advocacy will work for the common good of the business. Sure, it helps you blast corporate messages out there, but does it actually resonate with your market? When employees are following employees, are you just talking to yourself? Does anyone actually trust or believe anything an employee says? 'They would say that', after all.

When I first started out on social media I used to work with a guy in public relations (PR) who had 1,000-plus followers on Twitter. A thousand followers is a 'platform' where you can start to form your own community.

But when I did an analysis of his followers, I realized it was 'just' colleagues and the 'usual' PR agencies. Great 'business as usual' stuff, but it wasn't a community, there was little inter-sharing, and little crossover with other communities, so little chance of growth. Nice network, but little community.

As mentioned earlier, the average person on LinkedIn has 930 connection, but they will be ex-colleagues and recruitment consultants. This won't be the very people that your salespeople are trying to sell to or the people that your human resources team are trying to recruit or procurement team are trying to buy raw materials from. Also, don't forget that salespeople come and go. In the connected society, social sellers will become the sought-after salespeople. Recruitment for salespeople with digital skills is now the norm. On the basis that you have a wonderful culture and great products, you will lose people and their communities. This is why you need your salespeople to create community at a macro level, as well as in their territories or at a micro level.

Social is about change

Let's stop a moment. If you are wearing a watch, take it off for me and put it on your other wrist. Notice how odd that feels; as you read this sentence you are thinking you want to switch it back to how you always have it. A number of you will have already moved it back by now. That is what we mean by change management. Digital and social require a new way of working and somebody needs to work with sales teams to help create that.

Regardless of whether you are a B2B company or you are targeting fly-fishing fans, people who love river cruises, or those who are Marvel comic fans, to build your community (and we talk about this in more detail in the following chapters) invite them to your site. Offer content that is specifically designed to fill their industry-specific needs. Hopefully they will start coming back for more.

In the B2B enterprise space that we tend to work in, the average salesperson we deal with has difficulty enough in understanding social. (The next chapter on personal branding should help you get started.) They have difficulty with the idea of being shared and are afraid they may make a fool of themselves. Some would even call them 'social phobics'. Anything about social sees them freeze and their eyes glaze over. If you are one of these people, even if you are a sales leader, then this book is a manual to help.

But we see in our training that, often, sales leaders and sales professionals say they 'get it', when in fact they don't. This is the area that is most dangerous to organizations. People who dabble in social and have not built community, even if they are seen as leaders in social, are not going to drive your business forward. They might talk a good story but if they could have, they would have. Again, just because somebody has a fancy job title, they too, if they haven't already created community, will carry on having just the fancy job title.

As we discussed in the introduction, the changemaker will probably have been you 10 years ago, and they may be on track to be the next sales leader. You must now give them the delegated authority to provide the leadership and the vision to take the next step and jump into social.

The organization needs to understand who their customer is. Yeah, I know we have sold to them for years and years, but do we really know them? That's where you are probably thinking, what we need is customer personas. But all of these things like personas, customer journey mapping and so on are built on the fact that I am building a process to sell to you. That isn't how it works today – today the buyer is in charge. For example, in the finance department there is the finance director or chief finance officer (CFO), financial accountant, management accountant and systems accountant. Each has different wants, needs and personal wins. In any sales situation you may well be selling to multiple people, but if you treat them as anything but individuals then you will lose. Marketers talk about personalization; when somebody hears that they think, 'I am being treated as a single human being.' We don't need personalization, we need context.

Finance people are often seen as continuous learners and like to be seen in organizations as the go-to for the latest information. They tend to see work as taking place during daytime boundaries. For example, if you send them a LinkedIn connection request at 8 pm, they won't accept it until the next working day. Finance departments tend to be fact-based, and perhaps less inclined towards infographics than a table of figures.

Marketing directors tend to see themselves as the 'new' society guardian. They will be connected at all times. Send them a LinkedIn request at 8 pm and they will accept it then, as they will still be online. There is a clear blurring of online and offline boundaries. Marketing directors tend to love infographics.

What community is not

Before we summarize the chapter, it is worth capturing what community is not. First and foremost, community is not measured in the number of followers you have. We are aware of people with 400 followers who, because of their niche, have been able to build a community. That is, people working for a common goal, sharing ideas and information, without expectation of financial gain. It is often a synergistic relationship, working for the common good. Salespeople need to do this within their territory.

As mentioned above, community has a true value when connections – people, business and things – are not static followers but when they all start to interact with each other. The number of connections can, at low cost, create an effect that exponentially multiplies value. Give-and-take provides an active and dynamic network of connections.

People make the mistake of thinking that LinkedIn equals social selling, and it does not. LinkedIn is only 30 per cent of your social graph. Social is actually the act of being social, not using a tool. If you want to learn how to grow vegetables, learning how to use a spade is useful, but it won't teach you, what to plant and when. For somebody to be truly social and to build a community they need to do this across multiple platforms.

Summary

In this chapter we took you through why community is so important in the digital and social age. Tribes and community come naturally to humans, and brands must grasp community as a way to sell and control their market online. Any organization has competitors and you need to treat community as your competitive advantage; it should not be seen as some sort of fluffy concept.

To build community you need to embrace today's changemakers, and the board of your business needs to drive that change. Through a company's evolution to social you will see new leaders for the digital age; they might not be senior in your organization, but they will stand out as leaders in the world of social and digital.

A CEO'S VIEWPOINT – CHRIS MASON FROM NAMOS SOLUTIONS

I've been involved in selling in some capacity all my working life, and what I learnt about social selling blew my mind because it was simple and obvious but at the same time myself and my team weren't doing it. There was some scepticism from the team to start – but those that have embraced it have seen the results of their efforts. There is still more we can do and learn but social selling is now a key part of our selling strategy.

COMMUNITY IN A COMMERCIAL ENVIRONMENT IN ACTION –
ERIC DOYLE

Why would you want to create a digital community, and how would you go about it...? Social media has changed the world. In the B2B space we used to do things in a certain way and those ways produced results. Everything changed. Social media has grown into all area of life and is now dominating our professional and commercial lives.

So how do you achieve the results you had historically, in a commercial social media environment? The first thing to do is to reframe the question. First, establish how things are now working and examine what you do in line with that. In most cases this will require a rebuild. Let's take networking as an example. Think of how you used to network – events, conference, working groups, trade gatherings, seminars etc. – all now in question. For so many these were crucial routes to market, so how do we network in the digital age? We look at how networking is happening and re-craft our position.

In the summer of 2020, I decided I wanted to start running live stream broadcasts on LinkedIn. So, what is live streaming? In basic terms it's a live broadcast of an event on a social media platform but, looking at it through the lens we described earlier, it is way more in terms of opportunity. Live streaming is a way to connect with an audience directly. It allows audiences to interact directly.

I thought about this and took it further:

- It could be a place where people can feel they belong.
- It could be a place where people can feel safe to express themselves.
- It could be a place where people can really see and understand other people (qualified relevance).
- It could mean a new way to network.

We put together a great team of hosts and The Big Live Breakfast Burrito was born. A weekly LinkedIn Live streaming show broadcast at 7:45 am every Thursday morning.

We created a mission:

- Do something unique.
- 'Funetize' not monetize.
- Create a digital space where professional people can relax and have fun.

- Create a community of support and togetherness.
- Make it all about the audience not the presenters.

And one last mission element:

- Try to redefine 21st century networking (no pressure…!).

We ran our first show in August 2020 and a few people watched. Cut to now and we have almost 40 shows under our belt. We have hundreds of viewers. We have merchandise and a social media group formed known as 'The Burritoneans'. The Big Live Breakfast Burrito allows people to find an anchor point. It has something for everyone: music, games, stories, poetry, puzzles, competitions, prizes, good news stories…all things that people love. It is centred around the audience, so they are regularly brought onto the show to take part and one of the main pillars of the show is interaction. There are sayings and calls that thread throughout the show and there is a real sense of community, all done on a social media platform for professionals!

We have had people win work live on air and people have met on the Burrito and are now working together. Everyone involved has grown their networks and the show grows every week with new viewers and new content. There have been hundreds of individual pieces of content produced by the community, all natural and not forced. The networking element is becoming stronger and stronger. We receive regular messages from viewers telling us that they connected with someone they met on the show, they checked out their profile and found that they could help each other. This has also happened to the hosts: 'Hi ****, I checked out The Big Live Breakfast Burrito and really enjoyed it. I checked you profile and think you might be able to help us'.

We have businesses that approach us to sponsor the show prizes and become part of the community. All professional people, all networking in a new way. All finding new people to connect with and expand networks. All finding common ground to share and open the space for conversations.

So, to answer the question, 'Why would you want to create a digital community and how would you go about it?' The why? Because it's important. As the world becomes more digital, the need to be able to create digital business communities will become more important.

The how? Think of something unique that allows people to anchor in, set it up and get going. It's that simple. We have to move and put energy into building and doing in digital.

References

Keltner, D (2012) The compassionate species, Greater Good. https://greatergood. berkeley.edu/article/item/the_compassionate_species (archived at https://perma.cc/8ZCL-6F9J)

Kemp, S (2021) Digital 2021: October global statshot report, DataReportal. https://datareportal.com/reports/digital-2021-october-global-statshot (archived at https://perma.cc/AZ4K-EUGQ)

Knoblauch, M (2014) Millennials trust user-generated content 50% more than other media, Mashable. http://mashable.com/2014/04/09/millennials-user-generated-media/#Bvohe6t8YgqD (archived at https://perma.cc/B39P-T9G8)

02

Your identity within social networks

In the previous chapter we looked at how community and tribes were central to us in the offline world and how key they are to us in the online world. In this chapter we're going to be looking at our own identity within the constellation of social networks that are available to us. In the last chapter we learnt about the importance of community, and being able to take a leadership position within that community. Now we need to start putting the things in place to achieve that. We will also look at personal branding and how you can set yourself up on a social network.

Throughout this book we're keen to impress upon you the importance of focusing on social networks and not spreading yourself too thinly; you have to go where your customers are. As of the time of writing, the best B2B platforms are, in our opinion, LinkedIn, Twitter and Instagram. This chapter will explain how to set up profiles on LinkedIn and Twitter. Importantly, we look at how to frame and present our identity in a way that is helpful to us, ultimately creating a leadership position within the community, as well as being appealing to customers.

Since writing the first edition of this book, our company DLA Ignite has worked with thousands of businesses to help them use social media strategically within their organization. It would be usual that a business can increase their revenues by 20 per cent and reduce their sales cycle by 30 per cent based on figures we have measured from our clients.

Opinion versus data

There are a number of books out there on social selling that talk about a person's journey or explain the interworkings of LinkedIn. This isn't either of those types of book. The other thing about this book is that what I am going to explain to you is based on our data and experience of working with clients. It is not based on opinion – just because somebody says something or writes it in an article or book this does not make it fact.

Is social somehow anti-sales?

The number one piece of advice I would give is to know your target markets, listen, engage and interact with them. When you build trust with people, they will also open their networks to you. In addition, there was that old adage that salespeople need to be proactive. I agree, you will only get out of social what you put in. Also, there is a 'hippy' sales fraternity who see social as a way of being nice and not as a sales tool we can use to create business, so don't forget to ask for the sale. I'm not saying here that you have to be aggressive, as asking for the business should just 'flow'. Often there seems to be a notion that somehow social invalidates everything we have learned in sales, which is why salespeople often are reluctant to use social. It seems that somehow we have to re-learn everything, but quite the opposite is the case – you will find that social is very similar to what we have always done. We want conversations, why? Because conversations drive sales. What I'm going to share with you is how you get those conversations. It's worth noting that posting brochures on social does not create conversations and therefore does not generate sales.

Is there a programmatic approach?

Twitter is for connecting; look for the signals, then switch to direct mail (DM), email or telephone. Once the person is connected, you can link to them on LinkedIn to stay in touch and nurture. You also get access to their networks.

We will now go through what you need to do to set up a LinkedIn profile. There are many books on personal branding and this is not a step-by-step process, but an overall vision of what a good LinkedIn profile and Twitter account should look like. In all of this you have to start from the bottom with no connect and no followers. That is fine, we all started like that – there are no overnight sensations. There is a famous Chinese proverb, 'The best time to plant a tree was 20 years ago, the second-best time is today.'

In all of this you need to start building your digital muscles. If you go to the gym the weights will be heavy, as you build your muscles the weights get lighter. The same with your digital muscles. Go onto social and watch what people are doing, or better still get yourself a coach. One word of warning

– there are a lot of charlatans out there in social media land, people who are willing to exploit your ignorance. My advice is to find a company that has been trading for a number of years and always check out an expert's social media feeds. Do they practice what they preach?

LinkedIn

LinkedIn have managed to get to a position where, if you're a professional in any industry (as buyer or seller), it's perceived that you have to be on LinkedIn. It's the 2020s equivalent of how it felt to have a business card in the 1990s – you didn't really have a job unless you had a business card with your job title on it. Today you don't 'exist' in business unless you have a LinkedIn profile. People from students to CEOs have LinkedIn profiles, because they can see it's a great way to find a job, get a job, sell, market, find your new team, retain your team, find and source new suppliers.

In the past, to get a message out as a CEO, you needed to talk to a PR company and they then spoke to journalists, and if anything was printed then you were lucky. Now a business can talk directly to its prospective customers, its customers, its employees, its alumni and future employees. There were a number of instances during the Covid-19 pandemic where this became useful and CEOs were able to pivot news as it happened. For example, the CEO of Accenture, during an outbreak of Covid-19 in India, was able to put out a message to support its 250,000 team members in the country. For the people who work at Accenture and are engaged, this gave them a feeling that the company cared, for people maybe thinking of working at Accenture it showed a caring culture. The same if you are an Accenture client or a potential Accenture client, that is a business that most people would want to be associated with.

While there is effort setting this up and running it in time, it is also 'free' PR. But it's not all about setting up a profile; LinkedIn can be used as your address book (people will always update their details so the addresses are never out of date) and it can also be used as a lead prospecting and nurture tool.

Getting started

If you unpick LinkedIn to the point where it is just a directory (albeit an international, universal one), your LinkedIn profile is your listing in that directory. It is an advert for you that anybody in the world can see and it's visible 24 hours a day, 365 days a year. Think of it as your shop window. There are millions of people walking past your shop window every day and what you need to do is to get people to look into the window and think 'That looks interesting' and then you get them to walk inside.

Your profile will be looked at by two audiences:

- People who have come to look at it because some signal from elsewhere has pointed them at it. For example, a friend or colleague may have recommended you and they've come to find you; you've asked to link to them and they want to know who you are; you've posted some content on LinkedIn or elsewhere and they want to know more about you.
- People who have come to look at it because they have found you in some search.

Those are two fundamentally different things – either someone is looking for more information (they're coming in warm), or they have no idea who you are at all (they're coming in cold).

Fundamentally, your listing is an advert, and like any advert it has to be engineered to get the viewer to take action. At a minimum you want them to follow you. At a maximum you want to be so compelling they contact you and ask to set up a meeting. This advert is your personal brand to the world. When people look at your profile they have a first impression of who you are. In the past a first impression would have been made when you were introduced; now because of the internet anybody can search for you and get that first impression. Wouldn't it be great if that first impression created a next action that got you an enquiry about your business or service, thus reducing the amount of proactive prospecting you need to do?

One of the underlying themes of this book is that social sellers have to be much better at marketing than traditional sellers. The traditional salesperson tends to rely on marketing to do a lot of the market-softening aspects of marketing for them (for example, cold calling, email, branding and advertising). In social selling, the market-softening aspects have to be done as part of the general sales process. Specifically in this case, your LinkedIn profile has to be an advert.

Your advert has to have the following aspects:

- a well-developed position – you want the person to walk towards you
- well-crafted, customer-centric (interesting to a customer rather than a recruiter) messaging around that position. Be human after all, that is how we get to know, like and trust somebody

- very little in the way of stuff the customer doesn't care about (it needs to be buyer-centric)
- a clear call to action

People jump to conclusions

FIGURE 2.1   Everybody jumps to conclusions

Let's imagine that you need to get to the airport quickly. Will you choose the bicycle or the car? You may live right next door to the airport, in which case you will choose the bike, but most people will choose the car. Now what if I told you the car was a prototype and it has no engine? Either way, we all jump to conclusions, we take a small piece of data and extrapolate it out, and that is what people are doing with your passive social presence, so your LinkedIn, Twitter and Instagram profiles and your active social presence. Your task is to get your prospects and your customers to get them to jump to the conclusion you want.

Gestalt thinking

FIGURE 2.2   Gestalt thinking

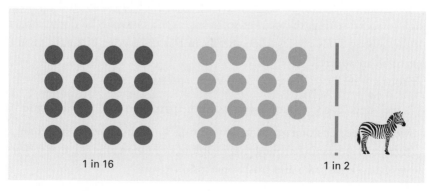

Gestalt thinking is where the human mind forms patterns. If you look the same as most salespeople you are seen as 'just another salesperson'. If you make yourself look different then you stand out and the human sees 'the crowd', and you. Psychology is then the choice.

Setting yourself up on LinkedIn

You should include a colour photo of yourself. This is a professional network and people are taking away a first impression of you from this profile. Don't put a photo of you in a bar in Spain – people might not see you as relaxed and social as you'd hope; they might just decide that you spend your life in a bar. Is that the impression you want to give? First impressions do count, so I recommend getting a professional shot done. You should use the same photo across all your professional networks – it's a personal brand after all.

You should show your full name, but in addition to this, any 'known as' names. For example, my birth name is Timothy, but I'm known as Tim. See also Michael and Mike, Robert and Rob or Bob, for example. This allows people to find you if they search by any version of your name, e.g. Tim Hughes, rather than Timothy Hughes.

Your LinkedIn profile is an advert for you. It is up 24 hours a day and 365 days a year. As we discussed earlier, the world has changed and buyers are now going online and researching what they want to buy. They are highly informed. Most buyers, when they go online, are doing so in 'salesperson avoidance mode'. To that end, if you look like a salesman then they will avoid you.

The key to this is the 'buyer-centric' profile. That is, a profile that appeals to a buyer in research mode. If your LinkedIn profile was set up a few years ago it is probably laid out as a CV so you can be found by head-hunters and get your next job. This, again, is old fashioned. In fact, head-hunters are looking for people with digital skills, so if you are looking for a new role you need to demonstrate those digital skills and get the head-hunters to jump to the conclusions you want them to.

To be 'buyer-centric' you have to appeal to the buyer if they come across you. You need to be intriguing, educational, supportive, helpful and ultimately encourage the buyer to take a next action, which is to contact you. The more human you are, the more people will walk towards you. Think about it – all your salespeople are running around trying to get people to like them, but are wasting time. By having a buyer-centric profile, buyers will walk towards you. That is transformational.

Check out this video on YouTube: https://youtu.be/9WQeRPpTCSI It is of Chris Mason, CEO at Oracle reseller Namos. Fast forward to 19 minutes 55 seconds where Chris talks about a $2.6 million win from being on social, after completing the DLA Ignite social selling and influence course. Let me walk you through this. The buyer has a business issue and was looking on LinkedIn for a solution. They found the chief revenue officer (CRO) from Namos and walked towards him and said, 'We have this problem; can you help us?' and then using all of his usual sales skills the CRO converted that in to a $2.6 million win. That's the power of putting the effort into having a buyer-centric profile

For example, if you sell filing cabinets, a traditional profile will show how many times you have made quota. As a buyer, I might think you are more willing to win the sale and make your quota than to get me the product that meets my needs. The alternative might be to put on your profile a blog article (written by you) called 'Top 10 things to think about when buying filing cabinets'. This helps and educates. It might be important to understand the differences between a foolscap size versus A4. The fact that I then make the right buying decision could lead me to recommend and become an advocate for you, bringing you more sales. You are looking to get people to know you, like you and trust you. When somebody trusts you, there is only once choice who to buy from – you.

People are also making decisions on what people are like based on their profiles. If, like me, you research people before you meet them, you will make a judgement just by looking at their profile as to how well a meeting will go and whether you even want to do business with that company. We often decide before a meeting how we think that meeting will go based on what a person's LinkedIn profile looks like. If you sell a product or service that is expensive or will be used by an organization for a long time, buyers are looking for long-term relationships, and will be seeking thought leaders and people they can partner with, not quota crushers. We will keep coming back to being buyer-centric.

If you Google yourself, it is your name and summary title that is visible and you want a buyer to take a next action and click on you. This summary title is the most visible thing about you (after you name) on the internet. You want your buyers to be curious and think, I need to find out more about this person.

The job title needs to be buyer-centric. It is understandable you are very proud to have built up your career over time to become a master principal consultant, or head of tax and that is probably your internal grade. But for the buyer it's most probably meaningless and does not sound like it can help them. The mistake people always make with the summary title is they write their 'what', rather than their 'why'. As in, they write *what they do*, rather than *why they do it*. There are many LinkedIn trainers that get you to write 'passionate about …'. This is utter tripe. The buyer reads this as: 'Salesperson who's been on a LinkedIn course'.

Your 'why' appeals to your limbic brain. This part of your brain does not understand language, it is all about 'gut reaction'. You want somebody to look at your LinkedIn profile and go 'Wow, what on earth does that mean? I need to look further.' Then if you write your profile in a similar style and also use storytelling techniques you will have pulled somebody in and they will be reading your profile and not the competitions.

To be buyer-centric, you need to think about your output – what is the business impact you make with customers? Do you make their customer services more efficient? Reduce inventory? How is it that you help them? What is it you think you can teach them? It usually takes time (and multiple iterations) to come up with something you feel comfortable with.

The next section is the summary. The summary also needs to be buyer-centric; it needs to be compelling and educational. What business issues have you solved, customers you have helped? How can you help prospective customers in the future? You also need to keep it human. Don't forget people are trying to find out about you, not your company and its products and services. The section should be 'output' based and also contain keywords that prospective customers might use to search for your product or services. Avoid buzzwords and internal jargon. Often in the B2B community we can be fixated on our own terminology, not considering that the customer may have no idea what we are talking about.

You should also upload some video/multimedia content below the summary. Some people add company videos, which is a 'cop out'. Corporate videos show your employer how committed you are, but they can make you look very 'corporate'. You are supposed to be helping somebody to buy, not just replicate your employer's website. You can create your own video content cheaply and easily – after all, what is a mobile phone for? Get a colleague to interview you, just using your smartphone, and upload that. It does not need to be more than five minutes.

We also recommend you have a background photo or picture, as this brightens up the profile. In my case I use a photo I took of the sun rising. The key thing is not to be one-dimensional but to bring the profile alive.

Your LinkedIn profile is a great way to start conversations. Where you went to school, the fact you did a sponsored cycle ride, maybe you did the Marathon des Sables –all of these things are talking points. They create conversations and it's conversations that will get you sales.

FIGURE 2.3   Your LinkedIn profile summary

A professional photo of your face, smiling and looking at the camera

A background image that creates curiosity in the reader and positions you as an expert

Your summary title, which is your 'why'. Again, create curiosity in the reader

Your summary should tell a story about yourself, your journey, why you are an expert
Tell us about yourself
This is NOT about your products and services.

Details of your job roles – not your objectives, but what you learned
How does this connect to your current role?

As a buyer, I want to see who you are as a human, what your expertise is, what you stand for, will and can you help me?

Think about the keywords your buyer will be searching on – avoid buzzwords

How to find the keywords to use

Go to Google.com (make sure you're signed out of Gmail and Google) and start entering words that you think people might use to find you, or your products and services. Google will auto-populate suggestions for searches. These suggestions are top searches performed on Google by other people. This should help you get a feeling for the keywords you need to 'bury' or 'build around' in your summary. Pepper these key words and phrases through your LinkedIn profile. Google sees a LinkedIn profile as a string of text, so you don't need to lump these key words all in one place.

One word on search. LinkedIn works differently to Google. Google works on search terms based on articles and websites it has indexed. It does not matter where the article is it will serve you the answer it thinks best fits your search request. LinkedIn will search based on your network. For you to be found by a buyer, you need to be close to them. This is why you need a wide and varied network. So, get connecting. But don't forget, don't sell, everybody hates a pitch. More on this later.

Once you have written your summary, may I suggest using a Word cloud application. Cut and paste what you have written into the word cloud app. It's a great way to give yourself a second view – is that word cloud the message you are trying to convey? Is that the conclusion you want people to jump to?

Completing job roles on LinkedIn

It may come as a surprise to some readers, but unlike five years ago where your LinkedIn profile was a copy of your CV as you were using it to get your next job, now it is being used by you to inform, teach and support your prospective customers. Don't list your objectives – tell me what you learned. In my LinkedIn profile I provide key facts (with keywords) and also back this up with recommendations. Recommendations are key, especially from customers or third parties you have worked with, to demonstrate this isn't just something you have thought up and put out on spec.

The way you describe your job should be output-based. What is it in your role that you do to support customers? We all have experience of jobs where things might not have worked out as we had hoped, but don't be negative – accentuate the positive. For example, 'I went to work at company X and I learned A, B, and C, which meant that in my next role I was better suited for E. But I did learn that small companies were probably not for me.'

Volunteer experience and causes

We certainly recommend that you itemize any voluntary work or charity work, as this shows the reader that you are a rounded and worldly person. I itemize all the sponsored cycle rides I've been on; life isn't all about me. You want to demonstrate to the reader that you have outside interests.

Education

Itemize significant educational achievements. In my case, I mention my university qualification. This does not mean you need to include every single swimming and cycling proficiency certificate. If you have achieved any training or qualifications as part of your role, such as sales or marketing training, first aid, languages, etc., mention them. You may find that the buyer went to the same university as you and then you are straight into a conversation.

Organizations

If you are part of any organizations outside of work then it would be worth mentioning them. Examples might be involvement with your children's school, or with charitable or professional bodies, especially if they are related to your work.

Skills and recommendations

Recommendations are different from skills on a LinkedIn page. Skills are used by recruiters to search for the people they want for a role. If you want recruiters to find you, it is worth spending some time working on which of these are appropriate for you. In addition, it is worth thinking about what the people around you, your family and friends, would think about you – whether you are loyal or trustworthy, etc. Again, you don't have to be 'corporate' and you can add and change these around to suit your own personality. I'm not saying you should, but I know people who want it to be known that a key skill for them is 'eating chocolate' or 'performing indie rock'.

Positioning and messaging

For a salesperson and a marketer, positioning is about having a clear focus as to who your customer is and what they want. Your job when developing a position is to get to a point where a human being understands your position and then wants to engage further. That necessitates someone seeing your position, which is what your shop window is. LinkedIn profiles are, in effect, shop windows, so it follows that the job of a LinkedIn profile is to get your position across.

Messaging is the execution of positioning. Positioning is the part you understand as a business – 'We want to sell hosted telephony systems to this sort of company.' Messaging is how you present the position. If you're a luxury brand advertising in a luxury magazine (e.g. Vogue), your messaging will be highly visual. On LinkedIn, our messaging has to be the written word.

The most important thing about a position is that it has to be focused. What kills sales and marketing more than anything (and, by extension, any commercial proposition depending on that marketing) is being too broad. If you sell hosted telecoms, a poor position would be to say that you can sell that to anyone. It's much better to have focus and say that you're going to sell to 'companies in or around London, in the legal sector, with a turnover of £x'. The reason for this is that it's easier to craft messages around a focused position. Consider 'We sell hosted telecom systems', versus 'Having worked as an IT manager for a London-based mid-sized law firm, I understand the importance of one-click dialling to you. That's why we've crafted this special solution using speed dialling.'

That said, it's likely you don't have a free hand in this market position, as the business likely already has one. Your job as a social salesperson is to fully understand the business's market position, and then craft a good message around it. But, let's not forget, people are not interested in your company or its products and services – people are interested in you. This is about you using your digital identity to position yourself, the human, the person that can help, that other people start to know, like and trust.

Buyer persona

Crafting a message is dependent on having well-defined personas. A persona is an expression, usually a written expression, of a sample customer. They are usually quite detailed and describe the person in professional and personal terms. Often they are amalgams of a small set of customers the company already has who are strategically important. If your marketing team hasn't yet developed personas, you will need to come up with your ideal customer criteria. A persona is the DNA of the person you need to target. Not just a job title, but the elements that make them up. Are they professional? What networks do they hang out in? What is the structure of their life? Are they visually or factually orientated?

By looking at human, emotional and rational factors, propositions can be based on two-dimensional rational and emotional reason to believe. In many cases people also layer on the purpose the company fulfils on a human or societal level.

Developing personas is outside of the scope of this book, but we will offer some pointers. Essentially, it's an imaginary person that you want to talk to. Write down who they are, what they do, what their pains are, what their motivations are, and how they need to be conveyed from being a prospect to a customer. You can have multiple personas. The critical aspect of this is that any messaging that you put together must be targeted to at least one of those personas. Effectively, you are writing for that person.

The purpose of doing this is that it carries the focus of the position through to the message, and by definition you'll only end up talking to people with whom the position resonates. It fundamentally makes it easier to put together messaging. Psychologically, we are all very good at talking to one person and developing a relationship – we all intuitively understand how to do that. The converse of this – talking to a group of people in the hope that some of them will come over to our way of thinking – is much harder and hugely counterintuitive.

Look at your existing clients – what are those people's beliefs, skills, abilities, behaviours and environment? The most common mistake that people make with LinkedIn is to talk about themselves in their profile. That's fine if LinkedIn is a directory, but we're trying to use our profile like a shop window. Presenting a market position through messaging that is seller-centric is the most basic marketing mistake that you can make.

For example, a salesperson might say they are great at creating relationships – in reality, a buyer does not care whether they are or not. Ironically, as a salesperson you already know this. You know that when talking to a customer you have to, above all else, listen to what they are telling you about themselves and their problems. Listen to who they are, what their struggles are, and what the impact of that pain is. Then develop with them a vision of what a solution might be and flesh out that solution. That approach works because it makes the customer feel understood and comfortable – it moves you both into a joint partnership position of trying to reach a common goal, rather than you as the salesperson imposing a solution on them. And so it needs to be like this with your positioning.

Is this a good message for a customer:

Twenty years' experience selling telephony solutions.

No – that's a good message for an employer. If a sales manager of a company that sold hosted telephony solutions wanted to hire someone for their team that's a roughly good-enough message. But the customer – someone looking to buy a hosted telephone solution – frankly could not care less about that. What about:

> Hosted telephony can be a great way to increase the reliability of your phone system.

OK, so now we have something that's not good for an employer, but is better for a customer. This underlines the importance of focus when it comes to positioning – is your profile for an employer or a customer? You can't do both – you have to have focus. In this case, we've focused on the customer.

With your developed market position and personas you can now go and craft your message within the summary box. You may well be thinking 'easier said than done'. Indeed, it will take some practice, some iterations and 'socializing' it with friends and colleagues ('socializing' in this context means circulating it, asking for feedback, and then taking that feedback on board). The important thing is to get something written, get some input, and then tweak. The only mistakes that you can make are talking too much about yourself, and not having focus. It needs to tell a story about you, what has inspired you, your journey and the more honest and authentic you are, the more people will walk towards you.

Calls to action

Your shop window needs a call to action (CTA). People viewing your LinkedIn profile have to be actively encouraged to take an action that you want, which is why marketers insist on having a clear CTA. Some people viewing your profile will do nothing, because it's not of interest to them. However, to some people, what you're offering (your 'position') will be of interest. The worst possible outcome is someone sees your profile, is interested, but then doesn't understand what the next steps are. An obvious analogy is of a fish wriggling off the hook as you're trying to land it.

Of course, what your CTA is may not be clear. We know people who put their mobile number on their profile and ask people to call them. We know others that want users driven to their Twitter account, or some other webpage. Think of the customer journey here; if somebody has taken the time and trouble to research you so far on the web, will they pick up the phone to you? It might be better to offer them a 'web' solution, getting them to connect with you or driving them to your blog, for example.

Whatever your CTA is, it has to be crafted into your summary section. When you've done your summary section, and you're socializing it around your friends and colleagues, make sure that your CTA is clear, and that you test it during that socialization.

News

Although at its core LinkedIn is a directory, it has a way of allowing a member to post news articles that might be of interest to that member's network. If you go to the home page in LinkedIn and you're logged in, you'll see posts from people that you have connected with, or that you follow. This idea is called content curation, and we'll talk about this in much more detail in Chapter 8 on technology.

The worst possible way of using LinkedIn

Most users' frustration with LinkedIn is that people use it as a channel for interruption marketing. It's very likely that you have experienced this. LinkedIn doesn't make money by you doing the above, which is why they try to get you to send inmails. Inmails are the same as a cold call or a cold email – you interrupt a person and pitch. Problem is, nobody likes being sold to, which means you won't get very far with inmails. As part of our social selling coaching, we don't recommend you use inmails.

Our suggestion to grow your network is that you send connection requests. The trick is to think about the buyer and not you. You need to know about them, and show how your life will be so much richer for having them in your life. As a salesperson, you need as wide and as varied a network as you can get, and you need the companies you are trying to sell to within your network. One of my team is connected to over 1,000 people in one of his target accounts. I'm not saying you will sell more by being connected to so many people, but you are more likely to sell in to that account than if you are connected to one or two people. More on that later.

FIGURE 2.4   The worst possible way of using LinkedIn – sending people spam pitches

Dear Matt!

Our companies work in closely elated fields and that's why I've contacted you. I noticed that you work for Influencer Insights

There is an opportunity to find mutual point of interest for both of us. Our main business is to provide software engineers to customers' needs. We have more than 200 developers and narrowly specialize in PHP, .Net, Java and iOS, Android and Windows Phone. The average price rate for a middle developer is 25 Europ per hour and 30 Euro for a senior developer. We can help your team to handle your software technology needs and assist in software development.

I'll be in your area on October 5th–9th and will be able to meet you to discuss some possible projects.

I would appreciated your feedback.

Twitter

As we said at the start of this chapter, social salespeople should be on LinkedIn, Twitter and Instagram. The objective of this chapter is to get your identity in these platforms sorted out. As we go through into other chapters, we will teach you how to use these to build up your community, as introduced in Chapter 1.

As we have discussed, LinkedIn primarily looks to model real-world connections, and does this through a directory metaphor. It assumes that people have already met, and just want a digital alternative to meeting in real life. Twitter, on the other hand, is geared towards letting people who don't know each other form relationships based on shared ideas and goals. What this means from a social selling perspective is that there are people out there ideating solutions to complex problems whom you can actually get at. Thus, you will find it significantly easier to find and engage with potential (not yet spoken to) customers on Twitter compared to LinkedIn.

The behaviour that you are looking for on Twitter is that, as a salesperson, you put something interesting out into the network, and that your actions will stimulate a user into doing something.

Twitter ROI

I'm aware of people that have spent £20,000 per annum on advertising for just a few hundred pounds worth of income. A connection of mine started to use Twitter, and for no expenditure other than his time he got over £2,000 of business in two weeks. He now averages £500 a month via Twitter. In fact we have a long list of clients that are getting business from social, that is, as long as you follow a methodology – after all, sales is a process.

How to be social – sharing ideas

With all social networks, the key is in the first word, 'social'. The idea is not to put out endless updates, but to get engagement and comment. The comments (or, better still, questions) are valuable in and of themselves, and because they are directly attributable to the author, and readers tend to attribute value and worth to the author. This makes it very easy to build thought leadership positions.

Your identity on Twitter is far more defined by your behaviour and how you present yourself than on LinkedIn. LinkedIn is a lot more sanitized and presents your 'shop window', whereas Twitter is considerably more 'human'. There is an advantage to positioning yourself as a 'purveyor of new ideas', compared to someone who just circulates other people's ideas.

Your Twitter profile

Users are attracted to other people on Twitter based on what that person posts, rather than who they are. However, your Twitter profile is important as people will often look at your profile before deciding whether to follow you or not. As we'll see in Chapter 5, it's important to build up your followers, and your profile will either help or hinder that process.

Your profile should contain a picture, a short piece of biographical information about yourself, a link to a website and a location. Your profile should be about you as a person, not about the business, and as a result the picture should be of you and not the business. A good number of people make the mistake of branding their Twitter account for the business and not for them as an individual. The whole point of having a social profile is to allow potential buyers to find you and then hopefully engage with you. People form an opinion of you from your Twitter and LinkedIn profiles, and if you have a photo of a corporate then they will think you are just that – a corporate. People buy people, after all.

The location is important as, although the network is global, you need to focus your efforts on where your customers are. For example, hosted telephony may be a globally applicable business, but your ultimate goal is to have meetings, and you need to be able to get to them. Part of this focus is being clear in your location information as to where you are. Our further advice on this would be to make this unambiguous. (In the UK, for example, there is a Sudbury in West London and one in Suffolk, so 'Sudbury, West London' or 'Sudbury, Suffolk' is better on a profile.) Further, putting your country on is also a good idea to make it very clear to potential followers where you are – for example, 'Sudbury, Suffolk, UK'.

Your bio should describe succinctly your leadership role in your new community, and the value that you intend to bring to people interested in that community. Of course, it should be aligned with your marketing position but it should also reflect you as a person.

In the bio, you can reference other Twitter handles, but any web links that you put in there will not be clickable. However, you need to consider your CTA on your profile. If someone is looking at your profile, you want them to follow you immediately, rather than get distracted and go off following something else. However, it's beneficial to use other handles to build brand and authority – for example, 'Helping people get the best from hosted telephony solutions. Co-founder of @MyHostedTelephonySolutions – ideas around hosted telephony' helps build authority, albeit at the expense of reducing the number of people who action your desired CTA of following your account.

Finally, there is the web link. This one web link will be clickable, but again remember that it will affect the CTA. On a company Twitter profile this should be the company website. On a personal account, the objective is less clear. You have to consider the action you want. Just dumping a user at the home page of the company website likely doesn't do anything particularly helpful – the user will consider the website, but seeing as most company websites do not have a clear CTA on that page you'll end up wasting the click. It makes more sense to send them to your LinkedIn profile. The LinkedIn profile will reinforce your position, and also has a clear-ish CTA objective in getting a 'follow' over on that side.

Structure of a Twitter profile

The fundamentals of a Twitter profile are the same as for LinkedIn – it needs to be buyer-centric. If a buyer looks at your Twitter profile, what is it that will make them want to follow you or even make contact with you?

You need a photo of yourself, as discussed above; this is about your personal brand. It is best to use the same photo across all your professional networks. Some corporate organizations make recommendations as to what an employee's profile should say, and if your business does you should follow them. That said, you don't want to look like a corporate suit; be original, funny even. But be professional. Say a little bit about yourself. Have a website people can go to for more information. The corporate website is fine, but this is also a great opportunity to drive traffic to your blog.

Decide whether you want to have one Twitter account for everything you do, or a separate account specifically directed to your company. In the United States it is the law that if you have gained followers during work time, they belong to your employer. For example, if you built up a large following and went to a competitor, the following that your previous employer had 'paid' you to set up could then be used against them. In the United States there have been situations where the employee has been asked to hand the Twitter profile back. While this is not currently the law in the UK, there have been high-profile cases where journalists for the BBC left to go to a competitor channel, and the BBC asked for the Twitter profile back. Of course, there was a mass unfollowing, as the people followed the journalist and not the BBC.

Some organizations suggest you need to add a disclaimer such as 'The views given here are my own and not representative of the business' into your avatar, but while this is standard policy, thinking has moved on. If it is a company account, you speak for the company regardless of what is in your avatar. There have been some suggestions that employees start using a hashtag so that the reader can see the tweet is from or represents an employee view and not that of the organization. This often happens when organizations are at a low level of social maturity, and they are trying to regain control of social media. Corporations need to understand that the genie is out of the bottle with social, and they cannot control the flow of information. IBM's social selling programme recommends that people should have one profile, so the follower gets a more 'rounded' view. A cynic might say that the IBM messaging might end up being more subliminal, rather than 'buy IBM', which I guess is what IBM want. I split my Twitter accounts up, and constantly remind whomever I work for that the accounts belong to me. They are not another channel to pump out 'corporate' content.

The key thing is to be interesting and educational, and I think my accounts are educational. I will also tweet competitor articles. My view is that social media in many cases is a ToFu (top of the funnel) or MoFu (middle of the funnel) activity, and if it helps to educate the buyer then that is great. My role is to support the community or to get us on the shortlist. Who wins the deal, and how, is not my concern; that is down to the salespeople – good old sales skills.

With my Twitter profile, my name is straightforward, and for my work account I would add my company name into the title so it is clear whom I work for. This isn't about selling by 'stealth' or not being honest about who we are. There is a short description, in which I try to show an element of a sense of humour, where I am based, and a call to action website, which in this case is my blog. Avoid putting your corporate website on here if you can, as it tends to be too broad.

Research shows that tweets with photos tend to get around 50 per cent more engagement than those without. It is not for this book to go in depth into how you craft a tweet, use hashtags, etc.

LinkedIn and Twitter can be used to find people that you would like to speak to, speak to them online, move that conversation offline and then form an ongoing relationship with them. Twitter as a social network can allow you to follow and be followed by people you don't know, whereas with LinkedIn you will probably know the person in some way. The key is to use both of these networks to complement each other and build your community.

The news feeds provide a way of offering content that your followers or future followers will find interesting and perhaps educational; better still, they will want to engage with you.

FIGURE 2.5   Your Twitter profile summary

> A professional photo of your face, smiling and looking at the camera – the same photo as in your LinkedIn profile

> A background image that creates curiosity in the reader and positions you as an expert

> Your summary title, which is your 'why'. Again, create curiosity in the reader – maybe use a hashtag so people can see what tribe you associate with

> Put in a link where people can find more information about you – maybe your LinkedIn profile
> If you link to your website, take people to the value proposition your cover rather than the .com

> Think about your 'pinned Tweet'. This needs to be something that is important to you right now

> Send me a Tweet at @timothy_hughes and say hello

Send a tweet

Have you managed to get your Twitter account set up? Please send a tweet and tag me @timothy_hughes. If you are feeling brave, send me a selfie of you and the book.

Summary

Changemakers are out there, building teams and looking to solve problems for their companies. To solve problems, look for new solutions – people are doing this by going online. While the obvious place to start would be a search engine, they are also using social networks to solve those problems. If you are in B2B enterprise sales, having a personal brand is as important as having a mobile (cell) – you don't exist without it. Personal branding is just level one; next we will explain what you need to do to use social networks to help you over-achieve your quota.

03

Talking to strangers

'Networking in real life' example

One of the first things our parents or guardians tell us from an early age, apart from not to be late home, is to never talk to strangers. Maybe that is why so many people find social media difficult; it goes against the parental messages that hide in our heads.

There is a video that does the rounds on social media every six months where somebody goes up to strangers in the street and starts following them. When challenged, the person says, 'I'm just being a follower'. The video also has a person going up to strangers and saying, 'Can I be your friend?' Why am I pointing out the absurdity of social media in a social media book?

As children and as adults, talking to strangers is something we are taught is rude, and is certainly something introverts will avoid at all costs. Networking is a term that has been used over recent years as the socially accepted way of saying, go into a room and talk to a bunch of people you have never met – strangers. Introverts generally won't want to talk to strangers, whereas extroverts usually will. But is there a way we can talk to strangers that will help us? I'm sure we can remember right back to our childhood when we first started school and we needed to talk to children we didn't know, but they soon became our friends. For some of us, they become friends for the rest of our lives. In my journey on social media, I have met and become friends with people from all over the world. I contacted many of these people when I have travelled to their part of the world, and we met up. It was Brian Fanzo who said 'social media turns the first handshake into a hug'.

In the world of sales, when we go for a first meeting with a client, we quickly need to create a connection between people as prospective customers and ourselves. That connection can be made from rapport, trust, mutual understanding and respect, and that all has to be built or created in a matter of minutes. Many of us recognize this in the offline world. Now we can (and have to) do this in the online world, as this is where our buyers in the connected economy are. Yes, our skills are useful when we have face-to-face meetings, but we also need to use social media, to help us get those meetings.

As we have talked about in the previous chapters, this book is about helping you and short-cutting the demand generation process. You need to build a community (a digital territory) so that you are already recognized as a thought leader and a 'go to' for knowledge in your specialist subject or niche. This gives you the credentials so that people might seek you out. In the online world, as you start to contact and interact with people they will want to make sure you are not a spammer, which is why you need a decent social profile, your shop window to the world. Building your online profile and community means you need to talk with many strangers; these people may be prospects, competitors and influencers already. We have discussed the importance of people and brands in building a community and owning that community. To build that community we need to talk to a lot of strangers.

The problem that many salespeople face is recognizing a potential prospect. There are, generally, three types of useful people you will meet as a salesperson:

- somebody whom will buy from you
- somebody whom won't buy, but will recommend you to somebody in their network whom might buy
- somebody whom might never buy, but they will amplify your message on a social network

In the sales environment we will meet many different types of people: decision makers, influencers (internal and external), user decision makers, and often, in the modern world, changemakers. As part of the selling process we need to work out whether they are supporters that will enable us to make a sale. Owning the community where these people need to work and thrive will help us, but we need to talk (and interact) with these strangers and build long-term relationships with them. We want our customers to become references and advocates, as it helps us to sell more. Plus, people move from company to company and we want them to take us with them in their new role.

When we say that we don't like cold calling, some people think we are being anti-phone. Not at all. We simply don't think that calling people up, interrupting them and then broadcasting a message has a place in the world today. Why would you start a relationship by annoying the person you want to sell to? As you will find in this book, there are far subtler, more efficient and effective ways of building relationships. Phones have their uses, at the right time, as do programmes like Zoom and Microsoft Teams. In fact, you job as a social seller is to nurture that relationship on social then take the conversation off social and onto some other form of communication method.

Let's assume we have just received an invite to a networking party. What do we do? We might take a friend, as that would ease the embarrassment of talking with strangers, but let's assume we go by ourselves. We might arrive, get a drink and either look around for a group that might 'look fun' or see somebody who is standing by themself and go up and talk to them. We don't walk up to people and pitch, we start a conversation.

If we take this example online, many people who I don't know contact me. There's nothing wrong with that, and I have built many a long-term business relationship with people I have met online but in fact have never met in real life. Some I do, but there are still people I have known for many years yet have never met them in person. What often happens is that people send me a message by direct mail (DM) and tell me about how wonderful their product and service is. No context. For example, somebody approached me and told me how great their telephone system is. I'm sorry, but I'm not currently in the market for a telephone system and I'm unsure I will be in the future.

Let's go back to the networking event. How about this for a scenario. I arrive, and before I get a drink I stand in the doorway and shout at the top of my voice, 'Hi, I'm Tim and I have this great telephone system!', then launch into my pitch... I'm sure this would silence the room for a few seconds and some people may stop to watch such a spectacle, or to see my embarrassment. It is highly unlikely I will sell anything, and even less likely I will be invited back! So, if you don't do that in the offline world, don't try it in the online world. In fact, going onto social and sending a person a message about your product and service, a pitch, is rude and is likely to get you blocked.

Another mistake that people make is that they don't consider how many people in a room might actually be decision makers for telephone systems. Or will be in the future. A presentation I listened to yesterday stated, 'Everybody at that party will be useful for you'. I'm sorry, I don't buy that. If you go to a networking party of 100 people, it's clearly illogical to believe that more than 20 people will be useful to you. I'm sure being the acquaintance of all 100 would be great, as they may know somebody who knows somebody, but it's a physical impossibility to get round everybody at that event. So how do you find the 20 people who will be useful for you and your community?

Previously we have talked about community, your digital territory. If you have people that are willing to amplify your message, this is like walking into that networking meeting and for people in there to turn to the person they are with and saying, you should be talking to that person over there. This gives you an increase in efficiency as you will talk to more people that are likely to buy and not waste so much time talking to people who won't.

Listening

Back to our networking event. Getting our drink, we decide which person or group we will go and contact. Once we have made our introductions, we talk about who we are and what we do. If we have approached a group, rather than butting into a conversation, which would be deemed rude, we listen to what other people are saying. We might nod in agreement or encouragement. We might offer up our own examples. As time progresses we might ask open questions (how, what, where, why?). After a time we might provide our own commentary. Often we will judge this by the body language of the people in the group. When trust is built, then often there is a swapping of business cards.

But how many times have you turned up to networking events and decided after a few minutes that the people you are talking to won't help you in your current goals and objectives? How long do you give it before you make the decision to 'go and get another drink', which is the polite way of dropping those people and finding another group, one that will meet your objectives? This is probably why speed dating became so popular, as it allows people to decide if there is a match within a couple of minutes. With the speed-dating concept the embarrassment of moving from person to person is taken away from you as you are forced to move on as part of the rules of the format.

There is a way you can talk to strangers and quickly qualify if they will be useful to you. In fact you can work that out before you contact them. You can do it on social media.

Before we dive into networking with hundreds of people on social media, let's talk about active listening, as it's different from hearing. When we are in a conversation with somebody we often hear what they are saying, but I'm not sure we actually listen to what they say. Why? In any conversation, while somebody talks we are thinking about what we are going to say next – we may even be trying to work out a way to move the subject away from certain areas. Our mind is in another place.

That is the difference between hearing and listening. Listening is where we hear and maybe even note down what the person is saying. I've often done this with customers where we have worked as a pair. There are two of you; one person asks the questions, then the next person, giving you both time to listen and hear what your customer or prospect is actually saying. Often you can use active question techniques and go back with, 'What does that mean to you?' or, 'What is that loss in $ value?'

The technique of 'active listening' can be used with active questioning. Active listening involves repeating back to the customer what they have said, not in a way that sounds like a trap. For example: 'This inventory loss sounds painful. If we could show you in a demonstration how we can reduce the shrinkage, do you think this would go some way to reduce the $ value of losses you are receiving right now?' Such techniques can be used in the online world of social media to help you network and group your community.

In the world of B2B sales we recommend that you focus initially on Twitter, Instagram and LinkedIn. The three have their advantages and can be used in different 'modes' for demand generation and through the sales process.

LinkedIn is ideal – and designed – for networking. Many people create their profiles, then meet somebody and receive a connection request. Many (most) people now research who they are going to meet by looking up their LinkedIn profile before the meeting. I will send LinkedIn connect requests before a meeting on the basis that people can 'check out my shop window' and therefore make the meeting more productive. LinkedIn, as described in the previous chapters, can also be used for searching for customers and prospects you don't know and approaching them.

Our usual approach is to use listening techniques when contacting somebody over social media and write: 'I noticed you were talking about XYZ – have you considered this?', 'I see that you have completed charity cycle rides, I have too', 'I see you posted about Star Wars, I'm a big fan'. There should be some content that the contact will be interested in, to drive the conversation forward. By encouraging and engaging (just like we would do in the offline world) we are able to quickly find the people we need to talk to and engage with them. For sellers this has major advantages, as you are able to accelerate the selling process and get your products or services in front of the right people quicker.

When I first started selling 25 years ago, it was explained to me that when I met customers I would need to build rapport. 'How do I do this?' I asked. When you go to meetings with customers they will have photos on their walls. They might be of fly-fishing, Formula One, or football – whatever it is that excites them. I was told to draw people into discussions about their passions, to listen and have a two-way dialogue, thus building rapport. Nothing has changed today, except that our offline world has moved online. We do exactly the same on social media.

Twitter works well for our methodology, as you can follow your prospects and customers and listen to what they are saying at the macro (company) level, and you can also find and listen at the micro level to the individuals you are targeting. This enables you to listen to what is important to that company, and also get an understanding of the individuals in your territory. What is important to them? If they tweet about walking their dogs, you know that their dogs are important. This is no different from walking into somebody's office and seeing photos of their dogs on the wall. Use it (and be authentic) as a way to build a conversation.

Your prospects and changemakers are out there leaving 'footprints' on social networks – you need to find them.

FIGURE 3.1   Listening on social – getting to know people

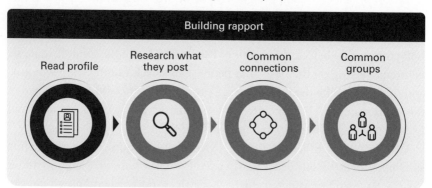

Social graph

The term 'social graph' was popularized at the Facebook (now Meta) F8 conference on 24 May 2007, when it was used to explain how the newly introduced Facebook platform would take advantage of the relationships between individuals to offer a richer online experience. The definition has been expanded to refer to a social graph of all internet users. The social graph in the internet context is a graph that depicts the personal relations of internet users. It has been referred to as 'the global mapping of everybody and how they're related'.

FIGURE 3.2   LinkedIn is only part of your social graph

While some people talk about social selling as just LinkedIn, this is wrong, as LinkedIn is only about 30 per cent of an individual's social graph. A person's social graph will cover all of the networks they belong to: LinkedIn, Facebook, Instagram, etc.

A friend of mine, Paul, was researching a HR director and couldn't find her on LinkedIn or Twitter, but did find her on Instagram, which is where she posted photos of her cats. He was able to build rapport and engagement with her through those cat photos, which led him to get a face-to-face meeting and he got to sell her something, which was his objective.

People often say to me, 'Isn't this stalking?' No. If people are putting photos of their cats on an open network, then they will be flattered that you have taken the time to find them and I'm sure they will like to talk about them. This is no different from our analogy above about a person's office, where they hang photos reflecting their interest. Engaging in conversations about these photos would be deemed as flattering, not stalking.

A colleague of mine was calling on a CEO of an organization. He did all the research and this CEO wasn't connected to any of his contacts on LinkedIn. What he didn't know was that this CEO was also the brother-in-law of a work colleague; that relationship didn't show up on LinkedIn, but it would have on Facebook. People often say to me that Facebook is for friends, family and photos. Maybe, but don't forget that it is also part of your prospects' and customers' social graph. I'm not suggesting that you start walking all over Facebook selling your wares, but if you cannot see your contact's Facebook connections you are missing a serious part of their social graph.

A friend of mine, Jon Ferrara, is the CEO of the social CRM product Nimble, a great tool that allows you to do research on somebody before a meeting. Jon set up a call with me a few years ago during which he was going to pitch his product to me. Some recent research showed that people were 40 per cent more likely to prefer going to the dentist than to receive a supplier pitch. I was sure Jon would be different, but I was knocked out by how different he was. Jon is based in California. Usually what happens when I have a call with people on the US West Coast (which is eight hours behind me in the UK) is that we have a conversation about the weather and what time it is. Jon was different; he had done his research about me and his first question was, 'What's your favourite vinyl record?' We then spent the first 15 minutes of the call talking about vinyl and the bands we had seen. This level of rapport knocked me out and if we are ever in vinyl record shops we send each other photos.

This, for me, is such a great example of somebody that took the time to research me and found out that I collect vinyl records. In the first 15 minutes Jon built rapport (he also collects vinyl) and we got to know and trust each other better through our appreciation for rock music. Jon 'nurtures' our relationship through that mutual interest by sending me photos of record shops or rare copies he has obtained. He and his product are then front of my mind.

While social is a revolution, it does not take away from what we have always done offline. We still need to have conversations with people and build relationships, but what social media does is enable us to build relationships quicker, sort the wheat from the chaff and then nurture those relationships.

Researching

There are many ways you can approach companies about your solutions and services. The most popular over the last 30 years have been mailshots and cold calling. I mention them together as they are tied in terms of measurement. They are both old-fashioned and require you to annoy people to try and have a conversation. When I started selling, this approach was described to me as throwing mud at the wall and hoping it will stick.

When I started work 30 years ago, we had a typing pool and I gave letters to the typists to type; each one had to be individually crafted and they got a pretty good response. Then came word processors and word processing software, and the belief was that if we could create more and more direct mail we would get a better and better response. Then came email and we switched from direct mail to sending as many emails as we could. Why? We no longer need to pay for postage and an email is 'free' after all. Our only restriction was the number of people's email addresses we had. A whole industry developed based on how to write headers that will get people to open these emails rather than just delete them, as most people usually do. As soon as we moved into mass direct mail and emails, we had to write based on the lowest common denominator to try to appeal to as many people as we could. Technology was developed by buyer companies to catch these emails before they 'filled up' your in-box. Junk folders and rules on incoming emails were all created to help you manage them and stop them cluttering up your day.

Research from right across the HubSpot client base shows that while the number of sales emails has increased, the response rate has fallen and keeps falling. The response rate from sales emails is down 37 per cent from 1 January 2020. Yamini Rangan, CEO of HubSpot, said in a webinar in 2020, 'We are inundated with email, especially busy executives and we are overwhelmed. So how do you cut through this, that is where the key is?' Kipp Bodmar, their CMO, said that HubSpot were 'sending less email' (Hubspot, 2020). HubSpot has also said that email marketing had a 98 per cent failure rate (Gillum, 2020). Let's not forget that HubSpot sell email marketing solutions and therefore have a vested interest to talk email marketing up.

The same goes for cold calling, telesales and telemarketing. In 2021, the Bank of America's Merrill Lynch banned cold calling and moved all their people to social selling (WSJ, 2021). Now, this isn't some trendy tech company that might have decided to do this on a whim, this is a very conservative financial services company that has made a decision based on data.

But surely cold calling has a better ROI than social selling? Not according to Merrill Lynch. 'They will also be encouraged to contact prospects over LinkedIn, which has a higher hit rate than cold calling'(WSJ, 2021). Because of the reduction in the return from legacy sales and marketing methods such as email and cold calling, companies have had to throw more and more mud at the wall and hope it will stick. If at any time direct mails or cold calling aren't deemed to work, the perception is that you just increase the number of calls or direct mails. Sales is a numbers game, after all.

The likelihood that your unsolicited email will be read is around 2 per cent, which is a 98 per cent rejection rate. The likelihood your LinkedIn inmail will be read is approximately 7 per cent, which is a 93 per cent rejection rate. Would you go to your board and tell them that you were going to put budget into something that had a 98 per cent rejection rate? I wouldn't. The same with cold calling – as soon as Bank of America switch away from cold calling, it was the final nail in its coffin.

Account-based marketing (ABM), also known as key account marketing, is a strategic approach to business marketing in which an organization considers and communicates with individual prospects or customer accounts as markets of one. It parallels the movement of business-to-consumer marketing away from mass marketing, where organizations try to sell individual products to as many new prospects as possible, to 1:1 marketing.

Let's not get too carried away here, as there are readers that will have multiple accounts. We are not saying you should just focus on one account. The idea is to increase your personalization to focus in on an account and individuals in that account. Like when Jon started the conversation with me about my favourite vinyl record, we want the approach to be appropriate and authentic, with context to that individual.

My friend Paul, who gets 10 C-level meetings a week using Twitter, is doing just that. He runs a networking company bringing C-level people together. But if you think about it, as individuals, once we have been to his meetings twice, we also have the network as we have met the people we want at the meetings. To get people to come back, he has to provide great content. He's always looking for great speakers.

When Twitter launched Twitter Spaces, a social audio product, Paul hit on the idea of getting the head of Twitter spaces to speak at one of his events, as that would be a great audience draw. He then went away to research this. Now he could have sent the guy a template email, probably like all the other template emails that people get. Instead, having researched the guy online he created a Word Swag using the app, and within an hour the guy had come back, they had a DM conversation on Twitter, and he agreed to speak at an event. Paul tells me he has a 90 per cent acceptance rate with Word Swags. More details on the application Word Swag and an example of it are provided in Chapter 8.

Now, before somebody thinks, I know, I'll create one Word Swag and email it out to everybody, the key is that one-to-one personalization gets a lower rejection rate. So let's go back to how Paul approached the human resources director who liked cats. He used standard ABM techniques on her, couldn't find her on Twitter and LinkedIn but did find her on Instagram. On finding her interest in cats, he created a Word Swag with a cat photo and a quote, and contacted her. It was highly personalized. From creating that connection and building the rapport he was able to connect with her on LinkedIn, enabling him to nurture that relationship. For example, any HR-related content that he posts on LinkedIn or likes, she will be able to see. This helps to continue to build and nurture his relationship and his leadership position in her eyes and also brings her into his community. Hopefully she will 'like' or 'retweet' some of his content, which will then ripple through her network. This amplifies what Paul is saying, but it may well also get picked up by other HR directors, who may then follow Paul if they are interested in more of that content, thus expanding Paul's network and community. They may even like or retweet it, too, expanding Paul's network and community even further.

FIGURE 3.3   Personalization

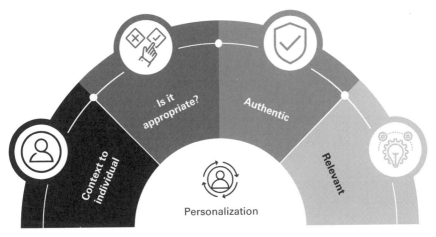

Talking

At the beginning of this chapter we discussed the need in social media to talk to strangers. But in a room of 100 people, how do we get to those 20 people we need to know, quicker? Then we considered the fact that we shouldn't just jump in and start trying to sell, but should listen to what our prospects and customers are interested in. Then we should try to build rapport and engagement with them around subject areas they understand or are passionate about, thus building trust and context, but also being authentic at the same time.

The next part of this chapter discusses how we can talk with prospects, customers and influencers using the techniques we have learnt so far. When people ask for my advice about Twitter, I tell them that the first thing to do on Twitter is not to tweet but to listen.

Many of us were taught at school that 'good behaviour' was writing pages and pages. The longer the essay, the better. Social media requires you to write in short sentences, and summarize what you want to say. This art, like many social media techniques, has been around for years; it is the art of the headline writer. Journalists and their subeditors needed to get you to read their article, and the way they did this was to write a headline that would draw you in. Some people call it a hook. It's about drawing you in so you spend time reading what has been written. When we read a newspaper, we don't read what we perceive as boring articles. If somebody looks boring we avoid them. So don't be boring.

In addition, don't be a 'corporate suit'. I know it's tempting to tweet or post on LinkedIn articles your company wants you to post. But come on. If you think they are boring, so will your audience. If your audience thinks they are boring then people won't follow you – they will in fact avoid you. Just like the person at the networking drinks who wants to talk about his double glazing, people will avoid you too.

FIGURE 3.4   Conversations, example 1

Nabeel, working at XYZ must be exciting and challenging. As the CEO of a fast-growing start-up, I'm looking to learn from the best. While we have not met, maybe we can connect? Tim

Hi Tim, Great to connect with you. Any chance you're a scout from Gryffindor? 😊

The conversation is over the fact my summary title is "Should have played quidditch for England", which is designed to create curiosity and create conversations in the buyer

Employee advocacy seems to be coming into fashion with big corporates right now. Employee advocacy is where you get your employees to post on social media. Your customers and prospects are not going to believe what your employees say, as they will also read the company material and say, 'Of course they are going to say that – they work there.' So, while your employees are a great way to increase your 'share of voice' (this is a measurement of how much muck you throw at the wall), nobody will listen and, more importantly, nobody trusts what the employees say. But the big thing that corporations like is the ability to control the message. Our research shows that people come to social media to be social, they don't come to social media to read brochures or brochureware.

Later on in the book we will talk about social media maturity models and how corporations have to let go of the message for customers and prospects to test it. The more corporations lose control, the more customers and prospects will trust them. This is a scary position that corporations are still trying to grapple with.

FIGURE 3.5   Conversations, example 2

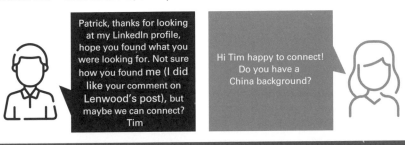

Previously in this chapter we have discussed how to approach strangers and accounts, to research them and offer a personalized message. This approach moves away from 'spray and pray' to invest time in focusing on an individual to understand them, before engaging. Just like we would if we were sitting opposite them in their office. By using active listening, we can also work with prospects, customers and influencers and personalize the message more. The more we personalize, the less rejection we get. This is particularly relevant when approaching influencers. Don't forget an influencer can make or break you – a clumsy approach could be tweeted for the whole world to see.

I recall a call with a senior social selling professional when they itemized their strategy. What would happen was an email would go out to each salesperson each day with a list of influencers in their area. It would be the salesperson's job to make contact with the influencer and offer them a piece of their content. My immediate thought was absolute horror. In the early days of the social selling project we would let people with little or no social presence make contact with seriously influential people, enquiring about the likeability of a certain product with back-up of a boring corporate white paper (note: nobody reads white papers anymore). This was a disaster in the making.

Contacting influencers is straightforward if you use the techniques mentioned above. You need influencers in your community as this helps to validate your brand and will bring you amplification and growth. You always need to talk to strangers, but you should also see organic growth, just like when you go to a networking event. The group that is laughing the most is the group people want to be part of. Successful communities will breed success.

If you want to connect with an influencer, don't just bound up to them like Tigger in Winnie the Pooh. Influencers will want a personalized message just like everybody else. Use your best active listening techniques. Read the material they write and when you connect with them, sell them the parts you like best of all. For example, tell them, 'I've read your blog and can really relate with the networking event theme.'

Influencers are always looking for good content, so if you have some great research or infographics, or both, then why not share with them? Don't be offended if they don't respond or don't think it's great – you can always try with something else another time. Don't forget influencers are not sitting there waiting for your approach; they are busy people trying to make a living, like all of us.

My advice is not to approach them and say, 'I've got a great website, what do you think?' or 'I've got a great app, what do you think?' We probably get three or four of those approaches a day individually. It's not original and just passes into the general noise of everything else. Think about it, is that personalized? Why do you switch into sales mode as soon as you have made contact? Why would I or anybody trust you?

A sales guy from a social app approached me by retweeting a few of my blogs, offered me feedback as to which ones he liked best, and even suggested a few areas he would like to see me explore. We would have frequent chats, and I even met him and helped him with his social media profile. It was at that meeting where he pitched his product to me (I knew it was coming). I would have done the same, if I had been in his place. As a social seller, you are using your social presence to create conversations. At some point you need to turn those conversations to something commercial and at some point you need to raise the subject of what you do.

If you are networking, sharing and engaging, people will spot you and hopefully be curious to look further and find out who you are. In many cases these people are 'lurkers', or they want something but are often too shy to make contact. One trick I use is that everybody that comes to my LinkedIn profile gets a note thanking them for making the effort to look at my profile and asking if they need any help. I have experimented with mentioning my blog, but actually keeping the message simple gets the best response. Maybe this approach drives them to a conversation rather than suggesting they move elsewhere. Of all the messages I send out, I get a 50 per cent response rate. Sometime it is 'You popped up in my network', and often they want to connect so they can keep up with my posts. It has also got me many opportunities in terms of podcast invites, which allows me to grow my reach into other people's communities and networks.

Wouldn't it be great if you could hang out where your prospects hung out?

Wouldn't it be great if you could drive to a market place or a mall, where a whole bunch of your prospects, are all in one place? All you had to do was go up to them and start a conversation? The $1.80 Instagram strategy (it actually works on any platform) to grow your business was created by Gary Vee (Vaynerchuk, 2017). This enables you to prospect at scale, for free.

HOW DOES IT WORK?

You will know the keywords that are relevant for your territory, industry or accounts. From that you can work out the hashtags your territory, industry or accounts are using. You then 'jump into the conversation' on a social network by leaving your pearls of wisdom on people's posts. Be positive, be challenging, but after all, people should recognize you for the insight you leave. As Gary says, 'You leave a comment with your very smart two cents.' This is how you become part of the conversation.

Back to Gary. 'They see your comment, they like it, they see your profile, they reach out to you. This is networking. This is the reality of the world. The overall process is incredibly simple. It's .02 cents, on 10 posts every day. That all adds up to $1.80.'

Summary

In this chapter we have looked at how many of the life skills we gained in the offline world can be used in the online world. How going to a dance or a networking event can help us as we continue on our social media journey. Making contact with people we don't know can turn them into contacts, prospects, customers and advocates. Better still, they help us create a community that we can sow and harvest to enable us to create leads and revenue.

Building on the social profile, our shop window created in Chapter 2, it is now down to us as salespeople to proactively go out and have conversations with people on social. Conversations can come about by sending connection requests, by creating content and dealing with the engagement we get. More on that later. Conversations can be either started online or you can join them online.

BUILDING A COMMUNITY TO CHANGE THE WORLD – CHRISTIAN JUMELET AND CHLOE HACKQUARD

My name is Christian Jumelet and I am the mentor to Chloe Hacquard and this is about Chloe's and my journey with social, and how we intend to change the world. We are doing this by building a global community. This community shares our vision and ideals and it is through this that one has become many.

HighChloeCloud was the brainchild of Chloe Hacquard and co-funded with me while Chloe was studying her Masters at INSEEC Business School in Paris. HighChloeCloud believes that social media has changed the world. It has changed society and it has changed the way we do business. HighChloeCloud believe that we can merge the benefits of the social changes and the business changes from social media to create social mobility for all. To empower and transform the disadvantaged across society and transform people and society for the better.

In 2015 HighChloeCloud was set up as a business entity to spread a global message of the use of social media to empower people regardless of where they are in society and to use social media as that enabler. Since that time HighChloeCloud has managed to inspire more than 30,000 contacts in France (where we are based), over 50,000 internationally and represented in 45 countries.

Part of this work to date has included running free seminars, so far mainly in French-speaking parts of Africa, to empower people in the ways of social media and how they can use it to sell locally and internationally.

References

Gillum, S (2020) Email marketing isn't working – what's a B2B marketer to do? The Drum. www.thedrum.com/opinion/2020/09/30/email-marketing-isn-t-working-what-s-b2b-marketer-do (archived at https://perma.cc/72NS-8G3E)

HubSpot (2020) Data trends and insights from an unprecedented year. https://offers.hubspot.com/adapt-2020-retrospective (archived at https://perma.cc/72QL-B8U2)

Vaynerchuk, G (2017) The $1.80 Instagram strategy to grow your business or brand. www.garyvaynerchuk.com/instagram-for-business-180-strategy-grow-business-brand/ (archived at https://perma.cc/NCT3-C4EF)

WSJ (2021) Bank of America's Merrill Lynch to ban trainee brokers from making cold calls. www.wsj.com/articles/bank-of-americas-merrill-lynch-to-ban-trainee-brokers-from-making-cold-calls-11621850400 (archived at https://perma.cc/BD9Z-5ZEQ)

04

Controlling influence

The objective of this chapter is to examine how influence works in social networks, and how the reader can manipulate influence in order to prospect, nurture those prospects and use social media as a way to close business.

What is influence?

In this chapter we're going to look in depth at the idea of influence, and why it's so important with regards to your social selling efforts.

Influence is one of those words that is mentioned a lot in terms of social networks and social media, but what influence actually is predates those technologies and goes all the way back to the start of commerce itself. 'Influencing', from a commercial perspective at least, is what a marketer does to an individual to make them reach into their pocket and pay for your service.

Throughout the last 30 years the advertising industry has chosen celebrities to promote products. The reason for this is that being recognizable as a celebrity drives influence. In essence, if a celebrity 'backs' something (like Fairy Liquid, or BT, or Cadbury's, and so on), we are more likely to ape that behaviour. I've used the word 'ape' deliberately here because this harks back, sociologically speaking, to tribal behaviour where we are hard wired to follow the behaviour of those of our peers that we deem to be successful.

Back in the 1930s when advertising was born, there was no internet, consumers got their insight about what products to buy from newspapers, and later from television. Advertising worked, because choice was low. You walked into a supermarket and purchased a product because you had seen your favourite star promote it. If they liked it then, it was certainly good enough for you.

We've already discussed how, back when we were living in caves, our tribes were small and static. We'd follow the behaviour of the alpha male and alpha female because we could see what they were doing was successful. Using celebrities in marketing in this way taps into this hard-wired behaviour. We tend to frame celebrities as 'alphas' (which is why we celebrate them), and hence we tend to follow.

In the pre-social networking days, using celebrities in this way was a top-down approach using television adverts to broadcast messages, looking to influence the behaviour of customers. It worked pretty well because there was far less distraction – in the UK there were four TV channels, and only two of them carried adverts. There was no Twitter, Facebook, texting, etc., to distract people. Today, things are very different. But the idea of using celebrities to hack hard-wired tribal behaviour in terms of influence still works; it just depends how you define what a 'celebrity' or 'influencer' is.

Celebrity

Television ads were and are all about B2C selling, and in this book we're mostly interested in B2B selling. However, ideas around celebrity are still important for B2B.

A celebrity, for the purposes of our discussion, is someone who can influence others without 'touching' them. Most of us as salespeople can influence people to buy from us by going out, meeting with them, and selling to them. We are influencing their behaviour away from choosing a competitor and towards choosing us. In this process we can be said to be 'touching' the person because we are interacting with them. We have a relationship with the customer. A celebrity can do that same job of influencing behaviour away from choosing a competitor and choosing us without having that relationship.

In reality, that relationship is implied. When we, and we all do this, 'celebrate' a celebrity, at some level we believe we know them and have a relationship with them because, from a purely sociological perspective, we only really understand our relationships with people as if we were in a cave and living in a tribe. In other words, if they are in our lives we have to at some level 'know' them.

The advantage of being a salesperson who has celebrity status with the customers is that you can achieve greater scale. We could all, with infinite time and money, go out and meet every individual in the market, 'touch' them, form one-to-one relationships and sell. We don't have infinite time and money – but we can gain celebrity and in this way bring customers to us, without us having to touch them.

In the first chapter we spoke about why it was important to frame your social selling efforts around the idea of community. The reason we need a community is because it becomes the centre of our influence. However, that's only the start of the work we have to do, as the job of manipulating influence to our own advantage is complex and multifaceted.

FIGURE 4.1   Brand vs personality – how influence impacts the buyer and seller

YouTubers

Let's take a diversion to talk about a key example of influence – YouTubers. If you have kids, you'll be aware that they don't watch TV. You can hardly get them interested in films anymore. If they watch anything, it's almost certainly YouTube. Most likely they'll be watching people playing Minecraft. Or more specifically, they'll be watching people playing with ideas around the concept of Minecraft. That distinction is quite important. It has been interesting to see the rise in sites like Twitch, which is where you watch people playing games.

What kids tend to watch on YouTube are not funny cat videos. They are generally not watching clip shows, compilations of *You've Been Framed* or *America's Funniest Home Movies*. What they are watching generally are 'YouTubers'. These are people who have their own channels, their own identities, but they tell stories and make programmes that look almost nothing like what older generations would consider a TV programme to be.

One such example is Stampy Cat. He has a series on his channel called 'Stampy's Lovely World'. He updates it weekly, and has been doing so for many years. In it, he builds things in Minecraft. Each week in his world he'll build a shop, or a house, or a game, and he'll explain how he's doing it. And his fans will watch him do this, for 20 minutes a week. The video he makes can get around 750,000 views. That's three-quarters of a million kids who have watched him in a week. And they'll come back the next week to watch him do the next one. For kids, YouTube has replaced television. YouTubers like Stampy Cat, iBallisticSquid, and Dan DTM have become celebrities who have tremendous influence over these children.

Notably, though, none of these YouTubers try to overtly sell to their audience. For example, none of them take a break 10 minutes in and say, 'Hey kids... Hmmm... I'm a bit thirsty. Time for a delicious Coke Zero!' They all could, and I'd imagine Coca-Cola Inc. would love to give them money to do it, but for some reason they don't and that reason appears to be more sociological than driven by regulations or ethics. It's perhaps that it doesn't occur to a 20-year-old or younger YouTuber to do that, as opposed to there being some structural reason why it's impractical. There is of course legislation that now restricts this and what you can do and say to certain age groups.

Aspiration also works differently in this context. Traditional *Mad Men* advertising works through aspiration – 'drink this drink and the opposite sex will be desperate to go to bed with you', and so on. For YouTubers, the aspiration is that the viewer will become better at what they like doing. By watching this video, little Johnny or Jessy knows how to kill the Ender Dragon, or build a model of a Creeper, or how to build a specific widget out of 'red stone'.

In the new world of celebrities that can influence B2C behaviour via their YouTube channels and community we see connected economy behaviour squeezing out commercial and corporate behaviour. Specifically we see that 'karmic, free exchange of ideas for the benefit of the whole group' behaviour that we discussed earlier. Or, to put it more simply, 'We're not here to sell to you, we're here to do something we enjoy as a group.' (That's not to say there isn't commercial influence over this new world. When the new LEGO Dimensions game was being released, all the YouTubers had the game and all the support they needed to push the message out to potential consumers in their communities.)

The reason why we have to understand YouTubers is because they portend what B2C celebrities will become as the current generation gets older and 'Generation Television' dies off. Specifically, celebrities become people who build up large communities of followers, and deliver valuable insights and information. Therefore, when we're looking at becoming a celebrity ourselves within our own little B2B domain, that's the angle that we need to approach it from.

From our experience of live streaming and community building over the last few years, your objective in the digital world is that this is all about your audience. The moment you think it's about you, you will lose. You have to help the audience and the audience will help you. They will help you by supporting you and spreading your influence. Community must always come before commerce. Now, some of you are thinking that this is anti-sales. It's not. I realize it sounds disingenuous, but by not selling you will sell more. We all hate being sold to, after all.

The structure of influence

It's helpful to understand what we need to do in terms of moulding pre-existing influence in our target market. Whatever market you are in, there will be pre-formed opinions and existing players. We have two jobs to do. First, our own influence needs to increase. Second, the influence of others who are not helpful to us needs to decrease. Controlling influence is also a constant process. We like to think of it as a little like moving around and shaping wet sand. We need to get it where we want it, and form a shape with it. But over time the sand will tend to fall back to being a shape we don't want.

It's very important that you consider that influence is valuable to both you and your competitors. Influence is something you need to think about as you build your digital muscles. Let's not forget that, from a sales prospective, influence is no different from having a digital territory. Similarly, gaining influence is a slow, careful process that has to be done constantly (although it's fair to say that once you have a critical mass of influence, it becomes hard for others to dislodge it).

Competitors are generally more important in social selling than most people realize. Although the principles of social selling are based on warm and fluffy connected economy ideas, the reality is that you still need to win, and in order to win you need a certain amount of aggression focused on your competitors. Most people don't do that, so a very easy advantage is available to you simply by being aware of who your competitors are and watching or listening to their activities. We'll talk far more about that later.

'Competitors' in this context is generally broader than your traditional commercial competitors. It's anyone who has influence over your customers. There will be non-commercial 'actors' in your space who have influence. Plus, there will be new, disruptive ideas and/or technologies that will also have influence.

There are generally six groups of personas that you need to consider:

1 your sales staff, marketing staff and others

2 sales and marketing staff at your counterpart and ancillaries at your competitors

3 'loved-up' influencers who advocate your offerings

4 'loved-up' influencers who advocate competing offerings

5 paid influencers who advocate your offerings

6 paid influencers who advocate competing offerings

FIGURE 4.2   The structure of influence

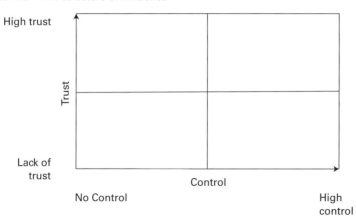

You can see that there are broadly two types of persona – those who advocate your offerings, and those who advocate competing offerings. Our objective is to make the people on our side more efficient, and to make the people who aren't on our side less efficient. Again, to reiterate, it's important you do both those things.

Cutting across horizontally, we have three types of persona:

1 sales, marketing teams and ancillaries

2 'loved-up' influencers

3 paid influencers

The job of sales and marketing teams and their ancillaries, in this context, is to build influence. They need to become celebrities in their own right within your chosen domain. In this way, they will be able to attract customers cold (i.e. customers will walk towards them), and they'll be able to sway customers who are being engaged by competitors. In reality, you need to build digital identities amongst your salespeople, marketing team and the rest of the business. This often terrifies marketing teams – 'What happens if people go onto social and they say the wrong thing?' It is your role in marketing to empower people so they don't do this. I hope you understand by this point in the book that social media requires a strategy and a methodology, not 'hints and tips' sessions. Social media, after all, is like any subject in business today, like health and safety for example, where employees are taught how to put up a ladder. The job of marketing is to place digital 'guard rails' around the business, so that your team can be authentic but within certain parameters.

Again, you need to consider your competitors. They will be reading this book as well as you. Over time they will want their sales and marketing teams to be the leading celebrity within your shared domain. We'll talk more about digital skills for sales and marketers later, but one obvious tactic here is that if your competitor's sales and marketing team does become really good, you can always poach them. The flip side, of course, is that they can poach yours.

All of these various actor types that we're talking about have a different way in which trust and control operates. You have ultimate control over what your sales and marketing team does because they work for you. You therefore don't have to trust them very much, in that they are unlikely to do anything unhelpful to you as a business. (Your sales and marketing team is almost never going to promote a white paper saying how amazing your competitors are and how useless you are – you can inherently trust them not to do that.)

The next type of persona is the 'loved-up' people. These are individuals who behave in what is easy to regard as quite a peculiar way – they will spend their own time, effort and money promoting a commercial product or service just because they like it. Finding and cultivating 'amplifiers' of your influence is important, as they will use their own time and effort to promote you. If you are new to social media, this may sound bizarre, but think about it, there are brands or people that we think are great. Importantly, they do not work for a vendor in the space. All they want to do is talk about how amazing XYZ technology is, and they'll end up with so many followers that even their dog has 50,000 followers and is regarded as an expert in its own right. These people are the YouTubers of B2B commercial influence space. They are classic connected economy individuals, sharing ideas and talking to people just because they want everyone to improve, and they don't particularly want to be paid for doing it.

Loved-up personas are both wonderful and dangerous, because you have no control over them. Therefore, have very little trust in them. They might spend years promoting your product only for you to find out one day they now hate the product and have fallen in love with your competitor, with all the attendant influence flowing from your product to your competitor's.

To the customer, loved-up influencers are highly attractive because they have no (perceived) bias. As we said right back in the introduction, customers operate in salesperson avoidance mode and hate bias. Loved-up influencers are therefore manna from heaven to customers. Which is another way of saying 'you need them', and we'll talk below about how to get them.

The final type of persona is paid influencers. These can be in two forms – loved-up actors who are being motivated with a cheque, or the effective equivalent of 'celebrity endorsements', i.e. people who are not paid-up members of the community, but who can fly in and say something to the community without being part of it.(Imagine Danny Dyer being paid to say something nice about XYZ plc's hosted telephony solution. Danny Dyer can be anyone here so long as they are generally recognizable to the community – they don't have to be a 'featured in *Hello* magazine' type of celebrity.)

In our opinion, paid influencers don't particularly work well. It is, after all, paid media, just an advert. Author and marketer Seth Godin once said, 'Advertising is a tax paid for by the unremarkable.' There is nothing wrong with paying an influencer, it's when the request of that influencer is nothing more than old-school advertising – you pay someone recognizable to carry the banner that says 'Buy our product, because we are great.' As discussed, customers don't like bias and they can sniff it out in paid influencers a mile away.

LEGAL IMPLICATION

It is worth mentioning the legal implication of paid influence. In the United States and United Kingdom, for example, you need to identify whether you are being paid to recommend something, and even if it isn't a legal requirement it's considered ethical in sales and social. Generally, you do this using the hashtags #Ads and #sponsored

Given that we have these six actor types, we need to move each of them around so that they are more helpful to us, and less helpful to our competitors. To reiterate, this is a constant process so it's not a case of doing this exercise once and then forgetting about it:

- For our sales, marketing and ancillaries, they stay with us and get better at what they do.
- For our competitors' sales, marketing and ancillaries, we can overtly move them by poaching them, but practically what we need to do is leave them where they are, but just make sure we remain better than them.
- For our loved-up influencers, the objective is to get a little more control over what they say. Ultimately this may mean turning them into paid advocates, or actually hiring them.
- For our competitors' loved-up influencers, the objective is to transform them into being our loved-up influencers, our paid advocates, or to hire them.
- For our paid influencers – this depends on how they have come about. The objective here would be to leave them where they are, or bring them in-house.
- For our competitors' paid influencers – the option here is to outbid your competitors, or hire them.

This is a dynamic system, and ideally you want to get into a position where you have some say in who goes where. What you don't want is to sit idly by whilst your competitor farms a collection of loved-up influencers selling their products, especially when you could be doing that yourself.

How do you create loved-up influencers?

It will be tempting to think that you can create loved-up influencers from scratch. It's obviously appealing to have people out there actively promoting your product for you, expecting virtually nothing in return, so why would you not take positive action to create more of those sorts of people?

Whilst it's certainly essential to 'lock in' loved-up influencers, and bring them closer so they don't become 'disloyal', creating them from scratch is almost certainly a non-starter. It takes a very special and, dare I say, unique individual, to love a product so much that they end up being a loved-up influencer. You won't find them – they will find you. Once they find you, you need to nurture those relationships. In the mean time, it's far better to concentrate on scaling your efforts as per everything else we've been describing in this chapter.

Control and trust

The different personas that we're talking about all have a different profile when it comes to control and trust. Understanding those profiles is hugely important when it comes to balancing risk in and growth of your community.

Your community is a business investment, so ideally you want to have total or near-total control over it, much as you would any other asset. Specifically, you want to control every message, every conversation, and so on. However, in terms of the people in your community there are only two classes that you can control – your sales, marketing and ancillaries, and paid advocates. If your community is only those people, you cannot scale. You can only achieve 'social scale' by giving up control. (Just to continue this thought for a moment, 'going viral' is the ultimate in achieving social scale for a given message, but when this happens you lose control entirely.)

Let me give you a real-world example. In a previous life Matt Reynolds, my co-author for the first edition of this book, used to be a 'loved-up' advocate for Microsoft. They never paid him any actual money, but over my time with them he used to get special treatment and 'treats', as a reward for him helping software developers understand how to use Microsoft products to build software. He managed to gain quite a following, and for a good while this worked really well for both Matt and Microsoft.

Then two things happened. First, Matt got a gig writing for the *Guardian*'s technology section. This took him from having a reasonable following in a niche market (software developers) to a massive following in a general market (anyone in the western world interested in technology). Second, Microsoft released what was widely perceived as a disappointing product: Windows 8. Overnight they went from having Matt being a loved-up advocate entirely on message, to having someone attacking a much more important product to a much, much larger audience. From their perspective, this must have been shocking. From Matt's perspective, he was doing the right thing – he spent some time honestly and frankly talking about how good some of their products were, and then he was presented with a new product, which in his opinion was terrible, and he spoke honestly and frankly about that. The point is that Microsoft had virtually no control over him.

If you have an employee or outside supplier working within the community, you can control everything they do. You can train them and coach them. Then, in the unlikely event that employee sends something that is off message, you can take them to one side and, essentially, make them delete it and/or make them take steps to control the damage (ideally, at least). But if someone in your community you have no control over does something you don't like, your only option is damage control.

The solution to this problem is 'relationships'. Given Matt's example above, what could Microsoft have done to stop him writing pieces in the *Guardian* that eviscerated their new product? Well, they could have asked him to stop writing and instead work with them on making it better.

Essentially it's your job as someone who owns a community to be able to bring people 'into the fold' where you can notch up the control you have over what they are saying. This works in both a proactive and a reactive way. Proactively, educating key members of your community as to what you are doing and why, keeps them on message. Reactively, having a closer relationship with those people means you're able to contact them and gently encourage them back on message. But you need to consider that, as we know, prevention is generally better than cure.

Trust tails off as we give up control. The important thing to remember is that it's a necessity to give up control in order to achieve scale.

Modelling

Social selling has a sneaky secret – everything you do, your competitors can watch you do. The nature of social networks is that the activities are all performed out in the open. So, whereas your competitors might not know that internally you're running a telesales campaign to poach all of their business, if you do that same thing on social networks they certainly could notice it. This assumes they understand and have invested in digital and social media skills in the first place. The flipside to this is that when your competitor is running a social selling campaign to poach your customers, you should be able to spot them doing that too. Or, to put it another way, the rules of the game are the same for both sides – everything happens out in the open, and that means there is a lot of information out there that you can take advantage of.

We've spoken about the importance of listening – now we come to talk about the importance of modelling this as a type of applied listening. This is where personality, having a social profile that is authentic but also human (through engagement) really pays off, because even if your competitor is doing similar things it will be about the relationship you have built and invested in over time

If you consider a given individual on a social network, they will have their own little universe of people that they talk to, and things they talk about. They also have a list of people they follow, and a list of people who follow them. This information is almost always public, because the networks fundamentally want you to see this information and trace down and follow paths of people who you think are similar to yourself. (We talk more about how social networks work in Chapter 5, and we spoke about this idea of tribalism in Chapter 1.)

If you also look at what people post, you can get a very good idea of their interests. They will usually have two types of interests – core interests, and niche interests. These themselves will subdivide into professional and personal interests, although for many people these are blended. For example, is my interest in 'entrepreneurship' personal or professional? It's probably both. However, you'll also see that I post not just about social selling, but also about leadership, innovation and the future of work.

By using the account-based marketing ideas that we've already discussed, you can build up a picture of an individual just by looking at their activity. You can use this picture to determine what they are doing, as well as how they are doing it. For example, if you examine the behaviour of a salesperson at a competing firm and see them striking up conversations with chief technology officers of non-profit/charity organizations, and trying to close them on downloading a white paper, you can infer that they are running a certain campaign and using a long-form content marketing strategy as part of that campaign.

You can then determine what you want to do about that. You can leave them to it, or you can actively work to ameliorate the potential success of their campaign in some way. For example, if you see someone engaging with a competitor's white paper, that individual is telegraphing that they are a good lead. Your agility here will be important in terms of which tactics you adopt, and we'll talk about this in later chapters.

The idea of using an account-based marketing technique to research people that you want to engage with has an obvious advantage – it's easier to engage with someone when you have some idea about who they are, and what they want. However, what we're suggesting here is that you scale this out in a structured way, and create a 'model' of your market comprising products, customers, competitors, partners and suppliers. The company that has the best model will win – simple as that. A model is a representation of your market, and it's self-evident that the company that understands its market best will be the most successful.

Summary

In this chapter we have discussed the importance of influence and why you need to get some in the digital economy. The debate has moved on from personal branding; this is not enough to differentiate you anymore. Salespeople and marketers reading this, you must not underestimate the need to own your market. You might not be a thought leader but you can control your influence.

Creating and controlling influence within your own territory/community will mean that prospects and changemakers will be attracted to you, which will in turn create inbound enquiries directly to you.

Everybody has influence, and as you build and flex those digital muscles you will see that you need a digital territory. There were always different players in an analogue territory; now that we live in a digital world, we need to be far more careful at nurturing a wide and diverse network and community. This community will help you spread your influence. You will never control it, but your job will be to feed and water it.

05

The mechanics of traditional sales

In this chapter we're going to look at the actual mechanics of social networks. Some readers may find this chapter a little technical, but it's worth powering through, as understanding the mechanism by which the market operates will help you to ultimately find opportunities, leads and close business.

We'll start by looking at the mechanics of traditional B2B telesales. This typically works by a salesperson having a list of people to call and 'interrupt', and then working through that list methodically. Some proportion of calls will turn into conversations. Some conversations turn into meetings. Some meetings turn into leads. Some leads turn into opportunities. Ultimately, some opportunities turn into sales. As we have said before in this book, it's conversations that drive sales.

That process is very easy for anyone to understand. Each stage involves taking a set of 'n' things in at the top, doing some operation to each thing, and ending up with a group of things that are discarded (people who wouldn't return calls, flat-out rejected the offer, 'you should have called three months ago', etc.), and a group of things that are kept and progressed on (people who agree to meetings).

Typically, managing this process involves conceptualizing it as a funnel, which is particularly appropriate because at each stage the set of things we're working on is whittled down. It's also possible to statistically analyse the sales operation such that either at a team level or an individual level, we know that a given set at any stage will likely reduce by a known given proportion. Most salespeople either intuitively understand, or alternatively actively manage, around those statistics: 'I need to make 20 calls a day, 100 per week, to get five meetings.' Sales is a numbers game, as salespeople often say.

FIGURE 5.1   Traditional sales funnel

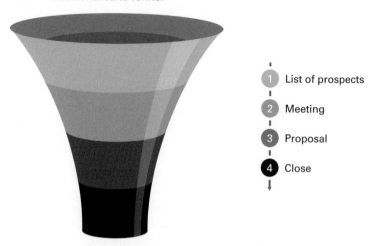

1 List of prospects

2 Meeting

3 Proposal

4 Close

The important point here is that it's easy for everyone to understand that if you stop running that process, you stop getting a useful end result. Or, more clearly, if you don't make calls, and prospect, you don't get meetings. (Or, at least, the meetings you do get arrive serendipitously because of prior actions – e.g. having a good relationship with a customer who moves to another company and finds an opportunity for you there that you hadn't explicitly chased down.)

There are also a number of very visible and very obvious supporting activities to this process. If a salesperson needs to call 100 people a week, they need a list of those 100 people. If a salesperson needs to attend a meeting, they need time to prepare, attend the meeting, transport to get there, etc.

Traditional B2B sales in this way is in reality highly mechanistic. Moreover, the structure of 'sales machines' like this is old but efficient, and is still prevalent in sales teams regardless of their industry. This means that whoever the salesperson works for and in whatever industry, the process is: make calls, set meetings, nurture opportunities, close deals. That is how it's worked for at least 30 years.

In social selling, we're using a number of techniques on social networks with a similar objective, which is to have conversations, to take these conversations to meetings and then to take these meetings to turn them into sales. Here at DLA Ignite we define social selling (and remote selling, modern selling, virtual selling and digital selling) as:

Using your presence and behaviour on social media to build influence, make connections, grow relationships and trust, which leads to conversation and commercial interaction.

Some people define virtual selling as being like cold calling (as described above), but doing it virtually. We define virtual selling in the same way as social selling.

The basics of social selling

There are three things you need for social selling:

- a buyer-centric social media profile
- a wide and varied network – this is your digital territory
- content

Let's look at each of these in more detail

A buyer-centric profile

Your social media profiles, as we have said before is your shop window to the world. Their job is to get people to be curious as they walk past and want to come into your shop. By doing this they will learn about you and hopefully they will jump to the conclusion that you should be the supplier to solve their business issues.

Let's not forget, if your LinkedIn profile is a CV, whatever conclusion can I jump to other than you are looking for a job? Or if you say you are a 'quota crushing salesperson', as a buyer I will jump to the conclusion that you will try and rip me off. This is why it needs to be buyer-centric; it is you working with a buyer, not you getting a job or you telling the world how amazing you are.

A wide and varied network

If you are to sell into accounts, then you need to be connected to the people in those accounts. You won't do this by saying 'I'm your salesperson and I would like to connect' or 'Buy my product because it is great.' We don't like salespeople and therefore if you connect to people and pitch, yes you will get a response, but it will be pretty small and you will burn through your target market and annoy people. It is your job to write a connection request that places the buyer at the centre of things and shows you are interested in them.

As I've mentioned before, LinkedIn works differently to Google. When a buyer searches for something on LinkedIn it gives answers based on their existing network. You are more likely to appear in a buyer's search if you are part of their network. The wider and more varied your network, the more likely you will get inbound. Inbound is where people walk towards you and ask you if they can buy from you.

Content

FIGURE 5.2   The DLA Ignite content hierarchy

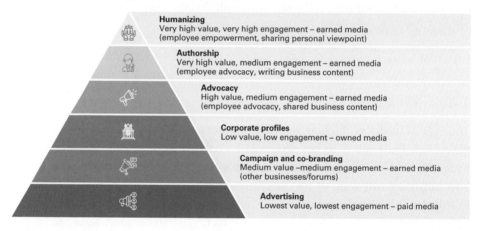

Humanizing
Very high value, very high engagement – earned media
(employee empowerment, sharing personal viewpoint)

Authorship
Very high value, medium engagement – earned media
(employee advocacy, writing business content)

Advocacy
High value, medium engagement – earned media
(employee advocacy, shared business content)

Corporate profiles
Low value, low engagement – owned media

Campaign and co-branding
Medium value –medium engagement – earned media
(other businesses/forums)

Advertising
Lowest value, lowest engagement – paid media

The final piece you need is content. Let's be clear here, any content is better than no content, but there is a content hierarchy (Figure 5.2). Remember, this isn't about 'posting and hoping'. This is about getting engagement with people within your target accounts. As soon as somebody engages on your content, first you know who they are, but second you have an opportunity to connect with them and have a conversation.

At the bottom of the hierarchy is advertising. We know that nobody likes advertising and we know that advertising says the same thing – 'Buy my product because it is great.' Which is why you will find little or no engagement via advertising on social. It therefore has little intrinsic value to you as a business and as a salesperson. To the marketer reading this and saying it's all about brand, I totally agree, but if nobody has liked it, you can guarantee that people have just scrolled past. You think the content is great as you are passionate about your product – it pays your mortgage and puts food on the table. Social media is a democracy; if people don't like your content they will just scroll by, and while you may love your product you are competing with all the other people who love their product.

As we move up the hierarchy, you will find that people won't have much interest in corporate content. Our research shows that people don't come to social to read corporate content. If you look at corporate content, most of it also says 'Buy my product because it is great' (or 'because we are great'). My background is in selling accounting systems and those suppliers are some of the worst for saying the same thing as each other. They have even invented their own jargon, such as ERP (enterprise resource planning).

The best content you can share if you want engagement is human content, content that appeals to your community and is empathetic to your community. Humanized content will get engagement, and engagement gives you the ability to have conversations. We often use a post that one of my team got from a humanized post that got 84 leads, six C-level meetings, two proposals and one purchase order, and it took 10 minutes to create. There is not one demand-generation activity that you can undertake – advertising, email marketing or cold calling – that can get response from that input of time. Hence why we say that social is more efficient and effective than any legacy sales methods you may use.

Often, people will say to us, 'But LinkedIn isn't Facebook.' We always ask people, 'So what do you do to get close to your clients?' The answer will be,' Take them to the sport or out to dinner.' I can guarantee that when you do this, you don't talk about work.

One final piece of advice is: don't put out humanized content all the time. When a person comes to your social profiles, they need to know what you stand for. Please come to mine and hopefully you will see I stand for social selling and digital transformation using social media. (I do hope you will drop by – I love feedback on the book.)

Technology adoption curves

The technology curve or 'adoption lifecycle' depicted in Figure 5.3 is used as a way of explaining people's adoption of new products or services. People's adoption styles will influence which approach/tactic you will need to employ to sell your product or service.

FIGURE 5.3   Technology adoption lifecycle

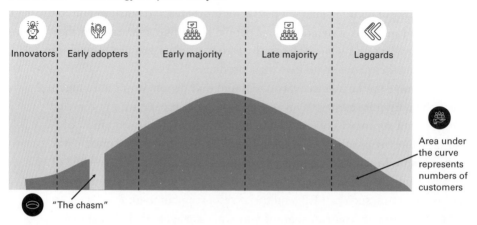

Innovators, you know the type, are the ones with the latest iPhone and always seem to battle through the technical glitches of a 'version one' product. Then come the early adopters, who like to see use cases before they will adopt technology, but still adopt it early on. The early majority are the greatest proportion of people; the iPhone is arguably now at this stage as so many people use it. Those people who are slower to adopt a new technology are the late majority or laggards.

The mechanics of networking

We've said throughout this book that social selling is much more like networking. Whilst structurally there is a great deal of overlap in this scenario, there is an important difference as to what networking events are actually for.

There are some salespeople who do all their selling through traditional networking. However, this process doesn't necessarily look that different to traditional sales. We'll call this traditional networking (where you physically show up at a room along with other people) 'in-real-life (IRL) networking'. From a mechanistic point of view, IRL networking replaces just the list-building part of traditional sales, and softens initial interactions. Someone who attends IRL networking will collect business cards, and then look to develop the initial meet by calling or emailing to set up meetings where further discussions can be held.

Thus far when we've spoken about the networking analogy, we've asked you to concentrate on the fact that the process of collecting business cards ('list building') has to be done using a listen–wait–interact method. Where this analogy breaks down is that salespeople at an IRL networking event are still primarily there to sell. That is not the case with social selling, where the salesperson's primary job is to build trust relationships and authority, and not to sell. We know that people hate being sold to; modern selling is about empowering people to buy. Surprisingly to many, you will sell more, higher and more often by *not* selling. Again looking at the mechanics, someone attending an IRL networking event is not traditionally operating in 'salesperson avoidance mode', which is the way we act in real life, typically because they themselves are salespeople and IRL networking is structured as a 'sales event'. They are an extension of traditional sales that has come about primarily to make list-building activities more efficient.

The mechanics of social networks

So what are people on a social network there for if it's not to buy and sell? Well, the clue is in the name: they are there to be 'social'. This is why we have stressed that you have to be perceived as being useful to people on the network. You do this by being a supplier of timely information, which in itself delivers insight, as opposed to just a supplier of goods and services. By building up a community and building up authority around the 'domain' of that community, you are able to create this insight. All of our research here at DLA Ignite shows that people come to social networks to be social and not to read companies brochures – we would go to a website if we wanted to do that.

All three types of system – traditional telesales, IRL networking, and social networking – have one thing in common, which is that in order for it to work you have to do something. If you don't make phone calls, you don't get meetings. If you don't go to an IRL networking event, you don't get meetings. If you don't interact on social networks, you don't get meetings.

In each of these systems, by doing something you are creating 'resonance'. Imagine you go to an art gallery. You go into a room and people are in there looking at the art, talking amongst themselves, etc. Now imagine you stand in the middle of the room and ring a bell. Everyone will turn and look at you. If you go into the room and don't ring a bell, it's unlikely anyone would notice you. When on social networks, it is essential that you create resonance in some way. Everyone on a social network is having their attention attracted by something – your job is to be the one who attracts it.

When we wrote this back in 2015 people laughed at us, but we have seen example after example of buyers actually walking towards social sellers, rather than running away. We have also seen social sellers getting higher faster with social selling and converting more of these high-level calls. It amazes some people that by not being a pushy salesperson and by providing insight, being supportive and even entertaining that this creates more sales. But actually it should not surprise us as that's the way we all like to be treated.

FIGURE 5.4   Social networks have high resonance

Integration with the sales funnel

It's important to remember that whatever you do on the social networks has to feed into your sales funnel. In order to transition people from your social network into your sales funnel, you have to be having private conversations. Essentially, what we are doing is replacing the list building and interruption aspects of the traditional sales process with social networking activities.

People do not discuss their needs – i.e. your leads – publicly (or at least it's very unlikely that they will). To get people to disclose leads, you have to meet with them privately. This means going through a process of deepening connections from 'I don't know him/her' to 'I'm meeting him/her for coffee next week'. Your objective throughout all this is to drive people through to a point where you are having meetings. The salesperson is doing this by connecting into the accounts you want to influence and sell to.

How many people should you connect to? Certainly, more than one or two. Gartner say that the average B2B purchase has 10 stakeholders involved in the buying process. We have helped transform a B2B supply chain software company and they tell me there are 100 stakeholders involved in a sale. At some point there is likely to be a meeting, where there is a discussion between stakeholders on which supplier to buy from. As sellers, we want them to choose us. Our job as social sellers is to have connected with each of the buyer team, to have had conversations with them on social, and it is better still if we can take those conversations off social and onto a face-to-face meeting, a telephone call or a Zoom call. We will continue to nurture these buyers so we stay front of mind, it reduces ghosting and will enable us to close the deal faster.

Follower/following

Most social networks operate on a follower/following model. You have some identity in the network, you follow people with a similar identity who you are interested in, and ultimately other people will follow you because they are interested in you, too.

It's interesting that LinkedIn doesn't quite fit into this model, yet a follower/following model is still essentially the definition of a social network. Twitter, Facebook, and others like Snapchat and Instagram, use the model. LinkedIn's directory approach predates this more modern social network structure.

It's generally true to say that the bigger the set of people following you, the better your performance on social networks will be, the more influence you will have. This is because the bigger the set of people following you, the 'louder' your bell will be when you ring it. You'll find that this is generally known as 'reach'. We're not going to use that term here particularly because, for us, the metaphor is the wrong way around. You are looking to do something that attracts attention, and 'reach' implies you're physically going out there and 'reaching out' and touching people to get their attention.

When you post an article on a social network, if you have 10 followers it will only appear on 10 people's timelines. If you have a thousand followers, it will appear on a thousand people's timelines. In that sense, having more followers is obviously good. Some people will say that you need to consider 'quality over quantity'. This isn't true. As long as you don't buy followers, an organically built list will have value that is to all practical intents and purposes proportionate with its size. Arguments like 'I have 10,000 followers!' 'Yes, but how many of those are quality followers?' are essentially navel gazing. While with Graham Hawkins in Australia, somebody said to him, 'There is no way that you can know all of the 25,000 people who follow you.' And he said, 'I don't need to, but they know who I am.'

Ultimately you will have two motivations here. You will generally want to build the size of your follower set and network, because having a bigger set is better. However, you will also have certain people that you want to have relationships with. Let's say you want to sell into XYZ plc. You will go and find people on the network from XYZ plc as part of your sales efforts. You have to be more proactive and definite in getting these people to connect with you and follow you, and from there to have private conversations with you. However, the principles remain the same, whether you are targeting specific people or the general population.

Let's look at the other side for a moment – what motivates someone to add someone to the 'followings' set? People follow people on social networks primarily because those followings deliver insight back to the 'follower'. To stretch the bell-ringing analogy, it's better to have a set of followers whose bell ringing creates nice campanological music as opposed to a deafening cacophony of off-key notes. What a follower is looking to do is have a set of followings that propagates ideas and information that is aligned with the follower's objectives. The follower will always drive efficiency around that point.

To be clear, having a bunch of spammy salespeople in their followings set does not create efficiency for the follower. Having a salesperson who's a leader in their community and is sharing practical information does create efficiency.

At this point you, the salesperson, want to be in as many individual following sets as possible. You already have some followers, and you want to have more. So, you need to 'ring your bell'. This is done by creating 'signals' in the network, as we'll now explain.

Since writing this book in 2015, I have seen many people understand the need for social, but it is still used as a tactic. I had a call recently with a company that actually sold a tool that found content to post. This sales leader was very proud of 'being social' because he was posting. I pointed out that he got no engagement on his posts. If you have no engagement, and no likes, it stands to reason that nobody likes your posts. In fact I would go so far as to say nobody cares. The sales leader pointed out that he had five likes on one post. But these five likes were from people within his team. He was talking in an echo chamber – nobody was listening, nobody cared and he wasn't influencing the people he was trying to sell to.

The ideal situation is where the people who are engaging with the content you are sharing are the same people you are trying to influence, or maybe know the people you are trying to influence. Many a salesperson is 'posting and hoping' – this is because these salespeople and companies see social media as a tactic. Hopefully you will understand from this book that using social media as a selling tool requires a strategy and a methodology.

Signals

Signals are typically expressed as notifications by the network. If you follow someone, that person will see a notification saying that you have followed them. This is a signal – it's the 'sound waves' from your bell reaching them. The point is that it increases the chances that they will follow you. If you're just sitting there in the network doing nothing, there is a chance that individual will find you and follow you, but that chance is very, very small. However, by proactively following them, and in doing so creating a signal, the chance of them following you goes up. The same applies to sharing content, or generally being active on a social network – you will be seen and will come front of mind for your prospects and customers. If you are not sharing content or active you are invisible, and your competition will be visible to your prospects and customers.

You can affect the chance of them following you by providing a better experience when they come to see who you are. This comes down to your messaging around your position, which we discussed earlier. If they come to your profile and it looks likely you will create insight for them (i.e. the efficiency of their followings set will be increased), the chance of them following you is higher. This is an example of backwards propagation through the network. There are two other ways in which you can do this.

The first is that you can 'favourite' or 'like' their post. Most networks support the idea of favouriting a post. When you favourite or like a post the person who posted it is told through a notification. This increases the chance of them checking out your profile and your offering and considering you for their followings set.

The second is that you can 'reshare' or 'retweet' their post. The idea of resharing is that you copy their post onto your timeline, but credit them as the original source. Resharing is hugely important, as we'll see when we consider forward propagation in the next section, but in this context someone will see you retweet something through a signal, and again this increases the chances of them checking out your offering and considering you for their followings set.

Backwards propagation is important because it's generally cheap (in terms of effort) and easy.

If you want someone to follow you, make sure your messaging is good and then follow them and favourite some of their posts. The chances of them following you increase if you do that.

FIGURE 5.5   Signals

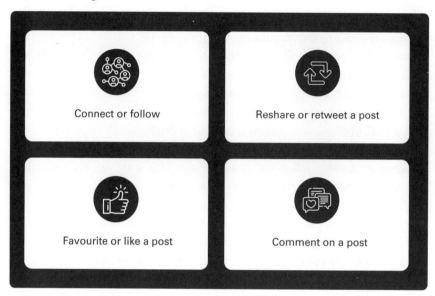

Forward propagation

Forward propagation is the single most important factor affecting the growth of your followers set. More than anything, you need to optimize around this.

If you're familiar with Twitter, forward propagation is 'getting retweeted'. Say you have 100 followers and you post something. One of your followers, who has 100 followers of their own, retweets it. Your message is propagated 'forward' through the network to a greater number of people than is in your followers set. In this example, your message ends up on 200 timelines as opposed to 100. This is where the term 'reach' does make a little more sense. You are 'reaching' a greater audience of people.

Similar to LinkedIn, if your post is liked or commented on, it is highly likely this post will show up in the timeline of the person liking or commenting. Let's stay on the Twitter theme for now. Following that retweet, the followers of this 'retweeter' have received a signal of your existence. The chance that each of those people will check out your shop window and follow you has also increased in each instance. Fundamentally, this is still all about signals – the more people who see your signals, the more people will check out your offering, and the more people will follow you.

Where this is more valuable than the backward propagation that we just covered is that the value you're sharing gets conveyed forward into the network. If you share a particularly salient or clever idea, as that gets pushed forward the value goes with it. Anyone reading it should say, 'Hmmm, that's a particularly clever/salient idea, who's that smart individual who shared it?' and from there, your association with it (and by implication your authority) also goes forward.

However, there is an association with backwards propagation here, in that if you reshare a post of someone else's, that acts as a signal. Coming back to our list of people that we are looking to connect with, by resharing posts of a particular individual, we are actively working towards the goal of having private conversations with them. Looping this back to the mechanical process of traditional B2B telesales, the same funnel idea applies here. You create signals (old world: a phone call; new world: a posting on a social network), and a proportion of those signals moves the story on (old world: a conversation; new world: a conversation).

The value of forward propagation is that it is subject to network effects. The point is that each follower of yours will have (probably) hundreds of followers themselves. And those followers will have hundreds of followers. And it keeps going. The reach (mathematically speaking) into the network can be enormous. As we have stated, the average person on LinkedIn has 930 connections. If somebody with 930 connections likes or comments on a post, this means your influence could be seen by 930 multiplied by 930 = 864,900 people. In the old world you may have had an email list and you sent out a newsletter – here you have a list of 864,000 people. In the old days, you could send out an email maybe every two weeks and anything more than that would annoy people. With social, every employee in your business can share insight, every day, with their network. The chance you will be seen by your prospects and customers is high. The chance you will be front of mind with your prospects and customers is high. The chance that they will get to know you, like you and trust you is high. The chance that they will place the next piece of business with you is high. In fact, we see many clients owning the digital share of voice, where they become the only choice, as they push out of the conversation all of the companies that don't use social or who use social tactically.

Optimizing around getting forward propagation is as easy or as difficult as you make it. If you follow the principles of good management of your social network activities (which we cover extensively in this book, but largely can be distilled to: 'Put out good quality information and build up authority around a community'), forward propagation should be easy to obtain.

Public conversations

Engagement is also another idea that commonly comes up when talking about social networks. Engagement is really public conversations, and public conversations are important because they are the last stage before private conversations.

It's very important that you engage with people who engage with you. For example, if you post something and someone has something to say about that post, you need to reply. And that's obvious because if you don't:

a you're being rude; and

b everything you have done becomes a waste of effort if you do not talk to them

Essentially, someone starting a public conversation with you is a huge buying signal, as it indicates they have received insight from you and want to get more.

When we look at your engagements with others, it comes down to backwards propagation of signals. By initiating a public conversation with someone (e.g. you see a post of theirs, and comment on it), you're effectively creating a signal, much like you do by following them, favouriting their posts, or resharing their content. However, that signal is much more overt, and carries greater cost for you as you have to consider and craft a starting point for the conversation, and then carry the conversation on. That greater effort does have an advantage in that it's a short hop from public conversations to private ones. We always recommend that you start public conversations, but you, as soon as you can take them private, because you never know who is watching. (As an aside, we have found competitors of ours 'surfing' our content, trying to create conversations with our prospects. The great thing about social is there is a simple remedy to this – we block them.)

Let's go back to having conversations on social. Interestingly, this is where most people struggle when considering how to do social selling, as they consider this aspect of initiating conversations with others to be the start of the process. Most people intuitively understand that just spamming out sales messages into social networks will not get good results, but then can't balance this tenet with the assumed need to initiate conversations. 'How can I have a conversation with this person I don't know when I can't mention that I'm selling something?'

Of course, this position is impossible. To make social selling work, as hopefully you are seeing by now, you need to overcome this by sowing the seeds of a community, growing that and your attendant authority by building the network using backwards and forwards signal propagation techniques, responding to inbound engagement, and initiating outbound engagement by listening first.

Summary

In this chapter we have seen how in a digital world there are new concepts around following, being followed, and retweeting, and how these can be used as signals to prospects, customers and competitors. As a social seller, you need to use these techniques carefully as you will leave digital footprints wherever you walk online. Once you have mastered this, these techniques are powerful ways for you to own your market and make your numbers.

We have also covered the three aspects you need to master to make social media and social selling successful for you: your buyer-centric profile, your wide and varied network, your content. All of this is used by you, every day, to create conversations, because conversations create sales. Business leaders often say to us, 'I don't want my sales team wasting their time on social media.' In fact, I hope you can see that, for your business to be a success today, you need to have your sales team spending as much time as they can in social media. But let's not forget social media and social selling is not a tactic. As a business, you need to drive social selling as a strategy, from the C-suite down.

MANAGING DIRECTOR'S VIEWPOINT – STEVEN RAFFERTY

I have been selling in the IT industry for over 30 years, from telesales, an external rep, a sales manager and managing director working across professional services, managed services and software. Selling hasn't changed during this time, but the platforms for sales engagement have. From the phone, a nicely written letter or a face-to-face meeting before the internet, to now email and engagement via social media platforms, selling needs to be about the buyer, not the seller. Most people forget this and just want to talk about themselves, their company or their product. However, customers want to build relationships; they want to know that you understand their business and you have solutions for their business challenges.

Tim continually demonstrates this and his teaching is all about engagement with multiple buyers across an organization and how to add value at the right time by delivering content that helps buyers make a decision thanks to the value you demonstrate. People get confused by the phrase 'social selling', thinking it's the way to sell on LinkedIn or social media. It isn't. It's about value selling, regardless of the platform. My win rates have improved since I met Tim and understood the power of engagement, content and timing.

06

Moving from an analogue to a social mindset

There are three concepts that were taught to me early in my sales career that seem to have moved into the digital world:

- Every day is a 'school' day, or the ability to be a continuous learner – The salespeople that I see winning and making quotas are those that are passionate about their subject. They are effortlessly knowledgeable about customers and the business issues that were solved when their product or service was implemented. These people seem to absorb information like a sponge; in fact they seek it out. These people's attitude is one where they treat every day as a day to seek knowledge. In her book *Mindset: Changing the way you think to fulfil your potential* (2017), Carol Dweck talks about two different types of people – those with a 'fixed mindset' and those with a 'growth mindset'. A 'growth mindset' sees failure as an opportunity to grow, challenges are there to help a person grow, feedback is constructive. These people like to try new things, they are inspired by the success of others. Whereas fixed mindset people see failure as the limit to their abilities. I'm either good at it or I'm not, when I'm frustrated I give up, I stick to what I know. They don't like to be challenged. I see this a lot in comments on social media such as LinkedIn, where it is clear people are not willing to try new things or they take the idea of social media and make fit their existing knowledge base.

- Prime selling time – This is the time during the day which you have as a sales professional to sit in front of customers, prospects etc. I was always amazed when a telesales agency I dealt with would book calls with me at 10 am. Surely this is prime selling time for them; it certainly was for me. I would always push the calls back to early in the morning or late in the afternoon. The concept of prime selling time no longer exists as social enables you to be online at any time of the day or night.

- Preparation – Whenever I have run internal competitions between salespeople there are a number of salespeople that consistently win. These are not the people that treat the day as a chore, a bit like exams, putting off doing any preparation until the last moment when it's too late. The winners spend time preparing.

In today's sales world, the average salesperson will have a mobile phone and therefore, just like their opposite number, the buyer, has access to data 24 hours a day, 365 days a year. The salesperson does not need to be physically present at their office. On planes, trains and (not driving) automobiles, they are connected to the office and sources of data about their products, services, customers and competition. The Covid-19 pandemic has compounded this, in fact we now live our lives expecting to be virtual and we expect our buyers to be virtual too.

FIGURE 6.1   Analogue interrupt marketing vs digital content

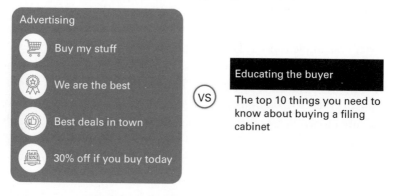

To be a social seller is not about how much you post and when. It is also not about how much of the company content you can throw at the wall in the hope that it will stick. A social seller is a helper. This is simple psychology – to know how best to work with the modern buyer and understanding what they are looking for.

Let's take a step back and understand the most important person in our day – the prospect, customer or buyer. A buyer may suddenly be put in a position where they need to research and draw up a shortlist of products or services for their company to buy. Let's say filing cabinets. Like me, they might not know anything about filing cabinets, so they need to learn. When they make an internal recommendation they will need to explain it. During the education process, they will get to understand their needs better. Do they need two-drawer or three-drawer cabinets? Will they want cabinets that only take A4 or Foolscap?

If you talk to a sales leader and ask them, what is a good day, they will probably say, good looks like my sales team out in front of customers having conversations. It will be different for different verticals and organizations, but let's say a good day for sales is that each salesperson has two meetings in front of clients. Because of travel time, you are restricted to just two meetings or maybe you can have a few more because you are using virtual software such as Zoom or Microsoft Teams. The difference is that, with social, your sales team can have conversations with customers back-to-back. While many sales leaders think that salespeople messing on social media is a waste of time. In fact, and it can be measured, every keystroke your sales team make on social can be attributed to social media. We have to change as sellers, as the buyer today is highly educated on how to use the internet and social media.

One of the things an educated buyer will do is avoid all the people out in the market pushing content that comes across as 'Buy my product now' and 'Isn't my product amazing!' In fact, that will put off many buyers. But wouldn't it be good if they came across an article that said: 'The top 10 things you need to think about when buying a filing cabinet'? Yes, somebody may have embedded in there some of their products' unique selling points. And the buyer may well say, 'Of course they would say that, they are a filing cabinet selling company.' But the fact you have taken the time to educate the buyer makes it more likely you will get on their shortlist. Better still, you might even get an 'inbound' call, during which you can use your best sales skills to close the buyer before they move onto the competition. As we say, social selling isn't just about playing on social media all day.

This is what we mean by helping the buyer, and you can do this through content creation. Now, any salesperson that has just read that and thought, that is marketing's job, will need to think again. As a professional salesperson who knows their stuff about filing cabinets, how long would it really take you to write an article about the top 10 things to think about when buying a filing cabinet? An hour, maybe two, then put it on LinkedIn and Twitter as a blog. It might be one of the best demand-generation pieces you write, and with a proper thought to search engine optimization and a fair wind you might get inbound from it. Once you start to flex your digital muscles, it won't take you an hour – it might take 20 minutes. In the modern world content is one of the ways you prospect. The blog I posted today was a change around of something I wrote six months ago, and it took me ten minutes.

But how can we be inspired to write content?

Some of the best places for content are your customer and prospect meetings. Good and bad. If you had a meeting with, say, a media company and they outlined their business issues, you would need to type this up and post it on the CRM as meeting notes. Why not also turn this into a blog (obviously not mentioning people or companies by name without permission)? Good meetings and bad meetings are ripe for content that you can post out on social media and that will appeal to your typical buyer.

My company was targeting a company so we wrote content that solved the business issues of that company. Now, it could solve the business issues of many companies but we were targeting just this one. We did our research and we found that this business wanted help in international expansion, so we wrote about that. Within a week, my salesperson had a call from the company's CEO and we had our first conversation. That ended up with us presenting to the board on the Friday of the same week and picking up a purchase order the week after.

Working with sales teams, I often see advice given out by so-called social media gurus that social selling is all about content. Content is the equivalent of talking in the analogue world. Talking with context is fine, but the best thing a salesperson can do is listen. There is an old saying that 'We have been given two ears and one mouth, and we should use them in that order.'

The first thing that a salesperson should do when they want to become a social seller is listen. Listen to your customers at a macro level (company and company executive) and at a micro level (employees). Listen to your competitors, the analysts, and the trade bodies.

In our roles as trainers of social selling to companies, we came across a sales guy who sells transportation software to supply chain and logistics managers. He had flatlined at 200 followers on Twitter and was getting little engagement. I guessed that the 200 followers were friends and family and he wasn't really getting 'out there'.

'Who's your trade body?' I asked.

'The Chartered Institute of Logistics and Transport Professionals – CILT', was the response.

So I found @CILTUK on Twitter and started paging through their feed. Just by scrolling down I found there was a young person's division, @CILT_YPF. I asked, 'Have you contacted them and asked if you could do an educational presentation?' 'I didn't know they existed' was the response.

@CILT were also retweeting (RTing) a number of thought leaders who were giving presentations. 'Are you talking with these influencers?' 'No, didn't know they existed.'

Each tweet that @CILT had tweeted was a goldmine of how the salesperson could get to know more about their industry and get involved. I pointed out that you could tell from @CILT's Twitter news feed that it was not a 'bot' (automation with no engagement) and that there was probably a person behind it. I also pointed out that maybe the salesperson might want to engage with that feed, to see if the person would talk back.

We talked in previous chapters about how to talk with strangers without coming across as weird or spammy. Why not retweet any articles that you think are interesting to your followers? Just by engaging with each of the different people on Twitter will increase your 'interesting' credit and might gain you followers. This will create conversations. We all have 20 minutes while waiting for a train, bus or meeting or sitting in a taxi where we have time for this.

Running some social selling training recently, I had a similar discussion to the one above where the salesperson said, 'Social selling is a waste of time, I cannot increase my following.' I looked at their Twitter feed and said, 'Could it be that you are boring?' 'But I post what the company tell me to post.' Just because the company ask you to post something doesn't make it great for your audience. This is about engagement to drive conversations.

A new follower to us recently contacted me and said, 'I follow you, as what you post is interesting. I don't read every article, but I'm able to build my knowledge by having you in my news feed.' This is the difference. Your Twitter feed and your LinkedIn profile belong to you. They are a reflection of you and a free advert for you that is online 24 hours a day, 365 days a year. How do you want people to think about you? As a boring corporate suit or as an interesting, insightful, funny and vibrant person?

The world has changed and so has the way we need to sell. With buyers online researching your products and services and making recommendations, how are you going to make sure you are found and get on those shortlists? You will need to drop certain 'analogue' habits and get digital ones. In the old days you may have gone to trade shows, but you need to follow your customers and while you may still attend some trade shows (let's be honest here, do they really work anymore?) you need to make sure you are partaking in the digital version too.

As a salesperson you must dedicate time to finding great content in your niche, absorbing it and sharing it on LinkedIn and Twitter. You may have many sources of corporate content, such as colleagues, partners and value-added resellers. 'Jump in' and engage in social; have conversations with colleagues, customers, partners, news sites and social media. Everything ultimately can be repackaged and shared. (We'll talk about specific tools later.)

The world has gone social and so should you. You need to get online and listen; find your customers, competitors and trade bodies and work with them to become the chief of your territory. Winners will be able to manage their time to build community, to absorb and create content, not only owning their market but also getting inbound. Nothing could be better than prospects walking towards you looking for help and advice.

What to listen for

All of my salespeople know that whenever we have a territory review, I will always look up the Twitter account or accounts of the companies they're targeting and ask them what the business issues are, or what is impacting those companies today. All of this is publicly available data, and it is more likely to be up-to-date on Twitter than on individual company websites. In addition, you need to be listening out for signals and using them as a way to get engagement. Who were the last three people that followed your competitors' social media feeds?

Typical signals to look out for

Listening (rather than posting) for social sellers is the most important skill in your armoury. So what are you listening for?

The types of signals to look for are dependent on the nature of the product or service you are selling. You need to think about what indicates how a customer or prospect may need your help. It is unlikely that somebody will come onto social media and tweet: '@Timothy_Hughes I need your help', so you need to think laterally.

Every product and service has its own signals but here are the typical ones to look out for:

- organizational change (e.g. new geography, recruitment drive or redundancies, mergers or acquisitions)

- leadership change
- market change (e.g. what is happening to their customers/end users, changes to markets or competition)
- external (e.g. legislation or regulatory changes, local community news)
- relationship (e.g. customer, partners, new markets)
- strategic (e.g. change of direction or focus)
- tactical (e.g. new initiatives, reviews)
- events (e.g. newsworthy, sharable events and awards, charitable contributions or sponsorships, incidents or accidents)
- new in post
- promotions
- birthdays

While we can always hope that somebody might tweet your name and ask to buy your product, it is more likely you need to listen on social media, find signals and then interpret them. There are different types of signals to look for on social media, and these can be expanded to cover four main areas.

RELATIONSHIP
This could be, for example, if a person has won a reward, giving you a reason to connect. The idea is to let them know you are there and not to use this as an excuse to sell. You are trying to start a conversation. For example, if the CIO of one of your target accounts wins a 'CIO of the Year' award, send them a note of congratulations. Do not start talking about your products and services. The congratulations are enough; the fact you represent an organization is enough of an advert.

RISK
It might be that you have picked up in the press that this organization has announced job losses. Still don't sell, but express your sympathy and highlight how you can help and support.

COMMUNITY
If you understand your prospects, their world and their competition, you can make contact explaining you may have heard an announcement from one of their competitors. Maybe they are expanding, or perhaps they have

been fined, and you want to share that with your prospect or customer and express the hope it does not happen to them.

SALES

This is where your prospect has positive news; for example, they are expanding, are part of a merger or acquisition (M&A), have had a change in management or have won a big deal. This gives you the opportunity to position your product as supportive to that news. Note I say 'position', I don't say 'sell'. It's key that you offer a short quantifiable business case and a reference to back it up. It's a pretty good assumption that your target will say, 'Where have you done this before? And what were the results?' before they respond or make contact with you, so be proactive.

Blogs

Blogs are an excellent way to understand the culture and direction of an organization. Three-quarters of B2B marketers are now using blogs as part of their marketing approach. A blog is digital evidence that you are an 'expert' in your field. It enables you to dominate over your competition, by providing digital position, which, if they have not read this book, will still be working in an analogue world and won't be connected to the digital buyer. Blogs are a great place to put keywords and key phrases that will be picked up by people searching on social media and Google. Over time you will build a library of blogs, which will become indexed and will mean you will show up more and more; this is how you can start becoming digitally dominant for your product or service and vertical.

News

It is often overlooked as a source of insight, but by definition news is information about recent events, and business news is insight into your customers and prospects.

Social media platforms

Join LinkedIn and Facebook groups that your customers gravitate towards. Monitor Twitter hashtags to identify people and companies that are associated with a particular topic, trend or concept in the markets you serve.

Use Glassdoor to give you an insight into what employees think of their company.

Make every minute spent listening a minute well spent.

Here are some examples of LinkedIn social selling triggers you need to look out for:

- Somebody has viewed your profile, so thank them; we generally get 50 per cent of the people that we contact coming back. This has also turned into business.

- LinkedIn connect request.

- Your connection request has been accepted.

- If your contact changes job, why not congratulate them, or look for a reason to work together and maybe reconnect?

- Contact gets promoted / has a birthday / has a work anniversary / has done something newsworthy – 'like' the update and congratulate them

- LinkedIn blog post is liked, shared or both – all great ways to connect and amplify content.

- Comment on a blog post; this is a great way to engage.

The problem with listening is, of course, that the sheer volume of information on social and digital networks can be overwhelming, and this makes the job difficult. There are almost 100,000 tweets, 100 LinkedIn accounts and 1,500 new blog posts created every minute. To quote Clay Shirky in his 2008 Web 2.0 Expo talk, the problem is not information overload, it is 'failure to filter'. Buying signals are occurring all day, but you can't spend your whole day listening (you have other work to do if you are to close that sale or retain that customer!).

Listening should be frequent but brief. This can be facilitated by using the right tools, which will cut through the white noise and can be built into your working rhythm to minimize the time you invest. In Chapter 8 we discuss some of the tools that can help you listen to customers, prospects and competitors.

What is your digital identity?

If you want to own your digital territory, do not make the mistake of thinking that all tweeting is good and any content is better than no content.

Wrong. As discussed above, you are what you tweet, and people visiting your LinkedIn page or Twitter page will make a judgement on you from that. What conclusion are you letting people jump to about you? People who are boring, over-tweeting corporate suits will be passed by. All of us use social media, we are all great scrollers, and we will all just scroll, scroll and scroll past people who are boring.

Think what it is you stand for. What is your personal brand DNA? What is your digital identity? You need to start making judgements about what you tweet. Does it meet that standard? For example, I avoid anything that I wouldn't want to discuss with my granny, so I avoid politics, religion, anything rude, talking about any things that cause addictions (drink, drugs, gambling etc.) – pretty much anything that might cause offence. I'm not saying don't post it; you might be running a Twitter account for the next President of the United States. But if you are posting articles that might offend your customers, guess what? When they find it, they will be offended, so don't. Open up another Twitter account for anything controversial.

Now I am going to balance that with saying you need to be authentic. One of my team members talks about being openly gay and if you have a problem with that she doesn't want to do business with you and you would never do business with her. My overall advice is to be careful. In the book *Thinking, Fast and Slow* (2011) Daniel Kahneman talks about how as humans we tend to have two types of thoughts, the fight-or-flight thoughts that we just fire off and thoughts that, once we slept on things, are a little more measured.

Understanding what you stand for and what your digital identity is critical. I was helping a guy that sells human capital management (HCM) software, and he was in a tailspin about all the content he could share. We sat down, had a one-to-one and talked about what it was he would stand for, what did he want to be famous for. He decided that the subject that interested him most was work/life balance. This, he decided, was to be an area where he would 'own the narrative'. He would find all the articles on this and write some too. After a discussion on hashtags he put on 200 followers in a week, just by people being able to find him, and think him interesting.

A business leader I work with sees his digital identity as 'Mr Encouragement' – every article he posts, every comment he leaves, should encourage people. He obviously doesn't call himself this online, it's just that when he turns up to social, he wants people to see him as positive and encouraging.

Figure 6.2 shows a digital identity Brentney Hutchinson created. She has pinned it up on the wall by her desk, and it provides her with a constant reminder. Why don't you take a few moments and sketch out your own?

FIGURE 6.2   An example of a digital identity

What is your online brand?
Your digital identity?

Content

Nowadays there are some amazing 'content curation' tools. They do all the hard work in finding articles for you. Products like Flipboard, Pocket, and Medium all have algorithms that will search for articles based on the criteria you put in them. For example, you can get articles on the subjects you want to be famous for; filing cabinets or work/life balance, etc. We mention a number of these tools in Chapter 8 on technology.

Once you have those articles, you need to filter through them. Which ones meet your own brand DNA or digital identity, which will your followers find interesting? Are there articles that might enable you to grow your following?

Hashtags

One of the ways to get found across all social networks is the use of hashtags. When Twitter first started up, the only way you could search on data was using hashtags. It has since changed that, and you can now search on any data (we often use Twitter to search for information rather than Google). Hashtags have now entered into day-to-day language, so much so that every brand will have a hashtag. I've seen organizations create mission statements, backed up with hashtags.

If you want to be found then you need to use hashtags that your customers are using to search for information. While some of this is trial and error, you can start to search for terms for your niche on Twitter to see what you get.

For example, I once tweeted 'The 10 best places in the world to buy chocolate' and then added the hashtags #food and #drink. If people were searching for articles on chocolate then it would be picked up as that word appeared in the tweet. But if people were searching on subject matter related to it then a nice summary would be #food. Therefore, people searching for food-related articles would also pick up that tweet.

Hashtags are used a lot on Instagram; in fact they are now used there more than on Twitter. It is only in the last few years that they have started being used on LinkedIn as people are searching for people and content. It would be usual to use no more than five hashtags on LinkedIn.

In a recent training course we gave to a large B2B enterprise company, one of the attendees had 600 followers but had flatlined there for months. Looking at his Twitter feed, which was informative and interesting, it was clear (to us) why the follower growth had stopped. Nobody could find him. After 30 minutes learning about hashtags, he put on 200 followers in a week and last time I spoke to him he was accelerating past 1,200 followers.

Twitter lists

As your Twitter following and the people you follow grows, I highly recommend that you start using Twitter lists, otherwise you can soon waste time and effort. You need to get organized. Lists are a way to start grouping subject matter areas or people into certain sections. The best way to think about Twitter lists is that they are similar to a library. How do you find a book in a library? If you want to find a book on fly fishing then you go to the sports section and in there will be a subsection on fly fishing. With

Twitter lists you can collect similar companies or people around certain subject matter areas. For example, big data, cloud, filing cabinets, desks; all the people or companies that talk on those subject areas. You might want to have lists on your customers or competition. You are able to fine-tune the subject areas.

You can also subscribe to other people's lists; for example trade shows and conferences will often have lists of attendees or people using the conference hashtag. Why not jump in and engage and retweet with these conferences? I've been itemized on leader boards at conferences that I haven't even attended, but they were in the niche I worked in and just by being interesting, I've picked up followers. You can also use lists to group your favourite sports teams, news channels or any interests you have.

Then, when you have that spare 20 minutes in your day, go through one of these lists and see if there is anything your following would be interested in, and if so retweet that. If there are articles you want to read later then like those. You can go back to them later on. You don't need to spend hours on this, but 20 minutes a day is an excellent time to invest in growing your personal brand.

It is often at this point in my training sessions that people ask me about automation. As one person said to me, 'Why don't we just automate this so we can go back to doing our day jobs?' Let's not forget that social media is based on reciprocation. You come to social media to buy and sell, and I come to social media to buy and sell. There has to be a buyer for every seller. If the sellers decide to automate then so will the buyers, and at that point all falls down. In Chapter 8 we discuss the pros and cons of automation and how it can help, but also hinder. Social selling is social. People come to social media to be social. People expect to be able to engage with you. Your Twitter and LinkedIn feed belong to you, and they reflect you out there in the digital world. Many people think that automation 'saves time' and think that it's all about how many tweets you can get out there. I'm sorry but if you use tools to post and have no time to engage, people will immediately recognize you as a robot/bot, and will soon lose interest and unfollow. (Don't forget, people can unfollow just as quickly as they can follow.)

The 4–1–1 content rule

Many people ask me what rules I follow when I tweet, or how I know what to tweet. My advice is to follow your gut instinct and tweet what you think is interesting and will help your buyers, followers and community. Or you could use the 4–1–1 rule for Twitter. This was popularized by Tippingpoint Labs and Joe Pulizzi, founder of Junta42 and the Content Marketing Institute (the earliest use I can find is from 2011). The rule states that:

> You share four pieces of relevant content written by others, one self-serving (about your company product or services) tweet and one tweet that shows you as a human being. Such as your football team, you walking the dog etc.

What's great about this approach is that it lets you engage in the conversation, build awareness, and keep in touch with your followers without coming across as pushy or too 'me' focused.

The 4–1–1 rule can also apply to your lead nurturing using LinkedIn. Formally, lead nurturing is the process of building a relationship with prospects that are not yet sales-ready by conducting an informative dialogue, regardless of budget, authority or timing. Less formally, lead nurturing is the art of maintaining permission to 'keep in touch' with potential customers as they educate themselves, with the goal of being top of mind when they are ready to move into a buying phase. This is where the 4–1–1 rule can apply. As you plan out the cadence of LinkedIn posts, try scheduling four educational or entertaining posts mixed with one 'soft promotion' (e.g. attend an event) and one human post (share something about yourself).

ADVICE FROM A MARKETING PRACTITIONER – PRISCILLA MCKINNEY

Posting on social media, I don't know what to write

When it comes to people not posting on social media, the excuse I hear most often starts with 'I don't know what to write.' That is followed by a close second with 'I don't want to sound salesy.' My response is, 'You do know what to write. You've already written tons. You simply don't know how to curate what you have and post with the right cadence.' And on the salesy front I just say, 'Well then don't be salesy.'

But when you're ready to post I find that my simple Rule of 15 is a great way to remove the anxiety and guesswork from social interaction. It helps on both accounts from not knowing what to say, to not wanting to sound salesy.

To be relevant on social media, as in any social situation, you must either be interesting or interested. In order to get the right mix of content it can be easy to curate your content into three groupings and follow my simple rule.

Be interesting

The bulk of your posts should strive to show you are interesting. Being in the know in your industry and network is a great way to stand out from all of the noise in the feed. Content that engages makes me think about something differently, question a going industry standard or demonstrates authority on a subject matter. Interesting posts provide street cred.

When people simply curate content from other sources or create their own predictable copy without concern about how interesting it is, let's just say they don't get invited back to the cocktail party! For every 15 posts you create, 10 of them should show you are tremendously interesting.

Be interested

The next four posts you create should show you are interested in others and in their success. Being overtly helpful builds rapport and is an easy way to include others in the conversation. By leading with downloads, articles, podcasts or guides that are overtly helpful to others you demonstrate your emotional intelligence and low ego, and invite collaboration and comment.

When people only think about how their content can serve them or create a spike in their personal brand following, they eventually do more harm than good. Granted, no one kicks the bore out of the cocktail party, but they do conveniently find ways to extricate themselves from the conversation and eventually the relationship. For every 10 posts you create that show you are interesting, create four that show you are interested in more than yourself.

For both of these 'buckets' you can mix and match with personal and professional content and you should. It can also be a mix and match of things you've written yourself or things written by others and carefully curated. While people may feel a bit awkward at first posting about their personal life, opinions or experiences, the truth of the matter is that social media is for humans, by humans and there is a big difference between sharing your deepest, darkest secret and simply showing you are not a robot. Also, robots don't get invited to cocktail parties.

The Rule of 15

The Rule of 15 simply states that for every 14 posts you carefully curate to show you are interesting and interested, you earn the right to pitch your wares: 10 + 4 + 1 = 15.

People don't like being 'sold' to, but occasionally they need a new car. When they do, you want to be considered because you have been considerate.

When they are in the market for what you do or what you sell, people need to be in the know. Being enigmatic and unnecessarily ambiguous about your profession just creates friction. At the risk of being salesy, many forget to simply let people know about their area of expertise. If you're a salesperson, there is no shame in being a salesperson. We have real revenue goals and offer genuine value to our most ideal clients.

Shame on the person who lives on social media all the time and never asks for the sale. People show up there specifically as a business in a professional marketplace, especially LinkedIn, in order to be seen and to see what's available in business. So, we do need to actually ask to do business with others. The reason it doesn't work for some is that they haven't done the work. In that case it seems too forward and slimy simply because it is.

Eventually, after four years of dating, it will eventually end the relationship if there is no proposal. Consider that next time you want to build a case for *never* asking for the sale. That is how social contracts work. There is a natural order that should be understood to inform our actions.

I often refer to the Rule of 15 as the Cocktail Party Rule. It's a very helpful analogy. It is totally rude to walk into a cocktail party and ask, 'Who wants to go home with me tonight?' But when we write only sales copy online that is what we are doing, in effect. Instead, it is wise to have a joke or two in your proverbial back pocket to show you are an interesting guest. It is also very rude to talk only about what you are interested in and have nothing of value to offer others in the conversation. That person corners people until they find an escape route.

Conversely, after a nice evening of getting to know one another and experiencing reciprocity, humans tend to want to pal around with other nice human beings. In the end, they like to do business with nice human beings. In the quest for making what can sometimes feel awkward socially into a highly fruitful experience, the Rule of 15 can provide much needed equanimity.

Online and offline community

With the move to social, there has been a creation of both online and offline communities. In the earlier chapters we discussed how creating a community or tribe was a requirement of a modern day salesperson. That said, social is a channel; you don't stop talking with people or engaging with people offline.

People say to us sometimes, 'Social selling won't work for me as I have to talk to my clients.' At no point have we said, don't talk to your clients. We are saying, don't interrupt them with cold calls, spam emails and adverts. We would expect you to prospect people on social, have conversations with them online and then want to move that to a virtual or face-to-face meeting. At the end of the meeting you would move back to social as you want to nurture the person online, to move the deal along and avoid being ghosted, etc. Social is a way to listen to the market, find the people and nurture them through stages until they 'pop' into the offline funnel or, as some sales leaders say to me, 'the normal funnel'.

The other things that sales leaders say to me is, 'All this personal branding is interesting, but where are the leads?' The leads are all in this community, they are there in the engagement at the top of the funnel for you to find. Personal branding, listening and using signals are all ways that you will find the leads, or better still they will find you.

It's worth saying that we get a significant amount of our business from inbound, and a lot of this inbound is without competition. That will be because of our digital dominance, literally 'shouting out' the competition, because the prospect will have filtered out the competition as part of their own online due diligence or because our content has made us the obvious choice for solving their business issues.

Social selling best practice

All good sales professionals research their target accounts (no different than we have done for the last 30 years) but now we can do this online. During this research we can listen to an organization, business issues, or news items. We can also research and listen to executives to target Twitter, LinkedIn or even Instagram. Wherever our customers are, we need to be.

Just as when you go to a meeting with somebody and they have photos on the wall of their office, so too can you find out about them if they are posting on Instagram. People often ask me, is this snooping? No. If people are posting photos publicly then in fact they want you to find them and engage with them.

One way you can engage as a social seller with your target accounts is to make comments such as, 'Noticed you were talking about XYZ; have you considered this?' 'This' being some content that the contact will be interested in to drive the conversation forward.

A friend of mine looked for signals to contact one C-level person, and tweeted to him, 'Great to see this technology being rolled out.' The executive replied and they got into a dialogue. My friend told the executive he had a presentation that might be of interest, so the executive then followed my friend back so they could have a direct message (DM) conversation. My friend shared the presentation.

With some good research and a degree of luck, you should get a follow back and then enter into a DM conversation. A direct message conversation is private, and as such can be used to directly identify leads, or as a precursor to that. You are not limited to 'salesperson to prospect' conversations; standard DM functionality allows you to add pre-sales or support people to bring in a specialist domain skill.

Word Swag is an app that allows you to create quotes against a pictorial background. This type of personalized micro content is getting a high-level response rate. Get inspiration for a Word Swag from listening to and researching your target across social media. Then send them the Word Swag as part of a tongue-in-cheek engagement.

In summary, use Twitter and LinkedIn to research your customers and prospects, both at a company level and for the actual people you need to connect with. LinkedIn say that for every enterprise sale, 10 people are involved in the decision-making process, so you need to go deep and wide. Use LinkedIn and Twitter standard functionality to suggest additional people, or people connected to those people (they may well be connected in person and influence).

Listen to what your customers, competition and prospects are saying. Use Google Alerts, Hootsuite, LinkedIn Sales Navigator, Twitter, Facebook, Instagram and LinkedIn as ways to do this. Don't forget that LinkedIn only accounts for 30 per cent of your social graph, and it won't show up family relationships; this will be uncovered on Facebook. The CEO you are calling on may be the sister-in-law of a colleague. It would be a pity to miss that 'base' just because you only use Facebook for family and friends.

Engage/share

Use the usual platforms such as Twitter, Facebook and LinkedIn. But you also should spread your sharing to Instagram, YouTube and SlideShare. SlideShare and YouTube are used by B2B and B2C buyers for (detailed) research into new products and services. Follow people, look at their profiles, like, retweet or comment on what your prospects, customers or influencers are doing.

Connect

While you can use LinkedIn inmails (best practice shows a 7 per cent acceptance rate; that's a 93 per cent rejection rate), we don't use them ourselves. A well-crafted connection request is far better. Send tweets or use something like a Word Swag. It is important to point out, this is not about selling or pitching. That will come in time, this is about you having a conversation. Again, it isn't about being anti-sales – this is about simple psychology, nobody likes being sold to.

Nurture

Have you ever contacted somebody and they have said, 'All very interesting, but give me a call back in three months.' At least you are now on their radar. You can then nurture the relationship. While there has been a fashion to do this through a marketing automation tool, nobody is interested in corporate content and brochures. You should do this through LinkedIn. Connect with them and then the articles you post will allow you to nurture them. This won't stop you calling them in three months, but if for any reason a project kicks off before then, they should know where you are, you will be front of mind; you may be the first person they call.

FIGURE 6.3   Developing the traditional sales funnel – engage, connect, nurture

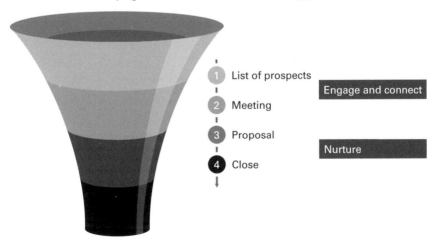

Social selling as part of the business planning process

As your business gets more skilled at social selling and you understand its contribution to the revenue generation process, you are going to want to bring social selling into your business planning process. How can social selling be weaved in?

When we are taking on a new client, I often ask, 'Why are you moving ahead with social selling? And what are your key drivers?' The response is nearly always that it is critical for the client for measurement, connecting social selling with revenue and profit, but also the need to weave social into the management of the sales teams and of the sales teams own management of their territory. In my days in the world of corporate this would be called a quarterly business review (QBR).

What is a QBR/account review?

This would often take place at sales team level, for example the team focused on selling into media, retail and distribution (MRD), or services, technology and construction (STC). I'm sure you have your own vertical make-up and three letter acronyms (TLAs). You can use a version of this process for account reviews (reviewing one account) or territory reviews (where people have multiple accounts).

While I've built and run QBRs for sales teams before, no man is an island, so I called upon the help of David Watts, who is a good friend of mine and helps companies run QBRs and account reviews as a living. My question to David was, 'What do you think a QBR looks like in a digital world?'

Account plan

1. OVERVIEW SLIDE OF KEY PIECES OF INFORMATION

Organizations, industry, size of business (number of employees, turnover), business drivers, challenges and timeline of previous interaction; who they are and who they compete with.

It is critical to understand the company and culture, but also what it has been like to do business with them in the past. For example, they might use external lawyers, which can add three months to the close date.

I would expect the salesperson to follow their accounts on LinkedIn and Twitter. I have often looked up the account on Twitter in the review and asked the salesperson 'What is the latest announcement from the business and how could we help them?' Always great to watch the salesperson's face and gets them to realize that leadership is serious about social.

2. WHAT IS THE REVENUE AND PROFIT AMBITION? THIS YEAR, OVER THE NEXT THREE YEARS?

Critical here – are the salespeople ambitious enough? Are they curious enough?

It always interests me if the salespeople 'just' cut-and-paste or if there has been an analysis of the company accounts. How is what we are doing aligned with the financial year business priorities? Also, how are we aligned with what the business is saying on social media?

A bit of forensic accounting does not go amiss as well as an understanding of the budget cycles.

3. DEPENDING ON ORGANIZATION SIZE: GIVE A SUMMARY OF THE REVENUE TRENDS BY TYPE FOR EACH PART OF THAT ORGANIZATION AND APPLICATION

For salespeople selling in cloud computing, what is the annual recurring revenue, what is the support, consulting and hardware opportunity?

It maybe that the business is decentralized; this will impact on who we are connected to where, and on the decision making process.

4. STRENGTHS, WEAKNESSES, OPPORTUNITIES AND THREATS (SWOT)

Out of any SWOT should be an action plan – how will you consolidate the strengths, mitigate the weaknesses, exploit the opportunities and snuff out the threats? This may require help from different parts of the business, so call that out.

FIGURE 6.4   SWOT example

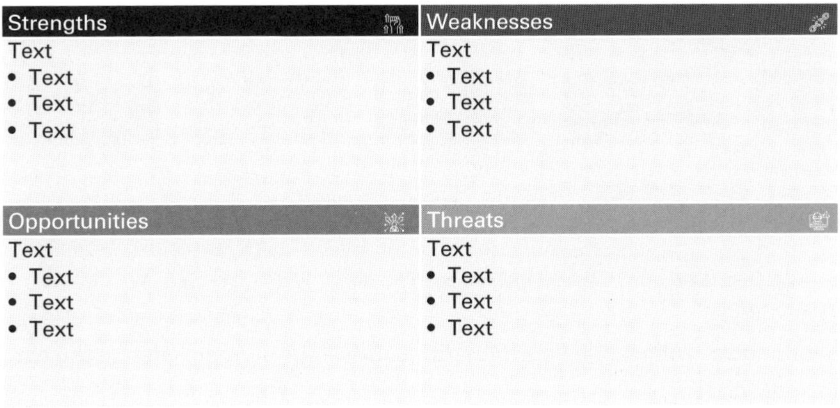

Strengths	Weaknesses
Text	Text
• Text	• Text
• Text	• Text
• Text	• Text
Opportunities	Threats
Text	Text
• Text	• Text
• Text	• Text
• Text	• Text

5. SUMMARY OF INFLUENCE MAP

This needs to itemize who we are connected to, who we are not connected to and how we intend connecting to them. Who we have had a conversation with and who we have a relationship with. This should, of course, be highlighted in the LinkedIn relationships. David makes the comment 'I am usually searching on my phone on the LinkedIn app at this point to check!'

In the past, legacy sales methods like cold calling and email have hindered our ability to scale across an organization. Now social selling enables us as salespeople to build relationships and have conversations right across an organization from the highest of the high to the lowest of the low.

If a sales team (note I'm talking team, not a single person) has fewer than 10 connections, this will raise serious concerns about the level of relationships in the business. Why? Connecting across a business is critical today, We are currently transforming a supply chain software company and they say 100 people will be involved in the decision making process. The sales team need to be connected to over 100 people per account in this case.

Don't forget that influence often comes from outside the company.

FIGURE 6.5   Relationship map example

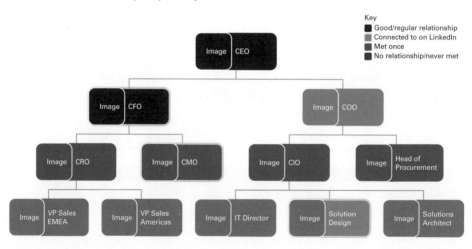

6. ACTION PLAN AROUND RELATIONSHIPS: WHO, WHAT, WHERE, WHEN, WHY (THE 5 WS)

While social will enable you to build relationships at scale, what is the plan off of social?

FIGURE 6.6   Decision maker/influencer map example

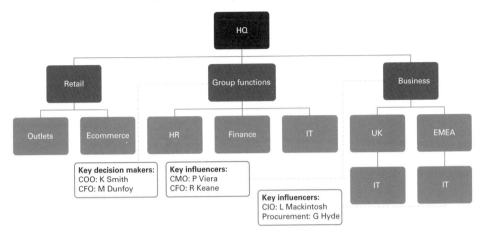

In the current economic climate, people's positions can be a little precarious, you therefore need to mitigate the risk of your economic buyer or sponsor leaving the business by having more than one. There would be nothing worse than getting all the way through the sales process only to find your project sponsor has left the business.

7. COMPETITIVE LANDSCAPE SUMMARY: WHERE THE COMPETITION ARE; HOW TO MITIGATE

This should also include a review of the competition from a social prospective. Are they social selling? If not then this gives us a competitive advantage which we can use. With us being able to understand the culture of the competition by looking at them on social, what can we understand about the competition?

8 BUSINESS ISSUES, CHALLENGES, DRIVERS VS YOUR SOLUTION

It is from this you would build out your opportunity map.

As well as understanding the challenges, what are the priorities? A company can see there is a business issue, but are they willing to put budget to it?

What are we going to do to create content that plays to these issues? If our sales team has deep penetration in the account, what content and themes will play in the account so that the business sees our content and this will then play out to our influence?

9. CROSS-SELL AND UPSELL SUMMARY

What are the cross-sell and upsell opportunities and the timescales? What are the relationships needed on LinkedIn and the support you need from within the business to help?

10. SENIOR EXECUTIVE ENGAGEMENT PLAN

What does the salesperson need from the senior executives? Word to the wise, social selling enables us to get higher than cold calling and email, so in the past sales may have expected senior executives to build relationships with each other. You should still do this as it consolidates relationships in an account, but salespeople need to be 'walking the digital corridors' and connecting and having conversations via social media at a senior level.

This engagement plan will also include the content that will be required to influence the senior executives team.

David's concluding words: 'Social isn't separated. It needs to be embedded in each of the areas!'

Summary

In this chapter we have taken you through the behaviours that you need to exhibit in the new digital world. We have looked at fixed and growth mindsets. Why you need to create a personal brand online, and what is it that you will stand for. What is your own personal brand DNA? What will be your digital identity? What subject matter will you tweet and post on? How often do you need to tweet and post and, importantly, how can you be found when you tweet or post?

Everybody, including your customers, is leaving 'digital footprints' on social media, and these are all signals that you can interrupt to engage and help your prospects or customers. We have itemized a number of signals as examples. Different signals require different tactics. But don't forget, this isn't about diving in and selling. This is about helping and teaching. Selling can come later in the buyer journey. How is it that you can use these 'digital bread crumbs' to start conversations?

We have also looked at how you can use social selling in your business planning process. For the companies that are already doing this they are seeing significant competitive advantage.

We then discussed some good social selling practice, or how not to be a spammer. Educate and inform your reader when you are on social, make them curious for more. Remember, buyers will know you, like you and trust you. Better still, get your reader to make a 'next action' to connect with you.

WHY SALESPEOPLE NEED TO USE SOCIAL AND HOW SALES HAS CHANGED – ROBERT TEARLE

Firstly... why salespeople need to use social.

When salespeople fail, it's because they've not sold enough. They missed their target. Why did they miss their target?

Sellers fail when the have too few opportunities

Social selling gives you a platform to open up more sales opportunities. And not just to create more leads but also to give you a platform to sell in a smarter way. Of course, social selling is no longer new. Do you know that LinkedIn was founded in 2003, Facebook 2004, YouTube 2005, Twitter 2006, Instagram 2010 and TikTok 2016?

The points I'm going to share with you are about B2B selling. If we were talking about B2C selling, it would be more of a marketing issue. This information isn't just for salespeople. My thoughts, ideas and observations are for you if you're in marketing, customer service, finance, human resources, procurement, research and development and so on.

You have your platform preferences; they're not necessarily the same as your customer's. Currently, LinkedIn's the dominant platform for business. However, you can leverage so much using other channels, notably WhatsApp, YouTube, Facebook, Instagram, Twitter, TikTok etc.

Why use social?

My objective is to give you at least one worthwhile insight that you can grab hold of. So, if you're a general manager, sales leader or sales executive why do you need to use social? There are three reasons: sales effectiveness, personal development and your broader career-based interests.

1. Sales effectiveness

If I started by saying it's an essential prospecting tool, you'd be forgiven for falling asleep. So let me put a marker in the ground and state that unless you use social, you'll never tune into a customer's persona. Even the police, intelligence agencies and armed forces feature on social, what with demonstrations, riots, cyber-attacks and confrontations making news on social, and of course, there are job ads. All providing business insight. Of course, your customers are more likely to be in banking, business services, legal, logistics, manufacturing, retail, tech, telecoms, travel & entertainment, utilities and so on.

Social allows you to tune into your customers business drivers and persona. If you do not understand your customer, you'll be at a disadvantage to your competitors.

- Your customers' customers are using these channels.

- Your customers' suppliers are using these channels.

- Your competitors are using these channels.

- Your customers' employees are using these channels.

- Your business partners are using these channels.

Social media gives you the opportunity to better understand your customers, their customers, competitors, employees, and business partners. Empowering you to excel and win more!

LONDON, MUNICH, PARIS, NEW YORK...

The working population in the UK is 32.5 million, of which 31 million have LinkedIn profiles. A similar pattern is repeated across major global economies. Social is a key customer profiling tool.

It's possible to profile customers using social, for example, where the business has operations and offices, how many people are employed in each business function, and in what locations, and where functions are based. How many people are based in these locations?

On LinkedIn, you can see patterns in headcount increase or decrease. And on Glassdoor, you can gain insights into employment stats, salaries, company culture and internal issues.

STAKEHOLDER MANAGEMENT

Using LinkedIn and Google, you can identify key decision-makers and chains of command. You can locate powerbases. And, importantly, you can quickly identify employment status changes, such as new starters, leavers, people vacating one position in a company and taking up another!

THERE'S A HIDDEN ROOM

Whatever perception you have of social selling, I'd like you to think about the concept of a hidden room. In this room, there's a ton of ideas and issues that you've missed out on or overlooked. Whether you're a social novice or an expert, the hidden room is full of goodies, and it keeps on giving.

We see the world through our own eyes. It's easy to think that others think as we do. To think that others see things in the same way. And to fall into the trap of failing to understand others, and if we fail to understand others, we'll fail to connect with them. And if you don't connect with people, you'll fail to build rapport and will likely miss out on selling opportunities.

But in the context of social selling, what's in the hidden room, gives you the chance to switch on a mass of opportunity, to tune into marketplace dynamics and, importantly, your customer sentiment. The hidden room on social is what other people are doing and saying, different types of people with different issues, priorities, desires, problems etc. And what different companies and organizations are messaging about, good and bad.

Sometimes you can see what a company or person is doing. You may think it's awful, and then realize your activity is much the same! What are the new things being said? Your prospective customer has an endless list of alternatives to your awesome offering!

By adopting a broader and open-minded approach to engaging on social, you'll be able to discover aspects and points of view that will enable you to better think through your strengths, weaknesses, opportunities and threats.

USE SOCIAL AS A TOOL TO GET THEM TO CHOOSE TO ENGAGE WITH YOU

You can use social media to develop prospects' awareness of you and confidence in your personal brand, enabling you to engage better and more frequently with them and with more relevance and greater sentiment. When you engage in a dialogue with a prospective customer, you'll be in a stronger position if you are on their radar, i.e. they are aware of you – you've connected with them on LinkedIn.

It is even better if the buyer feels familiar with you and even more wicked if they feel you connect with their issues and are knowledgeable and trustworthy. If you use social properly, you'll look to extend your network beyond your own community to gain a higher level and broader perspective.

Lots of sellers are connected to their colleagues, ex-colleagues, sales trainers, business partners etc. Too many sales execs publish postings about how they've smashed their sales quota, how they've had their best sales month ever, won the prize for 'Top Rep' or how they've just secured their place on the company's President's Club trip to Hawaii. Is this what you want your customers to be reading?

If you engage with more of your customer types, and with their industry associations, etc. you can start to better understand your customer, their issues, and needs, enabling you to make your social comments, postings more aligned with their business drivers, critical pain points and problems.

SOCIAL SELLING PRESENTS YOU WITH AN OPPORTUNITY TO DEVELOP A COMPETITIVE ADVANTAGE

Of course, if you can get visibility of your competitors, you can see what messages they're pushing out into the marketplace. Perhaps you can gain some competitive intelligence or use information in a benchmarking kind of way. If you're not already using social media to connect with people, identify and engage with decision-makers, and develop your accounts, I'd be surprised. However, what you need to do, is to do it exceptionally well... there's a ton of average, me-too content out there. Your customers will find that boring and mundane. Unless you use social well, you'll be at a disadvantage.

If you want to maximize your sales success, you've to prioritize social selling.

2. Personal development

Most business leaders look to hire and promote people who have a high level of emotional intelligence (EI). One of the characteristics of EI is self-awareness. An increasing number of sales leaders wish to hire curious people. Some will have curiosity featuring on their list of critical criteria. Self-awareness and curiosity go hand in glove. Decision-makers want to hire people and promote people who are open to new ideas from all directions.

Engaging on social allows you to expand your perspectives, particularly if you build a diverse network. Participating on social gives you insights into what other people are doing, providing you with the opportunity to see things in new ways, acquire new knowledge and ideas, and for self- and continuous improvement.

You need to be aware of what's become outdated, what the latest issues are and what's going to be happening next. What are the things you've overlooked and don't know about? Reading, sharing, commenting, questioning, and posting on social media will help you maintain an up-to-the-minute perspective and keep yourself relevant.

3. Your broader career interests

Using social is a must when you're in job-search mode, for ensuring you have visibility to key people in your existing employer company and for promoting your personal brand.

MAKE YOUR CAREER SUCCESS SUSTAINABLE

If you're in job search mode, you need to use social so that employers can find you. Even if you're not in job search mode, do appreciate that often the best times to make a move are when you don't have to! In such circumstances, you'll only move for a superior opportunity. In contrast, someone unemployed will more happily take up a new job of a like for like nature.

For most salespeople, it's a good idea for people in your company to have a good, positive visibility of you, without which you might be exposed if cutbacks and redundancies are to be made. If you've missed your number and no one knows of you or what you're doing, you're more exposed to being fired. You want to be seen as being active, doing constructive, positive things, as being pro-active. And when the best sales territories, account sets, leads, etc., are given out, you want to be visible so that you will be positively considered and ideally awarded the best work and opportunities.

Similarly, if you want promotion, you need to be seen as being successful. You need to be seen as being promotable.

YOU NEED TO BE READY TO CATCH THE NEXT WAVE

The reality is that the economy, industry sectors and what's expected of people are constantly changing. If you don't keep up, you get left behind. Most industry sectors are subject to trends. Products and service types often have a lifecycle. An industry sector can be created, go into growth mode, enjoy hyper-growth, then plateau and go into a state of decline.

The same applies to companies. If you think that your awesome current employer company is always going to be rocking, think again, a great many companies prosper, plateau and proceed into a downward spiral.

Most sellers' success will be determined by demand in the market for their proposition type and the strength of your offering. Employment opportunities and continued employment are generally for people with in-demand skills. A trap for people in sales and other occupations is to become outdated and no longer desirable. You need to be conscious to watch what's going on in your industry niche. You need to be ready to catch the next wave; otherwise, your career can go into a downward spiral.

Meeting people online, participating in discussions, chatting with others in similar and different job types and industry sectors, and different outlooks on life will help you think beyond your own limitations and better recognize the need for change. Using social is critical for advancement, career progression and to help you to make your career success sustainable.

How sales has changed

Customer side

Todays' buyer is more aware. He or she has data, insights and information accessible 24 hours a day. Not just access to information, but they'll also tap into their people network to see what other people are doing.

HAVE YOU READ THE NEWS?

News and advertising used to be in print and on billboards. News used to be consumed in a newspaper featuring yesterday's news, in which you'd find advertising. Today, lots of people read their news online on LinkedIn, Twitter, Facebook and share it on WhatsApp. Sellers and marketers need to interact and influence customers where they are at, online in a real-time virtual newsroom.

INFORMAL, TRANSPARENT AND BLURRED LINES!

Digital social media is no longer confined to social interaction. Social platforms are used for business purposes. Formal written and verbal communication styles, and dress codes have been displaced by a more informal, casual and transparent culture. Tech is cool, and business is dynamic – the world of work is more fascinating today than in the past.

The boundaries and barriers between work and home time have been removed. The buyer is more informed, which means that the seller must be so too. Timothy Hughes can be credited with the insight that 'today's buyer is already 70 per cent of their way through their buying journey before they engage with the salesperson'.

The seller faces many new challenges.

YOU NEED TO CONNECT IN MICRO-MOMENTS

The working environment is a non-stop one. People are doing more work each day, and they've got more meetings, more channels of communication and more apps to use. The intensity of work is at an all-time high. Your prospective customer has less free time, and their diaries are jammed. You need to connect with them in micro-moments.

YOU NEED TO BE HYPER-RELEVANT

Because they're so busy, you've got to be hyper-relevant when you connect with them. Otherwise, they'll look to switch you off or terminate your meeting early. Often the buyer is more informed than the seller, more so today than in the past! However, you need to understand that everyone is on a different journey, meaning that people may be ahead of or behind you in their thinking. And their agenda may not be what you think it is. It's easy to jump to conclusions.

The world is more sophisticated, and your buyer has more choices available to them. You need to understand your competition isn't just your direct competitor; it's also alternatives as to how they spend their time, money and where their motivations lie. You need to be relevant, be conscious that everyone is on a different journey, and you need to meet them where they are at. Engaging with new prospective customers used to be started with sending brochures, invitations to seminars and cold calling. Today cold calling doesn't have the same conversion ratios. Generally, they're low; however, they've been displaced by warm calling. A warm call is one in which, to a lesser or greater degree, you've got on the customers' radar, more about that to follow.

Whereas networking used to be associated with face-to-face meetings, events etc., today it's as much online – you can meet people, become acquainted on LinkedIn, become networking buddies and virtual friends using likes, comments, shares, messaging etc. Virtual meetings have made it possible to make sales without meeting in person. This was happening before Covid-19 lockdowns. In the US, the country is so massive this was taking place many years ago and similarly with international deals. Today's customer is digital savvy and not averse to doing business without face-to-face meetings. An increasing number of sales are being made end to end on Google Chat, Teams, Zoom etc. Similarly, there's an ever-increasing percentage of sales being made with no seller touch!

IS SALES AN ART OR A SCIENCE?

In the past, sales could have been considered an art; however, it's become much more of a science in recent years. The change has been that the buyer has become more informed, and every aspect of the world in which we work has become more sophisticated. Sellers do need to be creative, in so far as thinking of how to best approach their selling opportunity, and social can help with this by opening up your mind to new possibilities.

In recent years, social has given sellers an opportunity to promote personal and business brands online and significantly influence customer thinking. The meeting place, conditions and conventions have moved from face-to-face to online, from monitor to mobile, from text to video and from static to interactive and intuitive!

There's an emerging set of sales talents who are gaining mindshare and talents in content creation, copywriting, and comedy. They influence the marketplace not just with conventional text messaging but also in video and virtual meetings and conferences. Some sellers can captivate an audience, like a rock star, performing in different ways, some with straightforward authenticity, others with humour or personality. Today's customer is more informed, pragmatic, and can see through the BS. Never before has it been so crucial for you to be authentic.

NO LONGER JUST ABOUT SELLING MORE, SERVING BETTER, SAVING MONEY

In the old world of sales training, trainers would hammer home the need to sell benefits of 'sell more, serve better, save money'. However, today's buyer isn't just interested in those key triggers. They also want to engage with suppliers who have a responsible approach to all things environmental, social and governance, and align with their interests in this respect.

Employer expectations

Their expectations when hiring have become elevated, and likewise their expectations of existing employees.

They apply a greater level of focus on sales performance stats and cadence, and they're more accountable in their reporting upwards. Executives in the 'C' suite and managers seek to apply a better level of coaching to drive excellence and more closely track seller activity.

IS IT MICRO-MANAGEMENT OR SALES EXCELLENCE?

An increasing number of people buy into the concept that applying a robust process drives sales excellence. Is this micro-management? There's a bright new generation of sellers emerging, who buy into best practices, many like process, it works, it reduces risk and cuts down on errors. The world of selling has got smarter, more sophisticated, and new job types have emerged or become more commonplace in the last 10 years, notably functions like business development, sales enablement, customer success, etc.

Employee side

Picking up from that last paragraph, people can take up different types of jobs, presenting fresh challenges and new career paths. In the past, employers generally held the cards. The expression of a 'master/slave relationship' might be extreme. However, in the context of good salespeople with in-demand skills sets, demand to hire outstrips supply.

TODAY'S EMPLOYEE IS MORE INDEPENDENT

Different age groups have different expectations. They also have different abilities.

DON'T GET OVERLY CONFIDENT IF YOU'RE A DIGITAL NATIVE

Social is constantly changing. Wrapping up my piece, it seems that everyone wants to be an influencer, coach or leader. There are not enough such seats to go round. Social gives you an opportunity to be better connected, benefit from greater insights, and be hyper-relevant.

Whatever you do, kill your target.

References

Dweck, C (2017) *Mindset: Changing the way you think to fulfil your potential.* Robinson.

Khaneman, D (2011) *Thinking, Fast and Slow.* Farrar, Straus and Giroux.

07

Selling the idea of social selling and measuring success

Sales leaders say to me that 'This social selling stuff is all very well, but where are the leads, meetings and closed deal?' In this chapter we go through the common objections you will get to running a social selling programme, and how you go about getting sponsorship and with whom. Plus we look at how to measure such a project and the difference between different metrics.

At the start of the book we explained how the internet had changed everything. Our customers now use the internet and social channels to research and buy goods and services. The research is clear on this. In order to undertake social prospecting and to use social as a way to nurture prospects and to close deals, companies need to be on the channels where their customers are active. Social prospecting will give us the leads, and using the sales techniques that we have built up and continually craft we should be able to close these leads ahead of the competition, giving us the revenue at the margins we want.

In the book we talk about how to create community and use influence to control our markets. Community should not be seen here as a hippy concept, but a tool that can be used for competitive advantage.

The opportunity

Research from Gartner from 2020 states that '80 per cent of B2B sales interactions between suppliers and buyers will occur in digital channels by 2025'. In the same article Gartner state 'Sales leaders must adopt a digital-first approach and meet customers' new buying preferences'.

By our own behaviour we know the world has changed. If I show you a glasses case and tell you it's the best in the world, the first thing you will do is go online and research. Yes, you might think that all buyers start searching on Google, but do they? Simon Kemp (2021) has been tracking the world's search behaviours. He says: 'Social networks are now the second-top channel for online brand research after search engines, and amongst internet users aged 16 to 24, they're already the top channel.' This means that Google is not the first place people go to search, it's social media.

Once the buyer has undertaken their research they will usually come up with a shortlist of two or three vendors. The buyer of today is well informed and well researched, and by the time they have created a shortlist they understand each short vender's value proposition as well as price.

Note, we have also shared techniques so far in this book where you as a business can digitally dominate your space so that you will be seen as the only and obvious choice to your buyer, but let's assume you still have not created your digital muscles. If as an organization you have invested and implemented the techniques in this book and find and engage these buyers early on then your competition will be lower and there will be little price friction. If you decide not to change to the sales techniques of the digital world then you will be left to fight over what is left with all the other suppliers, creating, most likely, the need to drive your margins down.

In addition, research shows that the online buyer tends to choose brands as a shortlist. If, for example, you are a small- to medium-size organization, you are most likely to miss out, as these buyers will shortlist the bigger brands. But the good news is that small and large companies alike can use the methodology outlined in this book. That said, communities and owning the influence in your market can be obtained with little need to invest in big and expensive tools.

Common objections and how you get around them

'My customers are not on social...'

This myth is an interesting one. This goes back to salespeople talking about companies as if they are a single entity. I cannot believe that in the company you are selling to, 100 per cent of the employees don't use social. Even if you think that your customers are totally offline, what about your prospective customers? Your competition? There is a whole world out there that wants to connect and you are going to pull up the drawbridge and sit in your analogue castle?

Don't forget that social media requires a relatively low investment, but if used in line with the methodology in this book, it can have a high impact.

Your audience is freely telling you about themselves on their online profiles. You can use their social profiles to learn about their personal interests and what topics they wish to discuss. You can use this to target and engage with them. Why would you shy away from creating an expert reputation for your business, the go-to point for everything that your company sells, creating an online monopoly that wins deals, creates revenue and maintains good margins?

If a buyer team is 10 people, then you will find nine of them, the vast majority, are on social.

People that just don't 'get it' or don't want to

Presentation skills courses will often say that when you present, cast your eyes round the room and look to see who is engaged, who is falling asleep, etc. As we tour the world talking about how to make a change to the selling process one thing I notice is that often I see people's eyes glaze over.

While this could be because of my presentation skills, we often have the chance during question and answer sessions or networking to seek these people out (be warned!) and ask for feedback. Once, a person said to me, 'All this talk about social networks, sorry I have just no idea, I'm not on Twitter and have the minimum on LinkedIn. In fact you have got me thinking that I cannot wait for my retirement to come around.' We are certainly not being ageist here, as 'social blindness' infiltrates through all ages, cultures and backgrounds. However, we have moved into a digital age, and therefore people and businesses must move with this change if they want to remain competitive.

In many cases we've seen senior management give salespeople prizes for the number of followers they have, or the number of tweets they have made in the last time period. This for me is really scary, as it's clear that the management don't understand social. Of course it goes without saying that we always research a company's senior executives and the people within the company before meeting them. We then make a judgement (as do so many other people, potential customers, potential employees, your competition) on your organization based on your social profiles.

It's not just sales and marketing that is impacted here but the war on talent and the experience your customers have when interacting with you.

We guess that by reading this book you already 'get it', and even if not, by now you must have come to realize that the 'battle' for customers and market leadership has moved online and you need to be part of it. Or you might do what many companies have done, which is delegate it to a younger age group (although it is worth saying that I'm not suggesting you turn over your social policy to teenagers...). Our recommendation is to look for people in the organization that are young enough to understand social, but also have the business acumen to support the advice they give you.

We also recommend that if you have bosses or staff that don't 'get it', you simply buy them a copy of this book and give it out as a present. We have had sales and marketing leaders that have given this book en masse to their staff.

This social stuff is all 'fluff' – just go and get me leads and revenue!

We hear this from all the sales leaders and vice presidents that we work with. All this stuff on social selling and using social media is kind of interesting but what they want are leads, which convert into revenue (at good margin). In fact, when we first pitched this book to the publishers, Kogan Page, they said to us that they didn't want a book on personal branding; their feedback to us was 'there are enough personal branding books in the world'.

The objective instead has been to give you a platform to use social, but use it as a tool that will drive your leads (preferably inbound), and while we don't say that you need to stop cold calling, social should be used alongside this as a channel to cultivate prospects and customers. As a business, we have trained thousands of people and business, and are not short of case studies we can tap into and present.

It's worth breaking off from social for a moment to talk about cold calling. We have all been in the situation where we have that deadline to meet and we are creating a PowerPoint presentation or Excel spreadsheet for that all-important board meeting. We have scoped it all out and we have pent-up creativity that we just need to get out of our heads and into the computer. We are part-way through this amazing streak of creativity when the phone goes.

We all know this will probably be a cold call and most people just ignore it. (Sorry, salespeople reading, we know you will ring back.) If we do take the call then we know that the telesales agent will probably have a well-crafted script to take us through in order to get a yes. This just frustrates and annoys us and makes us feel animosity towards that company, the opposite of wanting to buy. We are so wound up that by the time we get back to our board presentation, we have forgotten what we were going to write.

Yes, we agree that 'interruption' cold calling is dead. As a sales guy said to me recently, 'I've just spent the whole day cold calling and got nowhere – surely there has to be a better way?' There is.

How do I bring social selling into my company when the managing director doesn't even have a LinkedIn account?

Often, leaders can be looking in a different direction. It may be because of their skill set or they are just busy elsewhere. That said, as business leaders it is our duty to stay ahead of trends in the market place. We don't have to implement them, but we surely need to understand what they are. A business leader that does not understand social selling today is fine, a business leader that does not understand social selling in a year's time is negligent.

If you are going to talk to a leader that has no social profile, it's important that you anchor your argument in data. You leadership team won't want 'fluff', they will want to know how they can increase sales, revenue and EBITDA. So make sure you have the latest data to hand – you are welcome to reach out to me if you want help.

Transforming your business to social is critical and sensitive, but this requires creating a platform for growth and a framework that is measurable, repeatable and scalable.

How to position social selling with your executive team

Social selling is a strategy that must be driven from the top. That's not to say that without C-level buy-in you needn't bother, but without it you will bounce along with what I call 'random acts of social'. See Chapter 9 on the digital maturity model.

To get buy-in you can (and we would recommend it) run a pilot. We take a bunch of volunteers (people who volunteer are usually partly social and early adopters). We then take them on a three-month journey to turn them into social sellers, offering a measurable journey (agreed with the management), so we can see that it is results-based. Finally we present the results and conclusions to the board.

We usually find at this point that one of the senior management will volunteer, and we work with them to help them become social so they can understand the journey we are proposing. Don't forget that 'one size does not fit all' and that different leaders have different motivations; you need to work with them around these drivers.

For example, marketers will maybe have more interest in brands, as well as leads. Sales will be interested in leads as well as using social through lead progression and closing. Don't forget that personal branding, employee advocacy and talent management can all have a social impact and that the human resources department may well be affected.

Some advice on how to make your social selling and/or digital organization programme a success:

1 Start with a strategy. Too many people start with tactics such as 'hints and tips'; this will get you nowhere fast.

2 As part of that strategy, you must create a mission statement, not for your business, but for this programme.

3 Get an external third party in to train the team. External third parties are more likely to be listened to by a cynical sales force.

4 Work right across the business on the corporate mindset. Talk to as many people as you can, show them the data, better still when you have the results from the pilot.

5 Use tools such as Slack so that people have a central hub on social. This will allow you to scale; social is a team sport and you need to create a content factory to provide the resources the sales team need.

6 Don't just train the team, but coach them as well. Everybody learns at a different speed and all members of the team will have strengths and weaknesses. By providing one-to-one coaching you are able to pick up on the strugglers fast and find and champion the people that are able to pick up and run with social.

In the next part of the book, we look at the different department heads and how you should position your pitch for a social selling project. This section covers the C-suite roles.

Chief executive officer (CEO)

When we talk with CEOs these are the usual concerns that they raise:

- How do they grow revenue, while maintaining margin?
- How do they attract and retain the best talent?
- How do they innovate and out-execute the competition, and what is the plan to still be around in five years' time?
- How can they enhance collaboration in the organization, and break down those silos?

So, how to position social selling with CEOs?

- Contextualize social selling as the key to top-line growth. Supply statistics about how social selling is connected to revenue, and position it as the future of the modern sales organization. Offer to run a pilot, which will have an agreed set of metrics.
- Highlight how social selling will separate you from your competition. Show how your competitors are relying on the old sales playbook, and contrast your competitors' efforts with your plan. Social selling will give you a competitive edge and enable you to control your influence and 'own' the markets you trade in.
- Talk about the performance improvements that you'll gain from knowing exactly which selling tactics are working and which content items are resonating with your buyers. 'We would see an increase of revenue of 20 per cent and a reduction in the sales cycle by 30 per cent.'

Chief finance officer (CFO)

The CFO, in most cases, is the person who 'writes the cheques'; often you need to convince them even when everybody else is in agreement.

We find the main concerns of CFOs are:

- Managing expenses: build a business case and show an ROI within 12 months, starting with a pilot phase to prove out the initial expenditure.
- Containing risk: explain where things can go wrong (change management etc.) and show how you will manage it.
- Planning for the future: once the return on the investment has been obtained, what then? Show how you can drive revenue (and margin) growth.

How to connect the dots for the CFO:

- Present your developed business case. You must always have a business case when talking with a CFO. We recommend you get an independent third party to 'cast their eye' over it, as the CFO will often go straight for the numbers and the detail.

- Use benchmark statistics to project how social selling will affect revenue. Your CFO will understand if you have to use estimates; simply note where you are using them.

It's worth saying that while we have many people and clients that have obtained results in days or weeks, social selling requires building relationships, communities and influencers, and educating buyers, so it could take time. Therefore we have to change the way we think about the costs associated with social sales.

In short, social selling is an investment. Your company incurs costs today, but social selling delivers benefits for many months and years to come. By investing in training, technology and pipeline today, you're setting your team up for success in the future. We come back to the pilot to show that while this is long term, there are 'quick wins' you can implement to show a return in the short term. Let's not forget that if you give your sales team new life skills they have them forever. The business returns we mention above are not for one year, they are forever.

It's like buying a house. The returns from buying a house are not immediate. They often come years down the road – when you go to sell your house. The same is true of social selling. Over time, when you have moved to being a digital organization and your sales and marketing are online, your investment in social sales will pay off.

Head of sales

Salespeople and sales leaders will always be thinking about the following things:

- How do they hit or exceed quota? Sales is a numbers game. How will they get a continuous stream of meetings to close? If the leadership think social is all about 'kids posting photos of lunch' then you need to explain how you can connect the investment to 'the numbers'. We have plenty of examples.

- How do they get an accurate sales forecast, which they can publish?

- Create references so that customers buy more or tell others to buy. Many want a lower cost and repeatable sales process, especially in the new world of SaaS.

- No sales leader likes being beaten by the competition.

So here's how you sell them the idea of social selling:

- Remind sales leaders that buyers are deleting emails and ignoring phone calls. By using social networks, creating communities and online knowledge champions your sales teams will stand a fighting chance of engaging their buyers.

- Show how social selling is a way to beat your competition. By reaching out to buyers before they approach your company, your sales team can start shaping buyers' attitudes early on, and in turn, your reps will win more deals.

- Highlight the ways in which technology will help you standardize best practices across your sales team, by using modern best practices such as lead nurturing. These free up salespeople to spend more time in front of clients.

- Use this book, the statistics and research reports available to you. Highlight the fact that buyers use social media when making purchasing decisions. Remind people what they do when they want to buy something. They don't dive in and ring a supplier; they go online and research first.

- Note that sales teams are more likely to attain their sales quota when they use social media. But this isn't about chasing vanity measures such as likes and followers; it's about using it as a tool to find new prospects. You can still measure people on meetings, revenue, or whatever metric you currently use. This is *not* about 'playing on Facebook all day', which is a common objection we hear. With the measurement of social today, you can connect every key press of a salesperson on their keyboard to revenue created by social.

- As mentioned above, being on social will enable you to create a position where you are digitally dominant and your customer should see you are the only choice to fix their business issues.

Chief marketing officer (CMO)

Here's what a CMO wants to do:

- Strengthen relationships with customers; it is easier to sell to an existing one than a new one. Plus, how can we work with the existing customer base to get new customers – isn't 'word of mouth' always the strongest sales tool?

- Build alignment with the sales department. It is important that the two departments don't 'throw stones at each other', but work together with a common goal and purpose.

- Measure and prove marketing ROI. This we have seen time after time – how can we prove that the leads we created were actually due to our marketing efforts? Are we measuring the customer journey or the last touch?

- Protect brand equity. With customers buying (or remembering) experiences, how can we make sure that we create and protect the brand and its DNA?

And here are a few tips for connecting the dots:

- Put social sales into context. Identify ways that the marketing team has evolved over the years through marketing automation, content marketing, moving the marketing budget online and other initiatives. Then, position social selling as a way of modernizing the sales organization. We often see social selling initiatives start in marketing (as it's seen as a lead generation tool) and then flounder as the sales department only see and hear 'fluff' rather than actual revenue. Don't forget, people will say 'Show me the money.'

- Discuss social selling as an opportunity to bring marketing and sales into better alignment. For example, the programme will empower the salespeople to generate their own leads, reducing pressure on marketing. It gives marketing activities greater visibility in sales so you don't get the 'you never tell us about your events' situation. Also by bringing sales and marketing closer, there is a greater understanding of what a lead is, so we move away from the thinking that 'marketing-created leads are rubbish'. Trust me, this can take effort, change management and constant dialogue; but it can be done – we have even seen sales leaders and CMOs start to send each other Christmas cards.

- Assure the CMO that the company's brand will be protected. Highlight your plans for social media training, and indicate that marketing can supply content and sample messages to the sales team. Sales reps won't be on their own. The big mistake that companies make is thinking that LinkedIn, Twitter etc. can be used just like Google and Amazon. No – we have never seen a 'How to use Amazon' training course, but setting up LinkedIn and Twitter to drive leads and revenue is different. It needs training (one to many) as well as, often, one-to-one coaching. You might say, well we would say this, we run a training and coaching company, but we have been in so many meetings where people say they 'get it' and they don't. People are frightened of admitting they don't understand social. One-to-one coaching will enable us to focus in on the particular issues somebody may have. For example, one person we coached put lots of effort into social but flatlined at 400 followers on Twitter (a common problem). Just by sitting with the guy for 30 minutes we enabled him to put on 200 followers in a week. How? He had been tweeting but nobody could find him, so with just a little coaching on how to use hashtags, within a month he hit 1,000 followers.

- Explain that social selling will not compete with marketing's social media strategy. Social media marketing speaks to large segments of buyers, while social selling offers an opportunity for personalized one-to-one interactions. Most of the marketing departments we talk to understand the difference and want other employees to help. Often they find they need help but don't know how to go about asking for it.

- Emphasize the idea that social selling will amplify marketing's efforts. Sales will rely on marketing's content to build relationships and check in with customers. More people will see your company's marketing assets without you paying for advertising. Creating a community will amplify the brand messages and get them to areas where marketing probably didn't have the resources to ever reach.

Getting a budget approved is infinitely easier when you have buy-in from other departments. Sometimes, your buy-in is literal, in that other departments will contribute monetary funds. Other times, your buy-in is simply support for an initiative. By getting the marketing and human resources (including training) departments involved, you increase the size of the budget.

Chief information officer (CIO)

It's not often we talk with CIOs, but when we do, these are their chief concerns:

- Controlling costs; they will want to make sure this isn't a back-door way of making another IT purchase.
- Innovating and evolving infrastructure for the future. Many IT departments suffer from legacy systems that use 80 per cent of the budget just to support them. IT resource is tight; CIOs don't want their staff distracted.
- Managing technology security, so that it meets the company's cyber and hacking policies.
- Most CIOs now understand that they must make investments that support the company's goals.

We find the following useful when working with the IT department:

- Paint a picture of the future. Show how sales teams need software beyond the CRM. They need mobile and social media tools as well. Life isn't just about adding the names and addresses into a CRM system; people need the social context. What is a person's network? Who are they connected to and who do they influence?
- Get buy-in from your marketing team, as well as sales and maybe even the human capital management (HCM) department. CIOs are more willing to approve technology if several departments are interested in it.
- Get the CIO to understand that Twitter and LinkedIn are standard social tools.

Revenue operations leader (RevOps)

Over the last few years the term 'RevOps' has emerged, which is the bringing together of all revenue-generating departments into one department, with a single set of objectives, measures, strategy and governance.

The Covid-19 pandemic has taught us that we have to find every deal for our pipeline and close every deal there is. Bringing all revenue creation departments under one leader creates focus.

The RevOps leader's chief concerns are:

- A single strategy for revenue generation across the business, no isolated pockets.
- A move away from legacy sales methods such as cold calling, email and marketing and move to use digital at the heart of the business.

We find the following are useful when talking with RevOps leaders:

- Re-emphasize that digital is about the people and process and not tools.
- Social selling isn't just about prospect, but the whole sales cycle, from 'land to expand'. For example, we work with businesses where the account-based marketing and renewals are drivers for new ways for selling.

Getting buy-in for social selling is not always easy. But if you understand your stakeholders' concerns and position social sales accordingly, you have a good chance of convincing your executive team. Don't forget, we are also available to help.

Return on investment (ROI) and criteria for success

To get approval for new projects, you need to establish criteria for success. In this part of the chapter we will talk about these. While some people still talk about measures that can be seen as 'fluffy', you should be getting hard advice on the impact on revenue and EBITDA. We will talk about the hard measures that will make a real monetary impact on the business.

We always get a business we work with to answer two questions:

1 How many meetings is the business getting from social media activity?
2 How much revenue/EBITDA is the business getting from social media activity?

There are just too many business 'posting and hoping' – that isn't good enough any more.

Since social selling is an investment, it may take time for your programme to pay off; even with a pilot you should still be looking at an ROI within 12 weeks or less. Revenue metrics will always be the best indicator of success in the short term, but these leading indicators can show whether you are on the right or wrong track. If a piece of content gets 10 likes, so what? No, this does not have a revenue impact, but it does mean that 10 people liked it (which is good, yes?) and you got distribution and amplification of the content over other people's networks (which is good, yes?). That is also 10 reasons to have conversations with people.

For this reason, to start, you may want to focus on engagement metrics. Think about numbers related to the amount of content shared by salespeople, network growth by salespeople and the number of conversations they are having, either from network growth or from sharing content. These are early signs that your tactics are working and that your team is on its way to building relationships and driving revenue. These signs give your business visibility of direction, way before things hit the CRM.

Different types of metrics

When it comes to social selling programmes, businesses can measure their progress in several ways. Below, you'll find three types of metrics. Choose the metrics that make the most sense for your objectives, your role and the maturity of your programme.

Training metrics

It's easy to get ahead of ourselves when it comes to launching a programme. We want to start as soon as possible, and we forget to take the time to build our foundation. It is too easy for employees (and it's usually the 'non-believers') to skip training, and this means that it will take you longer to show success. You will also get 'random acts of social' which are often off-putting to those who are struggling with the concept.

Training should be a key part of any social selling programme. Unless you train your team, you will never meet your programme and revenue objectives.

Here are several ways that you can measure training:

- average number of training hours
- average time to competence
- percentage of employees who are certified
- number of training sessions held for employees
- percentage of employees above competence
- percentage of employees below competence

We always recommend a certification process, as this means you know that the team has at least reached a baseline. This certification process, delivered by the management, shows that there is leadership buy-in. Otherwise, like any change programme, people will go back to their old behaviours.

Tactical metrics (they may be 'fluffy' but they do show momentum)

Another way to measure your social media efforts is through tactical metrics. To state the obvious, these measurements help you determine whether your tactics are working, your content is liked or disliked, and you are gaining the growth and amplification you need across your communities and networks.

Are your salespeople's posts engaging their followers? Are people clicking on their tweets? Are they retweeting your content? Are the accounts you are trying to influence (sell to) engaging with your content?

Here are different tactical metrics that you can use for the three major social networks.

LINKEDIN

- **Number of posts per day.** We would expect a salesperson to manage at least one.

- **Number of connections.** Any enterprise salesperson should have at least 500 connections, and at least 50 per cent of these should be across their community of accounts, contacts, influencers, etc. Each salesperson should be making at least 100 new connections a week, and should be getting at least a 70 per cent acceptance of these connection requests.

- **Number of comments, likes and shares.** Salespeople should 'share the love', and like and comment on their prospects, customers and the people who influence their prospects and customers. After all, these likes and comments start conversations. We live in LinkedIn; it is open all the time we are working. Unlike, maybe, Facebook where you can get distracted with cat photos, with LinkedIn you should be working 100 per cent of the time.

As we discussed earlier, getting your content amplified across people's networks is good. Don't fall into the trap of only being connected and only engaging with mates and work colleagues; grow and nurture your network on LinkedIn. If you have potential clients then maybe they will pick up on your content (and even make contact with you) when they start their research.

TWITTER

- **Number of posts per day.** Salespeople should be posting (and engaging) at least once a day.

- **Number of followers.** Salespeople need to have upwards of 400.

- **Number of @ mentions.** Salespeople should get one a day, and share the love by mentioning other people at least once a day. This is social media, after all.

- **Number of retweets.** Salespeople need to be interesting enough, with a big enough network, to be retweeted at least once a day. They should also be engaging enough to retweet themselves once a day. And please, not to just your mates, as you will end up talking to yourself. Salespeople need to know how, by using hashtags, they can get their content noticed by their audience.

- **Number of lists each salesperson is listed in.** Salespeople should want to own their territory, offline and online, and should want to be picked up on lists so their content is amplified.

- **Reach.** How many people saw your post? Salespeople need to get their material out not just to existing customers but also to people who haven't even thought about their goods or services yet.

FACEBOOK

Please don't think Facebook is just for 'friends and family'; LinkedIn only represents around 30 per cent of your social graph. There can be relationships on Facebook, for example brothers-in-law, etc., that don't show up on LinkedIn. You might call upon a CEO who didn't show up as having any connection with you when you researched them on LinkedIn. If you had looked on Facebook you would have found out that they are your brother-in-law's best mate. They play golf together. Certainly an important fact to know when you go to such a meeting. Yes?

While the measures are pretty similar to LinkedIn and Twitter, our advice is NOT to post the same article to every network. Facebook contacts will prefer non-work-orientated posts, softer subjects. You can be a thought leader, but leave the suit off and be more 'jeans and t-shirt'.

- **Number of posts per day.** At least one, but no more than two or you start looking like a spammer.

- **Number of friends**. You need to be pushing 200. Yes, it's OK not to be 'friends' with your boss, but still be careful what you say. Posting that work is rubbish will get you fired.
- **Number of likes**. Jump in and engage.
- **Number of shares**. This is a 'super like', people will still see posts that you have liked.
- **Number of comments**. Engage with people and don't forget, as posts are pretty much public, to be a beacon of niceness. Our advice is to not post anything that might offend your grandma, and, as you would with friends (or you lose them), keep off politics, religion, smut and profanity.

WORDS OF ADVICE

- **Number of posts**. The number of posts per day will vary by network. On LinkedIn and Facebook, you want to post between once and twice each day. On Twitter, you can post between 10 and 12 times per day without annoying your followers. *Do not* batch up posts and 'spray' them out to all networks via automation. This is *not* a time saver, and you will lose followers quickly.
- **Number of comments**. Some people will comment on articles just to comment on articles. Other people will comment only if they are prompted by a question or a specific call to action – something along the lines of 'Let me know what you think.' If you are seeking commentary, play around with different ways of soliciting remarks. Comments create conversations, and allow you to show people that you have ideas and thoughts in common. This is the basis to start having commercial interactions.
- **Number of link clicks**. If you are trying to get people to read your content, there are many factors to consider, such as your article's headline, whether you included a picture, whether you included a shortened link, where that link appeared in the post, the type of content and the social network that your content appeared on.

Experiment with different factors and figure out what works best for your audience.

Sales funnel metrics

With sales funnel metrics, you're trying to see how your programme influences your sales funnel. For example, are you generating new leads? More pipeline? More revenue? Sales funnel metrics are focused on money. These are the types of results that executives care about. But funnel metrics should not be the only numbers you analyse. Without a strong strategy and guidance to build communities that will pay, you'll never be able to influence your sales funnel.

Here are just some of the sales funnel metrics you can analyse:

- **Number of new leads and meetings generated from your social selling team.** Maybe use a campaign code in your CRM for leads created through social.
- **Number of social media touches with leads, pipeline and customers.** Where is your website inbound coming from? Can the sales team get inbound from LinkedIn and Twitter?
- **$ of pipeline generated from social selling activities.** Are the sales team driving and generating leads via the use of social?
- **$ of revenue generated from social selling activities.** Are they using social for lead progression, de-risking deals and competitive strategies? Are they using social to help close deals?
- **The average contract value of your deals generated from social selling.** Can you increase your deal size (ability to cross sell) with the use of social?
- **Sales cycle.** The average amount of time that it takes for your social selling team to close a deal. Can you reduce the time it takes to sell?

We often get inbound from social with no competition; this reduces your cost of sale, which increases the margin of sales from social media and is a great way to justify the investment in using social.

WORDS OF ADVICE

- **Social sellers vs. non-social sellers.** If you have a large sales team, you may want to run a pilot before you roll out a social selling programme to the entire sales organization. Compare the sales funnel metrics for the salespeople who are using social media to those who are not. See, for example, whether your social media team has a shorter sales cycle than your traditional team.

- **Be realistic**. There isn't a magic silver bullet in the sales world. If your current sales cycle is six months, don't expect to suddenly close deals in one week simply because you launched a new programme.

- **Be patient**. It's going to take your team some time to adjust to their new sales mentality. Being helpful and building relationships take time. Changing a salesperson's mindset and habits can be difficult. Some salespeople still think it's easier to deliver cold pitches and hope for the best. But, in the end, your patience and hard work will pay off, and you will generate more revenue. We recommend continual coaching sessions so that you can fine-tune the behaviours. Some people will pick this up and 'fly', but others will need support. It should be possible to build self-help groups within your organization, but then again, don't distract salespeople from what they are good at: being in front of customers. Social should aid not hinder that.

A final words on metrics

We looked at one small facet of a social selling programme: metrics. What you measure will depend on:

- your role
- your programme's maturity
- whether HR teams will care about training metrics
- whether curators and social media managers will be concerned with tactical metrics
- whether your executive sponsor will be interested in sales funnel metrics

In addition, the maturity of your programme will be an important factor. How long has your programme been running?

New social selling teams with long sales cycles may not see revenue growth for a few months. So, looking at revenue may not be the wisest move straight away. Instead, you may want to look at pipeline growth first, or you may want to focus on standardizing tactics across your team.

Bear in mind that, while metrics are an extremely important component of any social selling programme, they are not the only component. All sales programmes involve many moving parts.

After the pilot

Once you have completed your pilot there will be lessons learnt (given that all sales teams are made up of different individuals). There will be things that worked and things that didn't work. An open and honest feedback process should work out best practice and then work on rolling that out across the organization. The best people to do this are salespeople themselves. Our role has often been to organize and support, and the best way to sell the programme is to have the initial pilot group saying, 'I closed this big deal because of social, and you would be a fool not to do it.'

Don't forget to collate all the successes and communicate these internally – success all the way through the sales process, from the inbound, to the conversations that converted, right through the content that closed deals. Make sure you turn this into a report. You will need this for when you ask for more resource and more budget.

Pan-European projects

While I know some readers may be in small enterprises, for those in large pan-European or pan-global organizations, our recommendation is to run pilot projects in-country. With a project such as this, where there can be change implications and localized differences, a UK-centric or US-centric view of the world should not be imposed on other countries where the culture and use of social may be different.

Finally, some questions you should be asking yourself:

- What are the goals for social selling?
- Why should your sales team care?
- How used to change is your organization?
- Have you defined your target market personas?
- Could there be multiple personas? You may, for example, sell accounting systems, but there are many different people in finance you need to sell to. LinkedIn estimates that for every enterprise deal, 10 people are involved.
- What is the timeline in which you want to see a return?
- How does your company use social today? Is it integral to marketing?
- How does the sales team currently use social?
- Have you rolled out any social selling schemes to date?

- Has there been any training to date?
- What has worked? What has not?
- Do you have the resources to create your own content?
- Have any metrics for social been placed on the sales team?
- How does the sales team use content currently?
- Is there a culture (be honest) of building trust with clients online?

Summary

In this chapter we have taken you through the different ways you need to sell a social selling project internally. For each decision maker and persona you need to make a different case. Our mantra throughout the whole of this book is to try to keep the measure based around real data, such as the number of leads you will create, and therefore how much revenue. The temptation to get side-tracked with vanity metrics should be avoided.

References

Gartner (2020) Gartner says 80% of B2B sales interactions between suppliers and buyers will occur in digital channels by 2025. www.gartner.com/en/newsroom/press-releases/2020-09-15-gartner-says-80--of-b2b-sales-interactions-between-su (archived at https://perma.cc/535A-XKT4)

Kemp, S (2021) Future trends 2022: The evolution of search, Datareportal. https://datareportal.com/reports/future-trends-2022-evolving-search-behaviours (archived at https://perma.cc/568L-ETKN)

08

How to use technology to your advantage

One of the most common things we are asked when we are interviewed or when on the speaker circuit is 'What tools do you use?' This chapter is a round-up of the tools we use, as well as some tools which we know other people use to good effect.

We have placed this chapter later in the book so that you will have by now bought into the idea of a social selling strategy – the need to own and dominate your community by listening, contacting and engaging with people, influencers and competitors alike. It is only when you own the online world that you will enable yourself to gain a market-leading position. You do this by engaging, creating conversations and educating, but not by the old 'analogue' rules of sales muscle, large advertising budgets, email blasts and big discounts. In the new digital age, anybody with little budget (but time) can build a world-beating business that can own and dominate their community.

Grady Booch once said, 'A fool with a tool is still a fool.' In the next chapter on digital maturity we talk about 'random acts of social'. This is where some people in a department will start using a tool, but have no connection with the strategy. Tools will save you time, free you to do other things and bring more and better engagement. Tools also allow you to collaborate with other departments – sales and marketing working together for example. But if they are used outside of the context of the overall strategy, then these are just random acts of social.

We have broken the tools you can use down into four areas:

1 **Research.** How to use social networks as a way to find things out, such as your next targets for you to prospect.

2 **Scheduling**. How to post into your news streams for your niche and community in a way that will educate or evoke engagement. You want to do this outside your normal posting hours, for example. We advocate scheduling, not automation.

3 **Content curation**. How to find content (written by somebody else) that you can post in your social network news streams that will be interesting to your niche and community.

4 **Content creation**. If there is not the content then how you can create content that will attract people to your social networks and website etc.

Research

Talking to strangers – discovering more about people

In Chapter 3 we talked about the need to grow your network and own the community you work in. This means you need to talk to strangers. We mentioned how you don't just walk into a room and shout at the top of your voice, 'Hi, it's Tim, we have 30 per cent off this week', as many brands still do in the offline world. If you go to a networking meeting of, say, 100 people, it may be that only five are useful to you as a social seller. How do you find out before that meeting which five people you really need to talk to? We then explained in Chapter 3 about how you then go and listen to what they say, before joining in with the conversation.

There are a number of tools that allow you to do your homework and check people out before you go to a meeting. What are their passions? Did you go to the same college? Are there people you trust that you share in common? What is it that will turn that 'cold' conversation into a warm one?

FOLLOWERWONK – HTTPS://FOLLOWERWONK.COM
While I don't use this tool, it has been highly recommended to me. While there is a free version, you need to expect to pay money if you want to get real value from it.

It enables you to build your community by searching Twitter bios for target personas and allows you to search their contacts, networks and communities. This will enable you to find their influencers. You can analyse your followers by location, bio and who they follow, and contrast these relationships with your friends and competitors. By reviewing unfollows you can see what tweets people like and dislike, which enables you to fine-tune your content strategy. You can also follow and unfollow people.

Analysing your content

When you are taking the time and effort to post created content, is it the right content? There are a number of tools you can use to measure the response. In our experience, measuring what is good or bad content based on an unfollow is a pretty inaccurate science. People may be annoyed before-hand and just unfollow for the sake of it.

When building a community, you have to be mindful of your content, especially if you are trying to make an impact on key influencers or pick up on subjects that people are talking about, to raise your share of voice. In the projects we have worked on, we have listened to what people were talking about, then decided on what topics would resonate with the community and personas we wished to market to and influence. We decided that we would go along with two subject areas people talked about, and the third we would build from scratch and in effect create our own market place.

You can do some basic analysis of your content on LinkedIn as to which organizations have looked at your content, which job titles have looked at your content and the areas where the people that have looked at you content come from. As a salesperson you want to make sure that the companies and people you are trying to influence are reading and consuming your content.

Tools that schedule

The way to build community is to have high-quality content to educate, but it is also to engage. When somebody said to me 'Why didn't we automate social media and go back to doing our day jobs?' they were missing the point. One of the first subjects we get asked about as soon as somebody masters how to use Twitter and LinkedIn is how to use automation. The question usually arises as they don't really see they have time for social media, so they want to automate it and... you guessed it, go back to doing their day job. They then wonder why they don't progress very far beyond 150 followers. It is because they are being boring online. Why would any-body want to follow them?

This is where people can sometimes totally miss the point. Social media and using social for your work is not about banging out content and hoping somebody will pick up on it, or banging out more content than the competition, often called 'share of voice'. Content is there to help buyers; offering people an endless 'fire hose' of noise won't get you more leads or more sales. If we go back to that drinks party, does anybody like to hear someone talking only about themselves and their work? No. So why do it online?

Scheduling has its place as it frees you up to do other things. If, for example, you are running a conference, you can schedule tweets about the day. 'In 10 minutes, Tim Hughes will be talking about social selling in room 2B'; you can automate that. This frees you up to engage with people tweeting the content from the conference.

Social media is based on reciprocity: there are buyers on social media that the sellers can sell to. If one side of this equation decided not to turn up but sent a robot instead then the whole thing would fall down.

IF THIS THEN THAT (IFTTT) – IFTTT.COM

IFTTT is an application based on the idea that 'if this happens, then it will do that'. It comes with standard 'recipes' that other people will have written, that you can then use. These recipes do not need any programming experience; you just pick the ones you want in the app and connect the systems. For example, whenever I accept a connection on LinkedIn, this is automatically added to a spreadsheet in Google. Whenever the weather looks like rain, I get a text from weather.com reminding me to take an umbrella, which is useful in London.

It also allows you to get round certain issues. For example, Instagram gives you the option to post a photo to other social networks. If you post to Twitter, Instagram posts the text and a link to Instagram, completely losing the impact of the photo. By using IFTTT, you can post your photos from Instagram to Twitter and you can see the photo in full.

The use of IFTTT is limitless as more and more brands build out functionality. For example, there is an iPhone application that will switch the lights on when it detects movement. This can be used for burglar detection or deterrence.

You can also track work hours into a Google calendar, save the photos you have taken to Dropbox, send photos from Instagram to Flickr, etc.

Clearing your profiles

TWEEPI – TWEEPI.COM

In terms of social selling, Tweepi allows you to find users that might be interested in your brand. Once you have found them you can 'interact' by following or adding them to a list. By doing this your targets might just come and have a look at your profile, and better still they might follow you back. This increases your reach and amplification.

This is an app I use to manage my Twitter accounts. It allows me to see which accounts are not following me back, and which accounts have unfollowed me (I will then unfollow them). It also allows you to 'spring clean' your Twitter account. For example, you can unfollow inactive accounts (by number of days), users that don't have a photo, bio-less users, and followers who are inactive. This enables you to have a pretty spammer-free Twitter environment.

DISCOVER.LY – DISCOVER.LY

We interviewed the CEO of discover.ly for our blog, and they have a great story behind how the Google Chrome plug-in was created.

In previous chapters we have talked about social graph, a term that Facebook came up with, which describes your social network. Of course, as we use different social networks, our social graph is in silos. We recommend the use of LinkedIn, but it is only 30 per cent of the social graph. Many people say to us that Facebook isn't for B2B sales, and that they just use it for family and friends. Ted, the CEO of discover.ly used to be the product manager for the salesforce.com Chatter product. A salesforce.com sales guy called upon a CEO of a company, but what that salesperson didn't know was that CEO was a relation of Ted's. There was no connection on LinkedIn showing that the CEO and Ted were relatives, but there was on Facebook.

Discover.ly allows you to see people's other social networks as you surf LinkedIn, and it also shows you their last four tweets as well as insight into their Gmail network. This is all interesting if you are calling on a CEO and want to get some background information or points that you might have in common.

HOOTSUITE – HOOTSUITE.COM

Hootsuite and Buffer are tools that allow you to schedule your social posts. Hootsuite also allows you to listen to hashtags or certain words, and to schedule posts in the future.

Hootsuite has always seemed to me a great tool if you wish to have an editorial schedule over a few months or few weeks and need to create these tweets in advance. This has advantages; as we mentioned earlier, it can free you up to do other things or allow you to post them outside of your normal time zones. For example, 55 per cent of my followers are in the United States and I might want to post something I want that market to hear or amplify. Also, if you are running a conference or have a campaign with a whole stack of tweets, then maybe this is the tool for you. Be sure, though, that you don't just walk away from the tweets but make time to converse with anybody that engages. After all, it is the engagement that will bring you the leads and meetings.

The disadvantages are that tweets can be set up ready to happen but then something happens to disrupt it. There have been situations with super-markets where there was an issue that hit the news and then the tweets that were automated suddenly became highly inappropriate, causing the main news item to blow up even more. Joan Rivers, the American comedian, had passed away weeks before her Twitter account tweeted about her new iPhone (*Guardian*, 2014).

BUFFER – BUFFER.COM

We are big users of Buffer. The free version of Buffer allows you to 'buffer up' ten tweets in advance. In a usual day, I will buffer up ten tweets in the morning and then another ten tweets in the evening to pick up different time zones.

That said, I always build in time to go through all the day's engagement and comment, thank and take comments, maybe with direct mails (DMs). It is usually this that offers 'inbound' requests for work. Don't forget with any level of scheduling to find time for engagement. In B2C, customers now expect a one-hour response time. In B2B a response time of eight hours seems OK.

NIMBLE – NIMBLE.COM

We use Nimble as our customer relationship management system (CRM) here at DLA Ignite. The great thing about Nimble is that you don't need to type details of new contacts into the CRM – Nimble has a Google Chrome browser that enables you to 'suck' the social media profiles of these contact straight into the CRM. Nimble does this by having a Chrome extension where you can highlight the person on LinkedIn or Twitter and it will build a social profile for you, saving a lot of time.

Nimble has also built social selling prospecting functionality into the CRM. With most CRMs, when you register an account this then sits 'in' the CRM and you will then get questions from your leadership about what's happening. This means that salespeople are reluctant to bring in targets because of the ongoing inspection they get.

Nimble has new functionality where salespeople can have target accounts sitting alongside leads. This enables my team to have accounts they are targeting on social that everybody can see, so there is no conflict, as well as the pipeline, which is being moved through the various pipeline stages.

I often tell the story of a call I had with Jon Ferrara, the CEO of Nimble. As mentioned earlier, Jon lives in California and his time zone is eight hours behind mine. Normally when you get on a call with California from the UK the first things you discuss are what the time is and what the weather is like. On this call, Jon opened up with a question. 'What was my favourite vinyl record of all time?' He had taken the time to find out that I collect vinyl records, so the first 15 minutes of the call consisted of a discussion of the best gigs and bands we had seen. What a great way to start a sales call, building rapport.

Content curation

As part of your Twitter and LinkedIn news feeds you will need to post articles or information that will demonstrate your expertise and create curiosity in the reader (who is hopefully your next prospective customer) and they will respond or get in touch with you. Or they might think, this is an interesting person, when I next need those services I will get in touch. Either way, the way you work in the online world is not to put out this week's offer but to provoke thought and educate. In the B2C world, many brands are engaging with customers and hopefully prospective customers by using humour. The gambling sites are a good example of this.

So, how much content should you share and how should you do it?

The 4–1–1 rule

The mistake we see many people make today is using social as a way to push out as much content as they can. Often, corporations have content creation teams, and they see the employees as channels to push out that content. Employees are often given no training as to why or how to share, and will just do what they are told. Content without engagement means you are not prospecting. Research shows that people come to social to be social and not read brochures, brochureware and corporate content. Let's not forget that buyers are looking for insight, they are looking to be told something they don't know, they are looking to be entertained. They are not looking for boring brochures, regardless what marketing tell you.

This is where the 4–1–1 rule that we mentioned in a previous chapter comes in. We are not saying follow this rule religiously, but when you are first starting out it is a useful rule of thumb.

The rule is this:

4 – Post four items of information you have created that you think will be interesting or should educate your audience about your niche area. The key thing is these are *not* written by your in-house team. This is about demonstrating your expertise in the vertical or niche you work in.

1 – Post one item that is corporate or is written by your in-house team.

1 – Post one item that is human, funny or is personal to you. It might be a cat photo, a photo of your dog when you take them for a walk, a photo you took on holiday. This is designed to humanize your social media feed. It will be these posts that will probably get the most engagement and therefore the most opportunity for you to have conversations.

Which apps are available for content curation?

We use apps such as Flipboard and Medium to find content, especially Medium, as this is also an application that allows you to create your own content.

Flipboard works by users crowdsourcing articles, so they flip them into Flipboard, which indexes these articles so you can search on key words and strings. Flipboard comes with a number of standard magazines that you can follow, and you can also set up your own search words. For example, if one of your key terms is 'big data' you can use Flipboard to pull together all of the articles on this app that use the term. This then gives you a wealth of articles that you can decide to post through your various social networks.

Don't forget, don't just flip the article – add your own content. 'This article resonated with me as I can see how business is changing with the move to remote work' or whatever comment you can add to give the article some context.

In addition, as you have a readership that is hungry for content, you can then create your own magazines that people can follow and consume that content. Hopefully the outcome will be that readers will amplify the articles through their own social networks.

Some brands have tried to 'stuff' Flipboard with corporate articles, but because they are obviously sales brochures in disguise they don't get shared and often the brands give up as they don't get the followers or shares. Some brands have been successful at putting out educational material that has been shared. At the end of the day, the fact that an educational article has appeared on a brand's blog is enough to trigger the association or the 'like' for that brand. You do not need to be sales-y in the digital world.

Content creation

We highly recommend that salespeople start creating their own content. In the digital world you cannot rely on 'marketing' to create the content that will ignite the initial curiosity that a prospective buyer might have when starting down a road of research. In addition, we highly recommend that a salesperson creates a personal brand and wants to own their community ahead of all the other salespeople. We understand that this may scare many a marketing department, which is why we suggest using external third parties, who can provide the 'guide rails' and boundaries that people can work within.

Let's assume you are going to a conference and you walk into the drinks party the night before. In front of you is a crowd of people who are your prospects and your customers. As you walk in, you notice that each of these prospects and customers are laughing and joking with somebody. Would you want that person they are laughing and joking with to be one of your team or the competition? Content is your way of owning the digital narrative, owning the digital share of voice, owning the conversations and, as we have talked about before, being digitally dominant.

If, for example, you are selling supply chain systems into the process-manufacturing sector, surely you want to own that market? Be the person that other people turn to, or the opinion that is valued? In the past this was 'simple'; you called up your territory and found the people that might have been looking at that moment. In the B2B world this is usually about 5 per cent of the market. There will be another 25 per cent that will say, 'Interesting, but call me back in three or six months.' How can you do deals with these? More on that in a bit. But how can you cover that 70 per cent of the market that has perhaps never thought about your products or services, or may be just about to start out looking.

By being a thought leader, as a salesperson in your market it is highly likely that people will seek out your opinion, even if you work for a brand. It's better still if you are seen as an 'influencer'. In the digital world, anybody can become an influencer. With the right community, content and open attitude they can be a 'beacon' that attracts people hungry for knowledge and wanting to be educated. It is with that knowledge and education that they can go back to respected companies and start procurements. Hopefully you will be on the shortlist, or maybe you have used your analogue sales skills and already closed the contacts.

Your company is now a media company

In social selling, we know that our buyers are looking for content, they are looking for insight, they are looking for help, they are looking for real people to work with, they are looking to be entertained. We know this, partly because the research shows this, but also because it maps our own behaviours. None of us wake up in the morning and think, 'Looking forward to reading some brochures today.'

In the world of analogue selling, interruption and broadcast marketing such as cold calling, email and advertising all mean we don't have control of the sale, the control vests with the person we are interrupting. If you email somebody, they can just delete your email and ignore it. We also don't know who has read our adverts. We don't know whose read an article in a magazine. With social, buyers are actively looking for the content we are creating and we can see who has looked at it; and if they have dropped a like or a comment on it we have a reason to have a conversation with them. That places us in charge of a sale.

Content creation platforms

There are three main platforms for you to create or place content: LinkedIn, Medium and WordPress.

LINKEDIN
Many people are turning to LinkedIn as a place to put out content; usually this is in short form – about 500 words, so a single page of A4. This is a

great place to get subject matter out quickly and as it is published in LinkedIn it will go out to your network and hopefully your network will share it to their networks, etc.

LinkedIn is a platform (due partly to books like this) where people are very hungry for content and your blog should get shared pretty quickly and extensively. This will enable you to grow your community and following and start conversations.

Tips for LinkedIn blogging

- The headline and initial photo are everything. For people to find you and be intrigued enough to read and then share, you must give this a lot of thought. Somebody once sent a blog for me to read which had a three-word title, offering no reason for me to think I should read it. When I gave him feedback, his response was, 'Yes, but surely when somebody had read it, they would get the title.' He was correct, but I doubt anybody would read it.

- The first sentence is the 'hook' that will drive the reader to read on.

- Write no more than 500 words. Some people do write more than that, but I'm not sure if it all actually gets read.

As I write, LinkedIn is making the leap into mobile with its Pulse blogging platform, which should be a hit with LinkedIn users.

Why should we post content?

Simplistically, content is there to create commercial interaction – to sell something. But there are other influencing factors. To sell something, a person needs to have a desire to buy what you sell. Content can therefore help, top of the funnel, middle of the funnel and at the bottom of the funnel. That sounds like lots of meaningless marketing articles, but what does it mean in practice?

First, we need to demonstrate to our network and audience that we are the people to buy from. To do this, we need to show we are an 'expert'. All the way through my selling life, we have always walked into meetings and explained why the client should listen to us over and above our competition. This is not a sales pitch, this is giving us credibility. You social profile is your shop window to the world; content, by showing our expertise, gives us credibility. By writing this book, I'm not giving you a sales pitch. I'm demonstrating my knowledge and expertise and I hope you will walk away and think that I know what I'm talking about.

Content allows you to differentiate yourself from your competition. Who would you prefer to buy from? Somebody who you have got to know on social; you know them, like them and trust them, because they show their expertise and offer help and advice that you can use in your business? Again, like this book, or like the articles people write. Or some faceless person on social, who is clearly just another salesperson, who shares brochures? Of course, the authentic 'expert' sharing help and advice for your business is now what people called 'on brand', rather than the boring sharing of brochures that nobody reads.

Content, provides you with the ability to be found. By writing and using search engine optimization (SEO) techniques, for example, using keywords, or long tail search headlines you will be indexed by Google and found on search sites as well as being found on social. Note, the search capabilities on Google and social are different and we teach this in our social selling and influencing course.

Content can be repurposed. I put out a blog only last week that was a cut-and-paste from an article I wrote in 2018. Content builds a long-term library demonstrating you are an expert. Don't forget that the more content you post, the more likely you will be found and the more likely you will be the answer to somebodies business issues. I'm not talking about posting and hoping, content is about driving conversations and commercial interaction.

Blogs, LinkedIn articles and LinkedIn posts

Google loves to see a website growing and the best way of demonstrating this is by having a blog and regularly contributing. As long as you write in an SEO way, Google should index this article. The negative is that users on social media don't like being taken from the social network they are currently using, and having to travel to your blog. Not many people today will click on links. We have seen too many instances of hacking and viruses. Also, most social networks see themselves as 'walled gardens' and the algorithms don't promote posts that drive the user to leave that social network.

We still see marketers driving people to blogs to collect emails. The reason for this is that it's seen that the emails collected are the only measure of success. This is not the case, and I will come to this. There is a major problem with this – people don't like giving their email addresses. Why? because we all know we get a call from a salesperson trying to sell us something. If I recall, Salesforce reckon they will call you within 10 minutes of giving your email. Maybe they have stopped this, but it's creepy and anti-customer experience.

We've actually done research and found that, if you gate content, you will lose 50 per cent of the engagement and each piece of data you ask for you keep losing another 50 per cent. For example, if you drive 100 people to gated content, only 50 will register. If you ask for name, title and business name that 50 will turn into six. This does not seem like a very efficient way to build relationships with prospects. Is there another way?

If you post the article on social media, you can see the details of everybody that has liked and commented that social post. At that point you have the ability to have conversations that could lead to commercial interaction with these people. Now, of course, if you post content on the company LinkedIn page, you cannot have a conversation as it will seem creepy, which is why you must empower your team(s) to be on social.

Some people write excerpts of the post, others just place the 'introduction' on LinkedIn then take the readers who want to read the entire article to their blog site. This is often used as a way to get around the Google duplicate content rules. The problem with this is that it's seen as manipulative and you will get a high bounce rate – people won't follow the link.

LinkedIn posts are great for engagement on LinkedIn. The algorithm will promote them in your network's timeline, which is great for a dopamine hit. The negative is that Google does not index them and they have a six month shelf life on LinkedIn.

LinkedIn articles get less engagement than posts, so less dopamine. But they are indexed by Google. They will enable you to build up your expertise and create an online library that people can find. It's worth remembering that people don't know your article is any good until they have read it.

Duplicate content

Google isn't stupid – it is well aware that people will post the same content in multiple places to try and increase the content reach. This is duplicate content. Google is very strict about this and will ban blogs if it decides that there is duplicate content. Just be aware, it does not tell you that you have been banned.

Should I post on 'rented' sites (sites I don't own)?

One of the questions we often get asked is about LinkedIn and the fact that the real estate is 'rented', a blog you own. I have a friend that went all in on Google Plus, only for Google to close the social network.

What about the backup? What if, some day, LinkedIn changes policies and everything disappears?

If you are following the rules and writing about business, there should not be a problem. If you are writing about politics, religion, addictions, then yes, I would suggest you post on your own site. I have in the past posted on LinkedIn and then six weeks later posted on Medium, taking into account Google duplicate content rules, but I stopped as there are only so many minutes in a day.

MEDIUM

Medium has been created from the ground-up as a blogging platform to be read on mobile, which is probably where many of your future readers will consume your content. Again, they are often short-form blogs of 500 words, but many people put out blogs of 1,000 words or more. This is another platform used by people who are hungry for content and the blogs are made easy to share on social networks, giving you amplification. Medium allows you to follow people and to be followed; if you are followed then people are told by Medium when you blog.

WORDPRESS

I used to have a personal WordPress blog, but now use either our corporate website or social media. That said, some people like to own their corporate real estate and own their blog.

WordPress has a number of templates that a novice can use (many are free, some you have to pay for) with a quick start in terms of the overall look of the blog. WordPress say that they power 25 per cent of the World Wide Web. I cannot verify those figures, but many small companies use a WordPress blog as their first website.

While LinkedIn does provide some statistics for your blogs and numbers of shares, WordPress provides you with extensive statistics, such as where the traffic is coming from and then where it goes. This is important as you can focus on where you want to drive the traffic from, such as Google, Blogger platforms such as Medium, or social networks.

We highly recommend if you use WordPress or start down the road of blogging that you get into a cadence of publishing articles at the same time on the same day, regardless of the pressures to do otherwise. Why? This is good for Google and your Google rankings. Google has what they call spiders that go out and look for content to be ranked on their site and they are always looking for new content that shows engagement. If you are putting out content at regular intervals, sometimes the spiders might actually be waiting for you to publish.

Measuring influence and amplification

This book isn't about the details of these measures; we just want to point out that they are there and do have their uses. Since writing the first edition of this book, many measures have come and gone, because such measures have to comply with the European GDPR privacy regulations.

LinkedIn social selling index (SSI)

LinkedIn has the SSI, which is based on your usage of LinkedIn only. We have run a number of workshops for companies where we have used SSI as the starter measure, really as a way to get people comfortable to start posting, getting a buyer-centric profile, starting to like and share. For a beginner this is ample. As we mentioned above, LinkedIn is only 30 per cent of your social graph. Here at DLA Ignite we have developed our own proprietary measurement, which we share with clients.

Finding influencers

In Chapter 1 on building a community we talked about influence and how you find it. You can find influencers by just being 'out there' on social; you are always welcome to drop by and say hi to me. Twitter and LinkedIn are good places to find influencers.

On Twitter, find some time to look at the news feeds of people you trust; they will I'm sure tweet or retweet articles from their influencers. Then when you find those influencers, you can find who influences the influencers, and so on.

You will often see lists produced from time to time of usual places to find people of influence, but they come with a health warning. There is a well-known story of a person who wanted a job at an organization, so he created a list with people from that organization in the top 10. Just be careful, as often lists are created for an agenda.

Tools for finding influencers

We have ourselves used tools for finding influencers; you will need to pay for these tools.

ONALYTICA – ONALYTICA.COM

I have worked with the team at Onalytica since 2015 and they have a service that will allow you to create influencer lists. At the time of writing you will also see free influencer lists on the blog on their website.

As you grow your network and community you need to find the right influencers that can impact your business and your buyer's decision-making process. This may be the 'usual suspects' but also you may find people like ourselves who have influence but are not multinational companies. As you build your influencer network, you will need to gain insights on your influencers and plan initiatives that will let you work together.

It was suggested to us once that influencer marketing was easy – find the influencer and then send a salesperson off with a white paper under their arm to make contact with them. We had to challenge this. You have to remember that influencers are just that. What happens if they tweet, 'I've just had some idiot from XYZ company come to see me with some boring white paper'? That's a PR disaster and then all your competitors know what you are up to.

You must have an influencer programme (a programme is a project with no end) and develop focused, value-add relationships with your influencers. Use metrics to prioritize outreach, measure the impact of your engagement and report on the efficacy of your efforts.

It's worth stating at this point that influencers may be both online and offline. Don't forget to find and nurture the offline ones. Often you will find that journalists are still very offline. For example, they will have some online presence but their channel is really still newspapers and magazines. They still have influence, so don't just stick with the tools online and think that's it.

Other tools

WORD SWAG – WORDSWAG.CO

Word Swag is an app that allows you to create quotes against a pictorial background (see Figure 8.1). This type of personalized micro content is getting many social sellers a 90 per cent response rate, which is only a 10 per cent rejection rate. Compare this to LinkedIn inmails, which give 7 per cent acceptance and 93 per cent rejection.

For example, social sellers will research a senior influencer, but in some cases might not be able to track them down on email or the phone. Having researched them on LinkedIn and Instagram, they can create a Word Swag as a different way of making an approach.

Do your research, create a Word Swag and increase the likelihood of getting a response.

FIGURE 8.1   Presenting a tweet using Word Swag

WE HAVE NOW REACHED
A TIPPING POINT WHERE EMPLOYERS HAVE
A DUTY OF CARE TO THEIR SALESPEOPLE TO IMPLEMENT
A SOCIAL SELLING PROGRAMME!
- @TIMOTNY_HUGHES

Summary

In this chapter we have taken you through the applications we are using today to help us in our social selling endeavours.

We have also talked about content. People often find it difficult to start writing content, which is why we recommend getting an independent third party into your business to provide your team with a methodology and a framework your team(s) can use to create their own content.

Due to the nature of technology advancing so quickly, it's worth noting that these platforms are likely to move in and out of use, but the intention of the chapter is to show the theory of how these concepts increase sales, advance opportunities and complement each other efficiently from different perspectives, rather than how to use these platforms specifically.

THE WORLD HAS CHANGED AND SO SHOULD YOUR CRM – JON FERRARA, CEO, NIMBLE

Business brand and network relationship-building, the right way

The rise of social media over the past decade has changed the way we work, buy and sell and the pandemic showed us that the age of social and digital business is here to stay. We also learned that it is possible to create new relationships and nurture current ones online. It is important to have the right tools and the knowledge to do it right.

Developing digital business relationships is similar to developing relationships in real life. It takes time, as you need to try to connect on areas of commonality to build intimacy and trust. Developing a real, long-lasting relationship is a marathon, not a sprint. Remember that it takes most fuel to get a car up to speed and much less to maintain that speed. Same with relationships.

Scaling and nurturing your network and brand using technology

In order to be successful in business, you need to stay top of mind with your prospects, customers and, ideally, their influencers. The best way is to establish yourself as a trusted advisor in and around the areas of promise of your products and services by sharing educational, inspirational content on a daily basis. That way, when people need your products or services, they not only pick up the phone and call you, but they also drag their friends with them.

If you do all this the right way, you end up with hundreds of people in your network. Luckily, there's technology that can make managing, building and nurturing your business network fun. Before we get into that, let's better understand the issues with today's CRMs.

Why is CRM broken?

The way business professionals interact with their prospects and customers has changed. Unfortunately, the tools we use to manage relationships like CRM systems seem to be stuck in the dark ages. 'I know a thing or two about this, having pioneered contact management and CRM before Outlook or Salesforce existed, as a founder of GoldMine', says Jon Ferrara.

CRM stands for customer relationship management. Most business owners rightfully fear this acronym and most salespeople hate using CRM systems. The reason is that CRMs have traditionally been designed for sales managers for reporting purposes. Many salespeople think the acronym stands for 'customer reporting management'. Traditional CRM is great for sales and marketing managers, but lacks the contact management and sales force automation (SFA) features salespeople need to effectively engage. This is why many salespeople refuse to use CRMs. There are 225 million global businesses and less than 1 per cent use any CRM. Most people's CRM is a spreadsheet, email inbox and now social.

The truth of the matter is that CRM should not be for sales managers only and not even just for salespeople. The entire company should be using it collectively to manage their company's relationships.

The Nimble way to CRM

FIGURE 8.2   Nimble enables you to see the social media profiles of your clients as well as interactions and activities.

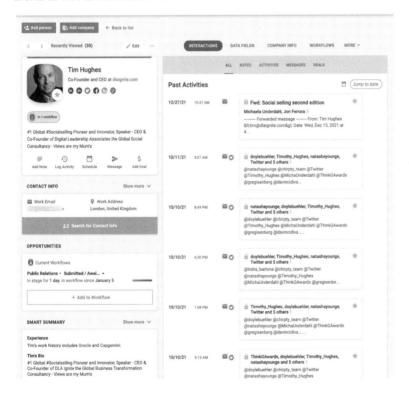

Nimble has re-imagined relationship management for the new social and digital era. The first step to success is to have a unified relationship platform that's cross-departmental. Today, you have sales, marketing, customer service, accounting – and Nimble can co-exist with those by unifying contacts and working back inside them, as well. It can be used across departments, so you can see the history of interactions (see Figure 8.2).

Nimble is a relationship manager that can be used by the whole company: sales, marketing, customer service, accounting, business development, PR, influencer marketing, investor relations, etc. It is a platform that works with and for its users everywhere they work, including where they live, inside email and social, and the business apps they use the most.

A lot of people see CRM as a beast of burden that they have to nurture and feed, but imagine if it actually helped that business' people and their network.

CRM that works for you

Nimble helps companies identify the right people for their businesses, with the goal of turning conversations into mutually beneficial measurable results. Its vision is to make the job of all customer-facing team members easier and more effective.

The reality of relationships is that people buy from people they like, know and trust, and social media is the perfect way to learn more about somebody. You should prepare for every call and interaction by getting to know someone, and social context helps you do that.

People connect through the commonalities of life experiences that we share. 'I call it the Five Fs of life; family, friends, food, fun and fellowship. If you do your homework to learn about a person and their company before you connect, you can earn the intimacy and trust you need to get them to open up and share the details you need to find ways to add value. Ultimately your job is to add value to others, which in the end delivers value back to you,' says Jon Ferrara.

Many times in business, people put up walls. LinkedIn is like walking into a business lobby. You'll learn about their business persona, but people buy from people, not from businesses. This is what Dale Carnegie taught, and today we're just doing it in a new way, in the digital era.

Another example is today, before you meet with someone, you typically Google them. That's you working for your CRM, and it's a waste of time.

Most people work for their CRM – it doesn't work for them. That's the biggest cause of failure for CRM. Even when you Google someone, things change, and that information will become stale. Your CRM should work for you and with you wherever you're working.

Today you might Google people before a meeting, tomorrow you will 'Nimble' them!

AI as your friend

Nimble automatically synchronizes your and your team's contacts, communications, calendars and certain social interactions into one easy-to-use solution and then allows you to take it with you into your inbox, social media like LinkedIn, the cloud business apps you use or any browsers. On top of that, it also enriches your contact records for you, saving you time on research and data entry.

FIGURE 8.3   Nimble allows you to highlight your customers in, say, LinkedIn and the Nimble Prospector tool allows you to pull the details straight into the Nimble CRM.

Most people have thousands of connections, and you need artificial intelligence (AI) to listen to signals and surface the ones that matter. Then you need a nudge on your shoulder to follow through to connect and reconnect with people. AI is like a second brain that helps you follow through and stay in touch with the right people at the right time and place.

With Nimble, you can highlight or hover over a name anywhere on the internet and Nimble will either surface an existing contact record or help you to create a new, rich record, within seconds. Nimble automatically builds contacts on the fly wherever you engage and then enriches them with the details you need to effectively engage. Most importantly, it enables you to follow up and follow through right where you are engaging.

So, imagine you are having a conversation with a prospect on Twitter or LinkedIn. Instead of having to open a new tab, log into your CRM and start typing all the information in manually, you can just hover over their name and Nimble will create a record for them, search for additional social profiles, find and capture contact information, and allow you to add notes, schedule the next steps, assign tasks to yourself or anybody on your team, etc.

From contact creation to a mutually beneficial relationship

Nimble makes it easy for you to set up custom 'stay in touch' reminders and will remind you every time a contact is due for a follow-up or a touch point. This can be in the form of a simple social interaction, which can pay off big time. Imagine that you come across an important contact's ask on social media regarding their need to promote their new book, write a review for it, or help them make an introduction to somebody. If you understand that service is the new sales and always approach developing and nurturing relationships this way, you will always be on the lookout for these tasks and will do what you can to help people out.

These are all great features and tips for ad hoc engagement or the type of engagement you do on a regular basis to stay top of mind with your contacts without necessarily having an exact goal in mind. Let's also focus on how you can utilize Nimble to perform a very targeted outreach and track your progress as you move people through a process or a funnel.

Workflows for the win, for the entire company

Nimble's Workflows were designed to help everybody in the company to manage their relationships with customers. Nimble offers dozens of templates with predefined custom fields to help capture specific information.

This feature can also be used by sales professionals to declutter their sales pipelines. As you know, there's a lot that needs to happen in order for leads to become properly qualified. Many times, the beginning stages of sales funnels are filled with leads that have not been reviewed yet and it's easy for things to slip through the cracks. And this can result in some serious loss of business.

One use case for Nimble's Workflows is to use its Kanban style board to visualize the progress we are making with our leads and, once properly qualified, turn them into a deal with the click of a button. Some leads fall off our funnel, which is normal and completely ok and can be for a variety of reasons. Nimble allows you to create a list of some of the most common reasons, select them, remove leads from your board, and then run searches on it later. So, for instance, you can go back to all the leads that were not ready to buy or it was not in their budget and reach out again in three months, six months, or even later. You've already invested in the relationship and it's worth it to stay top of mind and following up to see if now might be the right time to do business together.

FIGURE 8.4   Nimble has workflows, in this case it's the unsuccessful recruitment of a candidate.

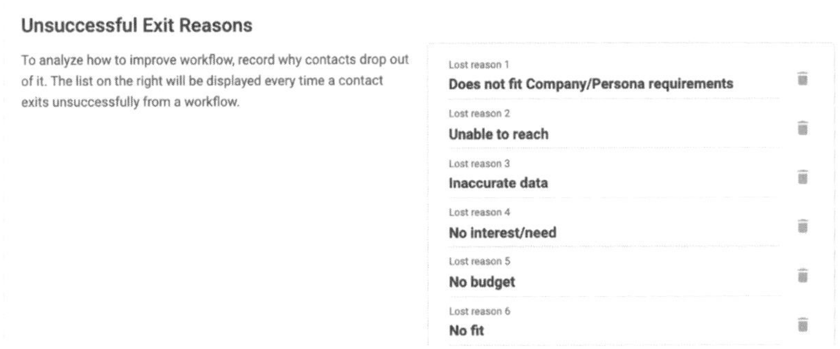

Unsuccessful Exit Reasons

To analyze how to improve workflow, record why contacts drop out of it. The list on the right will be displayed every time a contact exits unsuccessfully from a workflow.

Lost reason 1
Does not fit Company/Persona requirements

Lost reason 2
Unable to reach

Lost reason 3
Inaccurate data

Lost reason 4
No interest/need

Lost reason 5
No budget

Lost reason 6
No fit

Manage repeatable business processes from anywhere

Another use case is to use Workflows to manage your processes. No matter what industry you are in or the role you hold in your company, Nimble has the right template for you. Let's demonstrate this use case in another example. Imagine you are hiring a new team member. You have job postings in multiple places and the person responsible for hiring has to manage all the resumes coming in, all the cover letters, manage the interview process, and coordinate additional interviews amongst the team.

Usually, this will require a lot of back and forth within the company as everybody's feedback needs to be captured. Well, imagine that you can hover over the candidate's name, have Nimble create a rich profile for them including their various social media sites, upload their resumes and additional documents, and easily capture and store all information such as current title, previous employment, salary expectations, notes from previous interviews, etc.

FIGURE 8.5   Typical recruitment workflow in Nimble as an example.

Instead of sending links or actual files to your colleagues as attachments, you can just point people to a Workflows board within Nimble and create custom fields for any specific information that you need to capture. Everything will be in one place and everybody will be able to quickly review what they need as well as to submit their own feedback. Candidates are then moved through the board until they are hired or you decide that they are not the right fit. You can select the reasons why it didn't work out and keep their contact information stored in your database for future reference.

Reference

Guardian (2014) Joan Rivers posts from the grave: 'I've just bought an iPhone!' www.theguardian.com/technology/2014/sep/19/joan-rivers-apple-iphone-6-instagram (archived at https://perma.cc/65NE-XLXC)

09

Digital maturity

Different companies will have different digital strategies, and these will be impacted by how mature they are digitally. It is not always the case, but in our experience the digital maturity of an organization is connected to the digital maturity of the leadership.

From the outset of this book we have said that social selling is a strategy that requires top-down support and leadership. We showed in the previous chapters that the business benefits that a social media strategy can bring, not only in terms of internal business efficiency but also in terms of the subject of this book, which is more sales and therefore more revenue.

That said, to quote the visionary management consultant and author Peter Drucker, 'Culture eats strategy for breakfast'. The argument goes something like this: strategy is on paper whereas culture determines how things get done. Anyone can come up with a fancy strategy, but it's much harder to build a winning culture. Moreover, a brilliant strategy without a great culture is 'all bark and no bite', while a company with a winning culture can succeed even if its strategy is mediocre. Plus, it's much easier to change strategy than culture. The argument's inevitable conclusion is that strategy is interesting but you need culture. This chapter will go some way to explain the strategy for becoming a digital business – it is then down to you to build that culture.

We can propose a strategy but this has to be driven from the C-suite, by C-level people who understand why they need to move from an analogue to a digital sales and marketing way of doing business. This is where we get the 'I get it' syndrome.

Many C-level people we meet were top of the class at school and college and nothing has beaten them to date. When we get asked to talk about social at board level, there is a lot of nodding and comments like, 'I get it', but we actually find that, 'I get it' means, 'I don't get it, but cannot admit it in front of the other people in the team.' The forward-thinking nature of these people leads them to believe that, as they have mastered everything else in life, surely they should get social. Which is why we are often pulled in to offer our strategy sessions and one-to-one coaching sessions.

Social media is all about trust

A common objection we see at a leadership level in organizations is that 'social is for kids'. Many leaders see their children using social and think that is the only way it can be used. Leaders see their salespeople 'messing about on social' and see this as wasted time, whereas it's a highly efficient (high output for less input) way for salespeople to use their time.

The most common question we get when we present is, 'Is there an ROI in social?' We then talk about our friend who is getting 10 C-level meetings a week by using Twitter. He has been creating ROI for two or three years now, this is not 'messing about' on Twitter and LinkedIn, which is why we have discussed using real digital sales techniques, using community, and direct revenue-generating measures from social as key drivers for such projects. Since I set up my company we have literally transformed thousands of companies, and I've got a number of these to contribute to this book. Social media and social selling is driving revenue for many a business, and if your leadership is not supporting this then they are leaving money on the table.

So where does trust come into this? Well, actually, it is about companies exerting control. First we saw companies banning access to social media; now they want employees to use it but in a way that is controlled by the corporation. However, the 'genie is out of the bottle' and it cannot be put back in. More people are getting social every day, including our customers and competitors, and corporations must give employees the freedom (and this means they must trust them) to go onto social media.

Just think of the free advertising your company would get if you allowed your employees to talk passionately and authentically about working for you, the pride they have in your products and services, and how they like to serve and excite your customers. This passion will be infectious, it will help existing buyers to buy more, it will pull, like a magnet, customers over from your (boring) analogue competitors, and it will attract the best talent. You are then in a virtuous circle. The more passion within your organization, and the better talent and competitors' customers you attract, the more revenue and margin you make.

Alternatively, let's let things play out the way they do for your boring analogue competitors. In the 1980s, when I started to work, we had a typing pool. For those too young to know what that is, you scribbled out the letters on paper and handed them to a group of people called 'the typing pool', where they would type them up for you on manual or electronic typewriters. We then moved into the world of word processors, AmiPro and Microsoft Word, where the number of letters you could pump out increased. Then with the invention of email, you could pump out an infinite number of them at 'zero' cost.

The maths of this is simple. To increase your return on investment, you increase the number of emails you pump out. It's all based on the law of averages. We know the average percentage click-through rate, so we know how many email addresses to buy. As people click on emails less and less, you have to buy more and more email addresses. Where do you think this all ends? HubSpot research shows that email marketing now has a 98 per cent failure rate (Gillum, 2020).

In today's customer-led market, the sustainable advantage is in knowledge and engagement with digital customers – owning the community, listening to and engaging with customers and influencers and locking the competition out. The quality of your customer experience will unlock that in the digital/online world, where your customers are. I've talked before in this book about your business being digitally dominant and owning the digital share of voice.

It's worth noting that customers work and transact across different channels. If we stop to think about our own buying journeys, we might research something on mobile (YouTube, blogs) on the train to work, and then when we get to work we might look at a website and have a live chat session. Brands must offer these channels to customers seamlessly; you should not miss out on a customer touch point along that journey or you will be left behind.

In the path to digital, there is a clear dividing line between digitally mature and digitally immature. Digitally mature companies are looking to transform their business with a clear digital strategy supported by leaders who foster a culture to change and invent the new. Meanwhile the digitally immature are focused on discrete business problems, mainly throwing technology at them and hoping it will stick. We often see this as 'digital hope', that's a business 'doing' social with no strategy, hoping that somebody will figure it out or getting LinkedIn trainers in to do 'hints and tips' sessions.

Without a strategy, the business will waste a lot of money and miss out on the opportunity to be the digital market leader.

The digitally mature understand that they have to take people along with any change programme, and this will mean training or retraining. The digitally immature will let people 'self-serve'. They have a view that if nobody has to go on an Amazon course, why would you need to train people to use LinkedIn or Twitter? (Until somebody makes a PR mistake and the 'shutters come down'.) This is the talent challenge.

As a business, we train our staff on diversity, inclusion, sexual harassment, health and safety, and so on. We do this because we know there is good behaviour and bad behaviour and we want people to stay within the safety lines. Because the consequences can be devastating, the same with social media. We must empower the employees and sales staff to be authentic and human, but also on brand.

Before we are introduced to the digital team, we do our research on them. We know we are in trouble if we find they have little or no social presence. We are not saying that everybody has to be a thought leader, but being put forward as a digital expert when you have 150 followers on Twitter or no social presence does raise some questions.

The view from boards in digitally immature companies is often that social presence can be purchased, like the instant success of participants on the TV programme *X-Factor*. Press a button and you have 100,000 followers. As one senior manager once said to me, 'Why don't we just automate social media, then we can go back to doing our day jobs.' We explain that being social is more Bob Dylan than *X-Factor*. Putting in time 'playing to folk clubs with an audience of seven people' is a great way to find your voice and know instinctively what tweets and hashtags work to excite your audience and generate a next action.

In Figure 9.1 we show how trust in a business, the leadership and the employees can change over time. If you have read this far in the book, you will know that the modern buyer will only support a brand so much, as we all see everything a brand talks about as 'corporate propaganda'. Getting a leadership team on social is crucial to enable the modern buyer to understand the culture of a business. Will the buyer even engage with this business? And finally, the more employees we can empower on social the better. They all speak with a different tone and while one might not appeal to you, there surely will be one that will resonate.

FIGURE 9.1   How trust can change over time for brand, leadership and employees

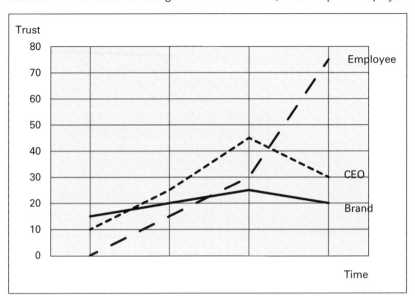

Social selling maturity

So far, we have discussed how social selling is the way to sell in the digital world and while I'm not saying revolution, you do need to start your evolution and start the journey to move your work ethic and that of your company to the digital way of working. As we have mentioned, this requires engagement with social selling both at a strategy level, and within the culture of your organization.

How to implement a social selling change programme

Making the changeover to digital selling will not happen overnight. You cannot just 'flick a switch' by putting training courses on the intranet or even hiring a trainer. Social selling requires sales professionals to change the way they do business every day. Changing behaviour is the biggest challenge that sales leaders face – social selling, after all, requires a mindset change and a habit change.

This social selling maturity model has been developed based on experience of social selling projects – what has gone right and also what has gone

FIGURE 9.2   Social selling maturity model

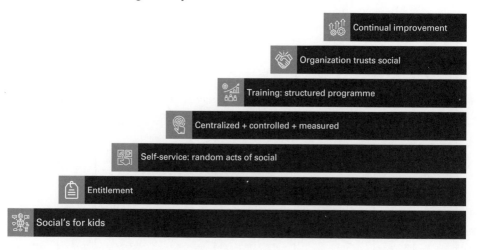

wrong. It would be great to try to get in at the top, but sometimes you have to learn and make mistakes to reach the greater goal at the end.

For example, if you have children, most people's goal is to give them life experiences and make them more rounded. One step in their development might be to climb a tree. We all know they are highly likely to fall; some will bounce, others will break an arm. But we have to be there for them and sometimes the broken arm is part of their long-term development.

Stage 0: Social's for kids

We get pulled into many organizations where well-meaning people, usually at 'shop floor' level, want us to sell the idea to management that they have got to get social. We usually find that the management has no social presence and end up presenting to a bunch of people with folded arms and glazed eyes.

It is in these situations where you need to provide case studies of where businesses in similar industries are using social media for business purposes and are gaining business benefit from it. The leadership need to experience the fear of missing out (FOMO). Our advice would be to present a comparison of the business's social profiles with those of the competition.

You should also present examples about how companies have created conversations on social and turned that into revenue. The leadership team may not understand social and digital, but they will understand revenue. You cannot therefore talk about visibility or reach, you must tie hard evidence of business and gains in revenue and EBITDA. The best way to approach this situation is by having a group of sales volunteers forming a pilot to show the ROI.

Stage 1: Entitlement

At this stage, somebody has probably read about social selling in an inflight magazine or attended a conference, and a project is kicked off. Often it is kicked off in marketing, as there is a belief that digital selling is all about demand generation and not about the total sales process. Modern marketing has a whole bunch of terminology that companies have to get used to: MQLs (marketing qualified leads), BQL (business qualified leads) etc. This is great, as it means that now when we describe a lead, we are all talking about the same thing.

At this point, businesses will often bring in a company to do a 'hints and tips' session. This is still where a business sees social as a tactic and not a strategy. There are plenty of companies that will be happy to exploit your ignorance. We have all been on these 'hints and tips' sessions on all kinds of subjects and we know nothing changes after them.

Another option people go for at this stage is getting a 'done for you' service. This is where a business runs your LinkedIn profile. However, this is illegal under LinkedIn terms and conditions, and if LinkedIn catch you they will close your account, never to be re-opened.

The second thing about social is about conversations.

A managing director connected with me the other day and it was obvious he was using a 'done for you service' – he wouldn't engage in conversation, it was just about connecting to me. As we have covered before, connection on social buys you little. It was also obvious (to me as a native English speaker) that I was speaking to somebody for whom English was a second language. This managing director would have also been a native English speaker.

A friend of mine told me that they have decided to hire a 'digital expert' to help with their transformation to digital. The friend shared with me the name of that person, but it was clear from looking them up on LinkedIn that this 'digital expert' was not the person they think she was. Maybe she knew more than the recruitment team but she wasn't going to transform them. This is going to be an expensive mistake.

Stage 2: Random acts of social

At this stage, the management may run a programme or even tell the employees to be social sellers. Maybe standard LinkedIn courses are offered on the intranet. Little or no guidance is offered. Individuals create accounts on social sites such as LinkedIn and Twitter.

There is a complete lack of coordination (management are usually allowed to get away with not being social). The early adopters drive activity, but there is no organizational governance, coordination or risk management. With little or no education and training, we often see these programmes fizzle out; they are seen as yet another management fad and people go back to doing what they did before.

Digital selling is supposed to bring sales and marketing together. Some people call that RevOps, and at this stage it can often add to the cross-departmental 'stone throwing'. For many a business, due to history, social media sits in marketing and therefore social selling is often seen as a marketing initiative and tactic, rather than a board-level strategy. Marketing often have responsibility for demand generation, and as the social selling article on LinkedIn that the senior manager read was probably written by a marketer it will be about demand generation. As a senior manager recently said to me, 'There is no ROI in social selling, we tried it in marketing and it didn't work.' It was difficult remaining polite and not responding, 'Social selling – the clue is in the name.'

Often, you will find random acts of social duplicate and confuse, or even just isolate people. If people don't understand social, throwing buzzwords and jargon at them won't help.

From an overall standpoint the impact of social selling at this level is limited, without a formal programme in place. At this level, the organization will be selling the greater percentage of business through analogue methods and the narrative will be analogue. You will get some uplift of sales through social, but it won't be transformational.

Stage 3: Control

At this stage, people use social every day; it is omnipresent. With random acts of social spreading through the organization and the number of Twitter accounts proliferating, things can often get out of hand. There is the risk of a PR disaster. How long before somebody has a bad day and tweets something negative?

The response to that from companies is to offer 'media' training to employees. Only registered 'spokespeople' are allowed to talk to the media. Now anybody can say what they like.

There are also sites like Glassdoor, where employees and former employees anonymously review companies and their management.

For somebody trying to control a message, this is the stuff of nightmares. You mean, anybody can post anything? Yes! Then they need to be shut down.

You may recall from history at school the story of King Canute and the waves. To flatter him his courtiers told him that he was so wise and powerful that he could even stop the tide coming in. The story goes that King Canute was not so gullible and told his courtiers to take him to a beach, whereupon he would command the incoming tide to go back. Of course, Canute demonstrated he had no control over the elements (the incoming tide), and that 'trying to stop the tide' was futile.

What usually happens at this point is that the potential risks are realized and people step in to bring discipline and consistency to the company's branding and messaging on social networks. This stage is useful as often there is a realization that social selling will happen. The companies then write and distribute a social media policy. They establish a process to monitor employee use of social.

I've seen 'outlier' figures that have created their own social brand in Steps 0 and 1, and these are in fact often the social leaders of the future; they either come into conflict with the organization or get shut down. Many leave, often poached by the competition, who are a step further ahead in maturity. Organizations need to be looking for these individuals, working with them and nurturing such talent, as they will be the ones driving the digital selling programmes forward in the future.

It is also worth noting that policy and process imposed without training often confuse people. People have said to me, 'I stopped posting, as the rules allowing me to post are so tight, I don't bother anymore.' This defensive position has little direct benefit for sales performance, and could be described as 'taking one step forward and two steps back'.

We have hundreds of salespeople contacting us asking for help. They say, 'Management have told me to be social, but the leadership and I have no idea what this means.' These salespeople often end up following me on social – they are desperate for knowledge on social media, as they know this will help them, but get no leadership support. These salespeople often leave and go somewhere that is investing in digital for their team(s).

Stage 4: Structured programme

Having established a marketing, legal and compliance foundation, companies are now in a position to empower their sales team with a structured programme and methodology. This will take the form of training, but does not mean that the management are on board or 'walking the walk'.

The training at this stage usually takes the form of LinkedIn training in the belief (as with many social selling 'gurus') that digital selling equals LinkedIn. As we mentioned previously, LinkedIn is only 30 per cent of your social graph, so the salespeople miss the opportunity to build and own strong communities. If you want to learn how to grow vegetables in a garden, this is very different from learning how to use a tool such as a spade or a fork. That's the difference in learning to use a tool such as LinkedIn and learning what it means to be social.

The training often revisits the programmes introduced before, which is really a personal branding project, enabling the company to pump out as much company content as they can. This is often hidden under a banner of 'share of voice'. That is, can we compete with all our competitors, in an 'arms race' to see how much content we can pump out? This comes back to the history of the 'pile them high' marketing we talked about earlier. First we pumped out letters, then emails, and now we pump out content; in all cases we crossed our fingers and hoped it would stick. Hopefully, having read this book, you will see this isn't how you run a modern marketing and sales organization. It's not about throwing mud at the wall and hoping it will stick.

If the training covers more than personal branding and also looks at how to talk to strangers (etiquette for making new contacts), social prospecting, having conversations, content sharing, content creation and community building, then such a programme should start 'moving the needle'. During the programme, the leadership must signal their desire, perhaps an expectation, that salespeople need to use networks to sell. Marketing must provide sales with content that is vetted and approved to post and share. It is probably very 'corporate', which is why salespeople need to think about creating their own content, but that won't happen until we get to trust.

We would highly recommend the use of Playbooks at an individual salesperson level, which are created with the salesperson and the sales leadership to drive the change in habits and mindset change. There should also be pledges on behalf of the salesperson and an understanding of the type of leading indicators and measures. As with anything in sales, there needs to be an understanding of consequences.

Note that it is pointless creating content unless you measure its success. We talked in the previous chapter about how we can use metrics such as likes to measure impact, and there are tools that can help with this. For example, you can find out for how long people actually watch your YouTube videos.

Despite many benefits, impact achieved in the training stage can be limited by two factors: measurement and scalability. Managers must measure how employees are or aren't acting on the information communicated in the training. This can be done using leading indicators or even basic use of LinkedIn's SSI score. And training can be difficult to scale, especially where there is high staff turnover. Sales teams overcome these limitations when organizations move beyond one-off training and when social is woven into the fabric of the organization.

It is our recommendation that training starts with new starters, so that the new intake of the business understands the culture and expectations that the business is digital.

Stage 5: Trust

A social selling programme will not blossom until an organization places trust in its employees. I'm not saying that you can accelerate straight to this place; most often, as with any change programme, this is a journey people need to make.

Trust is the opposite of control, and organizations will want to control the uncontrollable. It is only when they have wasted many hours and dollars trying to push the genie back in the bottle that maybe they will realize that it cannot and will not happen. There is only so far you can go with empowering people and yes, progress can be made, but it is only when management trust employees that the full potential is achieved.

There must be many of you reading this who are saying, 'This will never happen in my organization', and this may well be the case. If so, as a business your board need to make a strategic decision to stay analogue and communicate that to the employees. We usually find that it requires a major catalyst to make the move to social selling happen, such as a change in leadership, usually (but not exclusively) to a younger, social-savvy person. Or where the CEO is driving a company-wide digital transformation agenda.

I am aware of a very large organization where it is working, but it took the recruiting of a (not so young) very charismatic leader to push it through.

SO WHY TRUST?

Organizations have to let go and trust people and the passion they have for their work. If you're not passionate, maybe you should go and do something else. We live in a society where we make purchase decisions about products on Amazon through reviews from people we have never met. We make decisions on hotels via Tripadvisor through reviews from people we have never met. Often the fact that a person is a friend of a good friend makes their recommendations more trustworthy for us. People no longer read ads; they would rather speak to somebody in their network who has used a product. This means that ordinary people can influence purchase decisions.

But – and it's a big but – companies that are controlling when it comes to social for employees just don't get it. When you hear an employee says how great their company is, the first thing you think is: 'Of course they would say that, they are biased, as they work there.'

This book isn't about social media, it's about social business. If you look at how business worked in much of the 20th century, it was based on the production line. Everybody had one. It was what you did with it, how you treated the people and the raw materials, that gave you competitive advantage. In the world today, it is not what you know, but what you share with the communities that you build. When you have a company that is sharing knowledge internally and externally then you truly have a 'game changing' situation. And there is the difficulty – how can you trust people to share knowledge outside the company and not give away all your trade secrets? How can you share to attract and retain customers and talent? Even though you trust them to walk into meetings and share knowledge about the business.

Don't forget, you are already paying your employees, and if they like where they work and are passionate about the company, then they can become even more valuable for your marketing programme. Of course, not every employee will want to assume this role, but giving those who have a passion for your company and product an outlet on public platforms such as social media can drive even more loyal and engaged employees. We are seeing that socially native people see blogging, tweeting and updating LinkedIn and Facebook as things they do every day. Many of us have moved our lives online and it is natural for us to live and work there.

From our own experiences, when customers can experience happy and engaged employees, either in person or on social media, this leads to happier and more engaged customers. Who doesn't want to buy from a company where the employees are proud of where they work and happy to say this publicly? So why not trust your employees to talk about the company? OK, you can offer guidelines and have disclaimers, but you cannot ignore their passion. You can, however, ignore boring corporately written tweets and posts. Nobody is interested in a brochure.

Companies have to start with the recruitment process. You will find your digital workforce online. Every time these people tweet something, they don't even need to mention their employer, as people already know they work there. Maybe it's digital product placement.

Every time your trusted employees tweet something, it's listened to. This is a win–win situation. It's a win for your employees' personal brand and a win for the enterprise as they get an authentic voice and not just press releases being regurgitated. Don't forget you pay these people already, so you don't have to turn to outside influencers. Salespeople must have a position on social today as this will drive conversations with buyers, and, as we have already discussed, conversations drive sales.

There are already companies whose employees are intertwined with their customers on social, or customers that have left the organizations you are selling to but still have an influence on that company through their network. It is very possible you need to call upon company B to sell to company A, as there is a previous employee of A working at B.

So where are these people? Often they already work for your company, and you just need the leadership to harness their abilities and trust them. If you had your employees passionately talking about your company, this would give you such a massive lift. If you also pull people into a community you can create an unstoppable force and move yourself to a market leading position.

In summary, a smart brand advocate programme can help turn employees into advocates, and happier, engaged employees can translate into developing loyal customers who become social advocates as a result.

Stage 6: Continual improvement

At this stage social is embedded in everything that you do. It's not an 'add on' but people are living and breathing it. There should be a culture of trialling new developments and apps and dropping or adopting them as required.

You will have a new starter programme where new employees are inducted into your digital strategy. There will be a continuous improvement process where digital as a fundamental building block of your business will give your team(s) boosters so their knowledge stays current and the digital culture thrives. We talked earlier about every business being not just doing what you do, like a Drones company, but also being a media company, knowing that content and the continued need to create it as part of your prospecting process. We have also discussed how social must be inbuilt in the business planning process and quarterly business reviews.

Building your business: A social strategy

Why you need a strategy

All business do something with social media. Usually social media sits under marketing and a company will use paid media such as advertising (when we know nobody looks at ads) or marketing will put a post out every few weeks and the employees will be asked to like it. These are tactics. I doubt 'social media' is generating anything for you.

How to create a strategy

Here at DLA Ignite, we work with clients to create a strategy, we don't turn up and impose something. We run a collaborative workshop so the clients are empowered to come up with the strategy that they want. Of course, we will share our expertise, and offer support and guide, but at the end of the day this is about all of the leadership team buying into (and executing) a strategy.

What does our strategy session look like? We can run them face-to-face over a day, or deliver virtually. I've created this pictorially in Figure 9.3. I have broken the strategy session down into three parts in Figure 9.4.

INTRODUCTION (60 MINUTES)
In a 40 minute presentation (with 20 minutes for questions) we explain the link between social media, and revenue and profit – how, as a business, you can see every keystroke of your team(s) time spent on social can be connected to EBITDA.

FIGURE 9.3   Process flow of assessment

FIGURE 9.4   Strategy: process flow of assessment

Drawing on research and established facts we talk about how we see the world and how social has changed it, how people are behaving and why, and how this impacts business now and in the future.

This is delivered (and recorded) the week before the workshop.

QUESTIONNAIRE (20 MINUTES)

Following this session we send out a questionnaire. This is about collating an 'as is' position. The questionnaire contains a dozen or so questions, including:

- Where are you now?
- What's your thinking around what social could do?
- How big can you dream?

WORKSHOP (2 TO 3 HOURS)

Then we run a workshop. In this workshop we create a set of deliverables. We discuss key issues with the client as we want to understand:

- What is your 'as is' position with regard to customers, prospects, partners and competitors?
- What is your 'to be' position?
- How crucial is social going to be (we score this out of 5 – see Figure 9.5)?

FIGURE 9.5   Leadership teams score the priority of the social media strategy

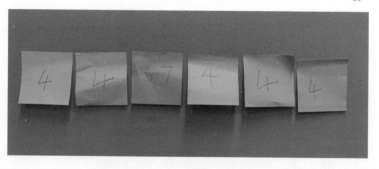

- What are the challenges to implementing?
- What to call this initiative, the initiative mission statement (see examples in Figure 9.6)?
- Pledges?

FIGURE 9.6   Examples of social strategy mission statements

To be seen as thought leaders. To be viewed as professional and not corporate. To be seen as problem solvers not politicians or salespeople. People want to work for us, because we make a difference

We believe that our journey on social media will make XYZ company the natural choice with technology leaders who have shared ambition to accomplish more: for themselves, their organization and their industry

With a dose of humour and humility, we make infrastructure legacy relevant for tomorrow, enabling us to be the most attractive place in the market

Following the workshop, we issue the client with a report. There is no restriction on the numbers who attend the workshop, but we would expect the senior management (C-suite) and their first reports to be there.

Optimization

We have stated many times in this book that social isn't a destination – it's a journey. Social is a changing space, with people bringing out new platforms, more people taking on digital as business as usual and the need for the various platform to evolve. Plus, the markets you work in all have an effect on the relative impact and usage in your organization.

The highest stage of social selling maturity is where actions are measured not to police the employees but to see what is working and what is not. Organizations will work in a closed loop, continually experimenting and innovating with employees and customers alike.

Good questions to ask yourself are:

- Where have we had success using networks and community?
- What relationships should we be using in the future?
- Which content is the most effective? Do we need to make changes?
- Do we use the terminology of the community and influencers or do we create our own?
- What target companies or individuals are under-represented or over-saturated?
- How can we work in our networks during the deal cycle to get the best coverage, wider and deeper?
- How can we affect influencers (external and within an account) to help us grow our share of wallet?
- Do we have the social graph of our accounts mapped out, showing internal and external influence? Do we have these bases covered?
- How many connections are our salespeople making each week, and how many of these are converting into conversations?
- How much engagement is our sales team getting on their content and how much of this is converting into conversations?
- How many meetings, leads and conversations are we having on social media?
- How much revenue, EBITDA, can we attribute to our activity on social media as a business?
- How much revenue, EBITDA, is a direct result of our actions on social media?
- How many new recruits do we get from our social activity?
- How many new employees do we get from our social activity?

Social initiatives

There are various social initiatives that will be kicked off at different stages of this maturity model, and we will now look at each of these to explain how they fit in, where they work and where they don't work. We look at:

- the importance of sales and marketing working together
- providing content that can be used in an employee advocacy programme
- clear delivery of messaging out into the channel so that channel partners, alliance partners and value-added resellers can use the same messaging

Sales and marketing – RevOps

In many corporations, sales and marketing just don't get along. Sales say that the leads that marketing create are no good, and marketing say that sales don't follow up the leads that are generated. This is often because the two sides are too busy throwing stones at each other to sit down and understand each other's wants and needs.

Defining a lead is a great place to start. How many meetings have you sat in where people have talked about leads, but they are really just talking about business cards from a conference? On the other hand, a lead isn't a company that is just about to sign for your product and service. Sometimes, sales seem to think that unless a prospect is about to put pen to paper, and effort is required, it's a waste of time.

We have seen the use of social internally as a great way of bringing the two sides together. Here at DLA Ignite we use Slack as an internal social network. Think of it as a corporate Facebook, corporate WhatsApp group, where an event can be a Facebook group. Only the people involved in the event are part of the group, and all sides can collaborate. It also reduces the amount of email traffic that gets pumped out to lists and never read, leading to better and timely cooperation on events.

Here at DLA Ignite we have a number of tools that we use to measure an employee's position on social media. This is like LinkedIn's Social Selling Index (SSI) but is our own propriety method. Apart from the fact that LinkedIn is a 'black box', and we have no access to how it is created, SSI only covers LinkedIn. At DLA Ignite, we have created a number of social selling tools; one of these plots an employee's/salesperson's social selling assessment against pipeline. Figure 9.7 is an example of an employee's social selling assessment score and Figure 9.8 shows an example of an employee's

FIGURE 9.7   Plotting employee DLA Ignite social score against pipeline: employee/salesperson's social selling assessment score

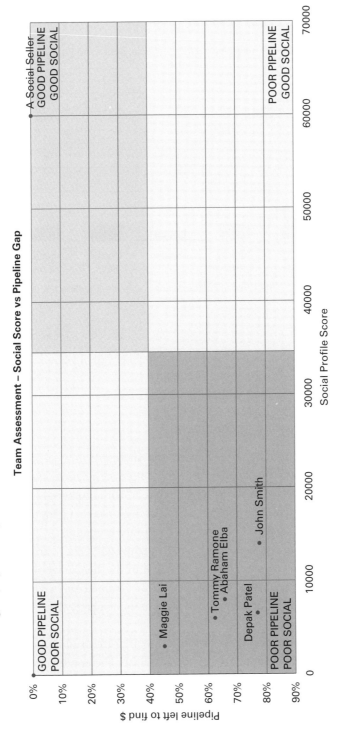

Team Assessment – Social Score vs Pipeline Gap

FIGURE 9.8   Plotting employee DLA Ignite social score against pipeline: employee's social media assessment and their pipeline gap

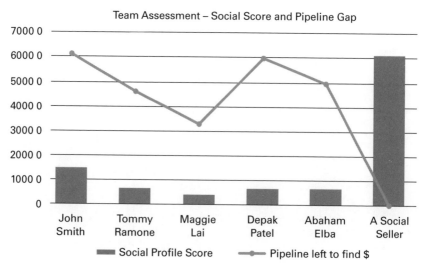

social media assessment and their pipeline gap. I've made the data and names up.

Employee advocate programme

This was partly alluded to earlier, and there are now suppliers that offer platforms that can be rolled out for employees. Often, these are seen by employers as ways of pumping out content, with no thought to its quality or the consequences. The problem is, research shows that people come to social media to be social and not to read corporate brochures.

The supplier's argument is simple – people will believe an employee more than a brand. Yes, sure, but we are back to the 'he/she would say that, they work there' argument. Unless people are trained on what good content looks like, and a structured programme is in place, then it is unlikely to move the needle.

In our experience, these programmes are often rolled out when companies are in the 'random acts of social' phase. The employees tend to have a follower count on Twitter and a LinkedIn profile consisting mainly of work colleagues or ex-work colleagues, now with competitors. Leaders are saying 'We need to be on social' but there is no structure, measurement or governance. You have this zero-sum game where content (and we have no idea if it's any good as we are not measuring it) is pumped out to other colleagues or into the hands of the competition. This is a waste of time and money.

It is not until we get into the 'structured programme' phase that people understand they need to grow their networks, and it is then that such programmes can be used to prospect and nurture. After all, content is great, but it's a means to and end, and the end is conversations that drive business. So often, the argument is visibility, clicks and views – this is a cost to your business and not a profit.

Channel partner advocacy

If you have a channel or value-added reseller (VAR) programme, these people are often too small to create their own content and would relish getting posts from the 'mother ship'. This does not stop the channel sales team from creating their own content. That is, the content can be created through a 'parent and child' relationship – the parent supplies official content and the children can decide to put this out through their channels. This means the parent can get content out through its employees, and the channel and its employees increase significantly their reach and amplification.

Now, the 'let's throw mud at the wall and hope it sticks' people will be rubbing their hands in glee. We have seen such programmes. I was once shown a report and told, 'Look how many partners we have signed up.' I agreed they had done a good job. Then I pointed out a column in the report, which was the number of retweets, and the figure was zero for every partner. No engagement had been obtained for the content and therefore probably few if any conversations and no revenue had been generated. As with the employee advocate programme, unless there is a clear training programme for all partners explaining why they are doing this, you are literally flushing money down the toilet.

Influencer marketing

First and foremost, an influencer programme has no end. It is a continued process of nurture and most likely a long game. There are different platforms that can offer a list of your influencers. Let's go back to basics here; today there are online and offline influencers. Journalists, for example, are influencers who will have an online presence but their main channel to market is through their newspaper or periodical. They are therefore still pretty much an offline influencer. So don't forget, the online tools look great but you still need to cover all your bases. The other 'gotcha' we see is that influencers are seen as sales targets, or an influence event is seen as a sales event. These are often run in an analogue format.

SO WHAT IS INFLUENCER MARKETING?

A primary objective of an effective marketing department is marketplace visibility. The team needs to build awareness for a product, company, or other positive change. The influencer is loved by their audience – if you stand close enough as a business to that influencer then that audience may notice you and check you out. But often awareness isn't enough. How can marketing move beyond mere visibility to engage customers, generate leads, or encourage purchase behaviour? One tactic for generating influence is to 'borrow' it from those experts or individuals who already have the ability to persuade or move customers to take action.

Successful influencer marketing isn't just about paying boldfaced names or social media stars, as that would be nothing more than paid media, or an advert. Influencer marketing has its own nuances. People love to have a third-party view on any discussion, especially if that person is independent. In the past people turned to companies such as Gartner or Forrester but in the 'new world' of social, a new independent person has emerged who has a viewpoint – the blogger. Bloggers are generally not connected to any major product or brand and are therefore seen as trusted advisors.

Influencer marketing is about getting influencers to say 'nice' things about your brand. Maybe you can co-create some content, maybe you can get an influencer give you a quote for the report you are writing. When buyers are in the buying process they may notice the influencer talking about your product or sharing content created with that influencer.

In a recent influencer campaign I took part in, there were five of us influencers. We were invited onto a panel to discuss the research the supplier had created. In the lead-up to that we all posted on our social media profiles that were taking part in this panel, giving it visibility. We took part in the panel, we all then wrote a blog about our key learning from the panel, which we then all promoted through our social media profiles. By using us as influencers, the supplier was able to 'buy' our influence and 'buy' the trust our audiences have in us.

We all make decisions based on trust, or how much we trust somebody, as part of our buyer process. From a marketing perspective, trust and control are at different ends of the scale. We place a certain amount of trust in a salesperson or an employee advocate, but we would probably think there might be a level of bias. That said, marketing may be highly controlling the message, which gives a lower level of trust for the buyer and a high level of control for the marketer. As we move up the spectrum of customer advocacy, the level of control for the marketer goes down, but as buyers we are more likely to trust customer comments.

The next level of marketing you should introduce is to get your channel partner to market for you. Again, the charge of 'they would say that' can be levelled against you, but often these partners may be trusted advisors at a customer or account level.

Customer advocates are a key component of the marketing mix. While you can expect people to support their decisions, sometimes the people who have advocated for you can turn and speak against you. But if managed properly, these individuals can be harnessed to provide input into product development and innovation, as well as saying nice things about you. I know someone who is a MicroScooter product advocate, and he is proud of the product and the changes he has enabled. He tells me about it all the time, and now I am telling you. That is great marketing.

Influencer marketing offers the highest level of trust for the buyer, but the lowest level of control for marketing.

In previous chapters we talked about going to a networking event and we asked whether we would stand in front of everybody and say, 'Buy my product!' No we wouldn't. But we've seen influencer programmes run in a similar way. 'How will you run your influencer programme?' I asked the global head of social selling. She told me she would use a tool to find the influencer and then give the salesperson a piece of content and ask them to make contact. It's worth mentioning that this company was in the 'random acts of social' stage. I'm amazed that an influencer didn't tweet, 'Some idiot from company XYZ has just tried to pass me off with some boring white paper'.

We have also seen influencer events that were actually sales events, run very much like events in the analogue world. A senior VP would be running the event, but they had no social profile. I'm sure the event generated leads, but did it generate influence?

I'm aware of 'independent' social media celebrities who are paid to say good things about certain brands. Influencer marketing is very real, but it is not for this book to go into its pros and cons. It's worth saying that in many countries it is now the law that if you use paid-for influencers you need to use the hashtags #ads and #sponsored. My advice is that if you use any kind of influencer, paid or otherwise, you make it very clear to the audience that there is a bias. The buyer won't mind – what they will mind is if they think a brand has lied to them or been manipulative.

Summary

In this chapter we have shared with you the maturity stages companies go through as they transform into digital organizations and implement social selling. Businesses are always looking for short cuts and silver bullets, but trust me, there are none.

Organizations have to realize that the move to digital and social is a change in behaviour. Such changes requires a strategy, a structured methodology, measures and governance and help in change management to embed the programme into day-to-day working. This, after all requires habit change and mindset change. This won't happen overnight, and a company shouldn't expect that employees will become social sellers just by saying they are. Change can take time and organizations should use the model to recognize where they are, and help accelerate their maturity by driving a strategy, rather than a series of tactics such as 'random acts of social'.

We have also looked at digital process over analogue process. In the world of analogue, which is something we are all used to, if you cover 50 per cent of the world, you get 50 per cent of the result. In digital it's made up of '1s' and '0s' – it's on or it's off. That means if you do 50 per cent of the effort you will get zero of the result – you must do 100 per cent of the effort to get a result.

Reference

Gillum, S (2020) Email marketing isn't working – what's a B2B marketer to do? The Drum. www.thedrum.com/opinion/2020/09/30/email-marketing-isn-t-working-what-s-b2b-marketer-do (archived at https://perma.cc/SU4H-M67H)

10

The digital organization practitioner

This chapter has been written by **Anita Veszeli**, *Director of Social Media and Advocacy at Ericsson. It shows how she applied the advice in Chapter 9 to her own working environment. You may want to make slight changes to meet the unique requirements of your business.*

Social media maturity

Nowadays, most companies have digital strategy and digital transformation plans, and these are quite impacted by their overall digital maturity. The Covid-19 pandemic accelerated digital transformation projects, as all companies were forced to quickly shift from office to fully digital, from in-person events to digital events. Some have been more successful than others in implementing the required changes. The ones that succeeded put their people and culture first.

Many digital transformation projects only focus on tools, automation and adaption, forgetting about people, the social skills they need and the culture that is needed to succeed.

Companies need work on their culture before strategy and execution. On top of culture, they also need a company-wide social media strategy and transformation plan to become a social business, where social media is embedded into every part of the organization. Individuals and teams (marketing, PR, sales, talent attraction, product development, etc.) use social listening insights, take part in discussion on social media platforms, build and nurture their networks, forming trusted relationships and ultimately achieving their personal and department-specific objectives.

A good social selling strategy includes digital tools, social media and skills training, enablement, along with behaviour change, and yet again culture is key. So much easier to come up with a new strategy or pivot an existing one, much harder to create and cultivate a growth mindset culture.

Embracing social selling in a company requires a culture with a growth mindset, where learning is part of everyone's daily lives, where innovation, testing and learning are celebrated. It also requires not only the buy-in, but the support of the C-suite, where C-level executives understand the need for adapting new approaches to how to do business.

Even though the pandemic turned our lives upside down and we all went digital and onto social media, still many CEOs say, 'yes, I get we need to be more social', but in reality they still don't get it. They have a perception of social media that it's for younger generations, politicians or social media influencers. They started to see that their peers are posting on LinkedIn, so they might feel that they need to do as well. However, they still don't understand what social media can bring to them and to the business nor that 'being active' or posting on social media without a strategy is just a random act and a time-waster.

Social media is all about trust

Nowadays, trust is the highest valued commodity. In the last few years, we've seen that people have lost their trust in governments, media and brands, but they trust people, experts and mostly their peers – this trend is here to stay. We've also seen that organic reach and engagement for brand handles is declining, paid social is a must. While paid social media ads have much value and the right place in any social media marketing strategy, they are less trusted than content shared by people.

A common objection at a leadership level is that social media is for the young generation, celebrities, posting selfies and pictures of their everyday life. The question that I've been hearing for the past 10 years or so still remains, 'What's the ROI in social?' When I show results of other brands successfully implementing social thought leadership and social selling into their strategy and culture, and how sales velocity speed up, the percentage of bigger-size deals, I see shocked faces. Is this really true? How do we get started? Leaders want to see the same results, right now.

There are some quick wins, of course, but a change of attitude and behaviour of the sales team requires time. If a company has been banning social media for a long time, the road to fully embracing social media and becoming a social business is long. It requires a company-wide social media strategy, including a social selling strategy, objectives, a transformation plan, training, coaching, internal community and change management. And, above all, it needs a winning culture.

As part of the culture and change, companies need to learn how to let go of control and trust their own employees. For many, this is scary and after totally banning social media, they usually turn to controlled ways of sharing. While this is a great start, once they start to share, you can't go back and you have to get comfortable that you can't control everything.

Just think about parenting. First you limit or ban certain actions of your kids – as they are growing you supervise all their actions, controlling what they can do and can't do. You teach them, you mentor and coach them along the way about what is right, what is not, how to do certain things. And the time comes when you just need to let go and trust them. Will they make mistakes? Of course they will. Will they learn from them? Yes, they will.

It is the same with employees. The best you can do is to take them along a social media maturity journey. Start from the beginning, share your social media policy/guidelines with them, set up their profiles, teach them how to grow their network, how to engage, how to listen, hold their hand while they are taking their first few steps, provide feedback, coach, train more and repeat. Soon they'll gain confidence, experience and you can let go of their hands.

It's important to realize that more and more people are using social media every day, including customers and competitors. Companies should give employees the freedom to be active on social media. Employees can be the best advocates for your brand – imagine the free advertisement you get through employees sharing about how they work, news, products, events and more. Employee voices not only help build your brand, but by standing out from the crowd, they help to attract the best talent, cultivate a learning culture and ultimately impact revenue.

Social selling maturity model

We've discussed how social selling is the way to sell in the digital world, and while keeping analogue practices you do need to start your journey in the digital and social way of working. This requires engagement with the organization's overall digital and social media maturity, a company-wide digital and social media strategy, a transformation plan within the culture of the organization.

FIGURE 10.1   Social selling maturity model graph

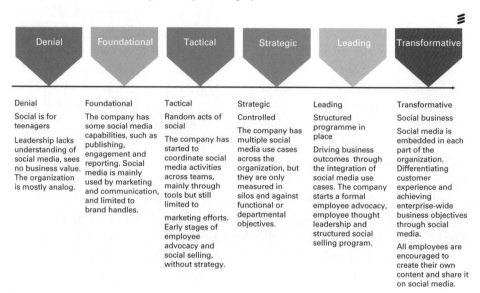

Denial	Foundational	Tactical	Strategic	Leading	Transformative
Social is for teenagers	The company has some social media capabilities, such as publishing, engagement and reporting. Social media is mainly used by marketing and communication, and limited to brand handles.	Random acts of social	Controlled	Structured programme in place	Social business
Leadership lacks understanding of social media, sees no business value. The organization is mostly analog.		The company has started to coordinate social media activities across teams, mainly through tools but still limited to marketing efforts. Early stages of employee advocacy and social selling, without strategy.	The company has multiple social media use cases across the organization, but they are only measured in silos and against functional or departmental objectives.	Driving business outcomes through the integration of social media use cases. The company starts a formal employee advocacy, employee thought leadership and structured social selling program.	Social media is embedded in each part of the organization. Differentiating customer experience and achieving enterprise-wide business objectives through social media.
					All employees are encouraged to create their own content and share it on social media.

Implementing a social selling transformation plan

Making the change to modern selling, embracing digital tools and social media will not happen overnight. Having tools in place, onboarding the sales teams to use them, hiring a trainer or having online courses are great, but they won't do the trick. Social selling requires sales professionals to change the way they do business. Changing behaviour is the biggest challenge sales leaders face.

The social selling maturity model is based on experience of how social selling or modern selling has been introduced and implemented in various organizations. It's a great way to assess where your company is and how to get to the top of the maturity curve. As mentioned before, getting to the top takes time and sometimes it is inevitable to make mistakes, learn, assess, change tactics to get to the top.

Going back to the parenting example, ultimately we'd like to prepare kids for different life situations and experiences. One step in their development is learning how to ride a bicycle. We know they'll most likely fall at some point; some will get away with bruises, some will break an arm or a leg, but it's part of their long-term development plan.

Stage 0: Denial – social is for teenagers

When leadership has no understanding of social media beyond what their kids, politicians, celebrities or social media influencers do, it can be tough to 'sell' the concept of modern selling. If they have no social media presence, or their profiles on social media platforms are outdated, you most likely found yourself presenting to a non-perceptive audience.

Even with the best-prepared presentation, full of data, statistics, proof points, your leadership will be sceptical. The best approach in this situation is to suggest a social selling pilot to show results (quantitative and qualitative) and possibly ROI. Note, your social selling pilot should be at least six months long, as change takes time. Set quantitative and qualitative goals for your pilot to see and show wins along the way, like network growth, SSI score improvement on LinkedIn, customers engaging with content, etc. The six months might not be enough for new deals, mainly in a B2B setting with long sales cycles, but will be enough to prove the concept, continue and scale the pilot.

Stage 1: Foundational

At this stage, the company has some social media capabilities, such as publishing, on branded social media accounts, engagement and reporting. Social media at this stage is mainly used by marketing and communication, and most of the time limited to brand handles. Someone at your company might have heard about social selling, might have seen a success story, a case study at one of the conferences, or came across an article or a book.

Most often, a social selling pilot is kicked off by the marketing department, to bring closer marketing and sales. The mistake that is often made is that social selling is seen as another demand generation tool, not taking the whole sales funnel and process into consideration. Marketing has a lot of terminology, like MQLs (marketing qualified leads), BQLs (business qualified leads), etc. which most companies and sales teams need to get used to. This is great, because sales and marketing will have the same way of defining and describing a lead, and this brings the two departments closer. We'll talk more about marketing automation later.

Stage 2: Tactical with random acts of social

At this stage the company has started to coordinate social media activities across teams, mainly through tools but still limited to marketing efforts.

Often at this stage, the company starts to encourage employees to be active and share on social media. It might even encourage sales teams to embrace digital. Standard social media courses are offered on the intranet, but nothing more. Employees create their personal accounts on Twitter and LinkedIn. There is no strategy, minimum coordination and leadership is not embracing social media. The few early adapters share, drive engagement and website visits, but there is no governance and risk management in place.

With the lack of strategy, governance and little training, these initiatives often fade out and people go back to the old ways of working.

Modern selling can really bring sales and marketing teams closer to work in a collaborative way. There are even terms describing it as 'Smarketing' or 'Smales'. At this stage, it is usually not so collaborative, rather 'stone-throwing' at each other.

Marketing is usually responsible for demand generation, hence trying to encourage sales to use social media and generate demand. However, this causes confusion between the two departments – who is responsible for what? With random acts of social, you'll just confuse or even isolate people. Throwing random training, buzzwords and metrics at your employees and sales teams won't help.

The impact of randomly sharing on social media, what I do not call social selling, is really limited. Just like with everything else, doing things without a strategy, goals and not being consistent, will not take you anywhere. If you don't see the results, you will just give up sooner or later.

At this stage, the organization might use digital tools, but business is still done through analogue methods. There might be some uplift of brand or even sales through social (random), but for sure it is not consistent, nor transformational.

Stage 3: Strategic and controlled

At this stage, the company has multiple social media use cases across the organization, but they are still only measured in silos and against functional or departmental objectives. People use social media every day; the platforms and why or how they use it might differ, but they are active every single day.

With random acts of social media across the organization at the tactical stage, more and more people are opening up social media accounts on

Twitter, LinkedIn, Instagram and other platforms, and things can easily get out of hand, leading to a PR crisis. Sooner or later, someone will have a bad day, be upset or just super-excited and share something negative, inappropriate or disrespectful before thinking of the consequences.

PR is a highly controlled area, producing carefully crafting messages that companies want people to hear. Many companies think about PR in the old, traditional way – no commenting or denying that anything is happening. There are usually a few, carefully selected 'spokespeople' who are media trained and are allowed to speak on behalf of the company to the media.

This approach can't be replicated on social media. Employees' social media profiles are theirs, not owned by the company. However, what they share might reflect back on the company in positive or negative ways. We also need to mention review sites as Glassdoor and Blind where current or former employees anonymously review companies and their leadership. For PR departments it can be utterly uncomfortable and scary that anyone can share anything on social media. Many times, their response is to take back control, or at least try to take it back.

At this point of maturity, companies realize the potential risks associated with employees sharing and participating in discussions on social media. To address this, they create a social media policy, along with processes and guidelines for employees to follow.

There are always a few early adopters who created their social media accounts and have built their personal brand while the company they work for is in maturity level 0 or 1. These forward-thinkers often come into conflict with their organization and get shut down or controlled. Some leave their employer due to the conflict or get poached by competition further ahead with their social media maturity. Companies must be looking for these individuals within their business, working closely with them, encouraging, nurturing their talent. Most often they'll be the ones becoming influential in certain topics or will drive social selling programmes.

It is worth noting that having a social media policy in place without proper communication and training is worthless. It's important how the policy is written and explained, otherwise it can confuse or discourage employees from participating in conversations on social media. If the policy is too restrictive people will stop sharing, being afraid of the consequences. A good social media policy should be encouraging, motivating, yet shed light on the risks, regulations and things to consider.

Stage 4: Leading – structured programme in place

This is the stage when companies start to drive business outcomes through the integration of social media use cases across the organization. When the social media foundations are in place, including legal and compliance, companies are ready to start a formal employee advocacy, employee thought leadership and structured social selling programme. Most of the time it will take the form of training and enablement. However, it doesn't mean that leadership is on board or 'walking the walk'.

At this stage, companies usually offer LinkedIn training, thinking and believing that social selling equals LinkedIn. While LinkedIn is a great platform, and thought by many to be the 'only' business or professional platform, limiting your sales teams to LinkedIn is a mistake. Focusing on only one platform means they'll miss the opportunity to build and own strong communities across different platforms. It's never a good idea putting all your eggs into one basket. Social media platforms change along with people's behaviour using them.

The training offered at this stage usually focuses on personal branding and sharing approved company content, such as news, products and deals. This often comes back to the overall communication strategy of the organization, when success is measured by share of voice on social media. Share of voice is easy to measure and compare with competitors; however, most of the time this means pushing out as much branded content as possible.

This comes back to marketing tactics again – pushing out as many newsletters and emails as possible, based on the law of large numbers. Now it's content, the more we push out, we hope more will stick. This might have worked before, but it is definitely not the way to do modern marketing and sales.

The training and educational series should cover more than personal branding. It should also cover the etiquette of making new contacts and connections, in other words how to talk to strangers on social media. The power of social listening shouldn't be left out either – just by listening and observing, sales teams can gain insights of the buying committee and can tweak their account plans accordingly. They can be better informed and have more productive meetings with their customers. Prospecting on social media is another key element. There are small tricks and tips that can make prospecting more efficient and impactful. Content creation and sharing is really the way to build a strong community. If all of these areas are covered in the training, companies usually start to see the impact.

During the structured programme, leadership must show their expectations that sales teams use social media as part of their sales strategies and tactics. Working closely with marketing is a key element here. Without content, all the above training is useless. Marketing usually provides the carefully vetted and approved content that salespeople can share. Almost all of the time, if we are being honest with ourselves, these are boring corporate content pieces, with an inside-out perspective and are 'globally relevant'. This is why salespeople need to start thinking about creating their own content that is timely and resonates with their customers and prospects. Getting to this stage, when salespeople are creating their own content, takes time and they must be trusted by their organization.

Good to remember – creating content is useless, unless you measure its success. We previously covered how we can use metrics, likes, comments to measure impact and there are many tools that help with measurements. You can see how many people have seen your video, read your article, blog, how long they've watched your video, etc.

At this stage, with a structured programme, companies can see some benefits. However, the impact will be limited by two factors: measurement and scalability. It is difficult to see and measure if and how employees/salespeople are implementing what they've learnt during the training. It is also difficult to scale, especially when companies have high staff turnover.

The only way to overcome these limitations is to move beyond the one-off training and weave social media into the culture and fabric of the whole organization. When social media is embedded to all departments across the organization, the company becomes a social business. Each and every employee uses social media as their everyday platform to share, engage, connect and take part in discussions.

FROM LEADING TO TRANSFORMATIONAL – TRUST IS A MUST

Employee thought leadership and social selling will not flourish until the organization is ready to let go of control, has an open culture and is willing to trust its employees. If you assess the level of maturity at your organization, you can skip a few stages and start here. However, for most companies it's a journey and they need to go through each of the stages to get here. Becoming a social business requires cultural and behaviour change and that takes time.

Trust is the opposite of control, and while you can skip some of the stages most organizations are so used to control that they don't want to let go. They only realize they need to trust in their employees after not seeing the wanted impact, wasting precious time and money controlling messages, content and behaviour. Of course, the organization will see some success at lower stages of maturity, but the full potential of social media can only be unlocked when leaders trusts their employees.

There are a few companies that fully embrace social media, and it's built into their culture and woven into the fabric of the company. Many of you might be reading now and thinking, 'This will never happen at my organization', and it actually might not. Companies who reached this maturity level usually had a catalyst who made it happen. It can be a change in leadership to a social-savvy person, or the head of social media might be a charismatic leader who can secure leadership support. A CEO can also be the catalyst if a company-wide digital transformation is part of their agenda and strategy.

WHY IS TRUST SO IMPORTANT?

Organizations need to create a culture of trust. They need to let go of control and trust their employees, their passion for their work, their judgement on sharing and collaborating on social media.

Every day we make purchase decisions based on reviews by people we have never met. We choose hotels and trips based on reviews, again by people we have never met. We opt for restaurants with good and great reviews by people we don't know. Our decisions are formed and influenced by other people, their recommendations on social media, their reviews on Google Maps, Amazon, Tripadvisor, Booking.com and more. People are getting more and more tired of ads and they lack trust in them. They would rather speak to somebody in their network, who has used a product or a service. Each one of us is influencing someone else through what we share on social media, the reviews we provide. People are influencing purchase decisions.

You might think this is true for consumer products and services and not so much for business-to-business purchases where the buying committee makes the decision. Today, there is no such thing as B2C or B2B, only P2P – person-to-person. We trust people, not brands, their PR and marketing teams. This is why trusting your employees to share and engage on social media is key to any company's success.

Companies who only allow approved messages to be shared by their employees and allow them to engage on social media in a controlled and restricted manner are missing out and will not see the full benefits of social media and social selling. When employees only share company news, press releases, company events, white papers, etc., their network's reaction is limited. They usually think, of course they promote it, they work there. While this type of content might get a few eyeballs and likes (mainly by colleagues), it doesn't open up for comments, discussions, and for sure it doesn't build trust and credibility.

Why should companies aim to become a social business? We already talked about moving from analogue to digital and today most companies have a digital strategy and digital transformation programme in place. But few have a company-wide social media strategy and social transformation programme. I'm not talking about social media marketing. If social media is owned by only marketing, the strategy will also only focus on demand and lead generation. Social media is much more than marketing. A company-wide social media strategy outlines what social media maturity stage the company is at right now and what is needed to become a social business. Being a social business is the highest level of maturity on the social media maturity model. It is when the company has a holistic approach to social media, and has programmes in place covering governance, training, enablement, social media listening, organic, paid social media, employee advocacy (executive social leadership, employee thought leadership, social selling, social talent attraction) and influencer marketing. Think about social media as a big jigsaw puzzle – each of the above areas is one piece of a puzzle and together they bring the big picture to life. In a social business, social media is embedded in everything the company does, with a social-first mindset. Each department knows how social media contributes to its success, and all employees are encouraged and enabled to participate in conversations on social media.

Nowadays, people are not interested in what you know, but what you share with your communities. When a company has a sharing culture, combined with a growth mindset, freely and generously sharing knowledge internally and externally, engaging and learning from each other, it is set to success and sustainable growth.

You might ask, why should I trust employees to share their knowledge outside of the company and not give away secrets? If you have a great company culture, your employees are most likely passionate about their work and your company and by sharing their knowledge and passion, they can bring much value to your brand, marketing, sales and talent attraction efforts.

Of course, not every employee is comfortable sharing and engaging on social media, and that is fine. It should not be forced on them. But there are those who would like to advocate on behalf of your company, would like to create and share their own content, engage in discussions and learn from others on social media. Socially native people see blogging, tweeting, posting on LinkedIn, Facebook and Instagram as part of their daily life. For others it's a challenge to build it into their everyday life. The Covid-19 pandemic made us move our lives online and it is more natural to live and work in this space.

From experience, when customers see happy and engaged employees in person or on social media, they are more likely to be engaged and happy with the products and services. Who wouldn't like to be connected and to buy from a company where employees are proud where they work and passionate about the products and services?

If they are already passionate and proud, why is trusting them so diffi-cult? Guidelines, training and enablement is needed. Help, support and guide them, instead of ignoring their passion or trying to control every single message. Do not force them to only share corporate tweets and posts.

When your workforce is digital and actively sharing and engaging on social media, they don't even need to mention your company – people already know where they work. Every time a trusted employee shares a piece of content, it's seen by others and listened to. It is really a win–win situation. It's a win for your employee's personal brand and a win for your organization as they get an authentic and trusted voice, instead of sharing corporate press releases. Your employee's voices are more trusted than any message or fancy brand video you post from your corporate social media accounts. External experts and influencers are also more likely to engage with them, so you don't need to pay for external influencers.

I often get the question, why put so much focus on employees, why invest so much in training, enablement and coaching? What if they leave? My reply is, what if we don't invest in their development and they stay? Happy employees are more likely to stay, but even though they leave and join other companies, your customers, their influence is still there. How they talk about your brand after they've left has a long-term impact.

How do you find these people? You can easily identify them as they will already be active on social media. All you need to do is harness their talent and passion, and trust them. If you already have employees passionately talking about your brand, supporting and guiding them will give them massive encouragement. If you create a community out of these passionate people, who are willing to learn and share their knowledge, you have an unstoppable force.

In summary, a well-crafted employee advocacy programme can turn employees into advocates, and happy, engaged employees can help to develop more engaged and loyal customers, who can also become social advocates for your company.

Stage 5: Transformative – a social business

At this stage, social media is embedded in everything that you do and your business is achieving company-wide objectives through social media. There is a culture of testing and learning, quickly trying out new things and pivoting based on the outcomes. All employees are encouraged to create their own content and share them on social media. They are participating in discussions with other internal and external experts, building their own communities. Social media is not a disjointed and added task for them, it's part of their life.

Optimization

Becoming a social business can and should be the goal, but don't forget, digital and social media transformation is a journey. Social media is changing day by day, with new platforms popping up, algorithms changing, shift to messaging and social audio. At the same time, people's behaviour using social media is changing and it is different market by market.

When it comes to social selling maturity, the highest level is where actions and impact are measured, not to control or to police employees, but to see what is working and what is not. Working in cycles, closed loops, continuously experimenting, innovating, trying out new things with employees and customers alike is important. Evaluating what is working, what is not and sharing findings and best practices with others in the organization creates the culture and behaviour that is needed for long-term success.

Here are a few questions to ask yourself:

- Which content is the most effective? Do we need to make any changes?
- In which communities we had the most success?
- Do we use the industry, customers' and influencers' terminology or do we create our own?
- Do we see any changes in the buying committee?

- Do we have target companies, job roles that are under- or over-represented?
- How can we work in our networks and communities during the deal cycle to get better coverage?
- How can we affect influencers (external and within the account) to help us extend the deal size and speed up the sales process?
- Do we have the social graph of our accounts mapped out, showing their role and influence (both internal and external)?

Social transformation projects

At each stage of the social media and social selling maturity, different social media projects initiatives will be kicked off. We'll take a look at the most important ones, where and how they fit in, whether they work or not.

- sales and marketing alignment and working together as one team
- content that can be used in an overall employee advocacy programme and in the social selling programme
- clear messages and clear delivery of them, so channel partners, affiliates, value-added resellers can use the same messaging
- how marketing automation can help salespeople spend more time with customers and potential customers

Sales and marketing – 'smarketing'

In most companies, sales and marketing still don't get along, they don't have shared goals or use the same vocabulary and this causes confusion and tension between the two functions. It's quite common that sales say that the leads coming from marketing are not good, and marketing say that sales don't follow up on the leads they generated. Many times, sales also don't see the value of marketing when it comes to key accounts and their buying committee. They are convinced they know all the key players, influencers and decision makers and they don't need marketing.

This often happens because the two functions are too busy doing their own thing instead of trying to understand each other's wants and needs. Defining a lead can be a great start. It's important to have the same definition and vocabulary so as not to get lost in translation. Mapping out a key account's buying committee, understanding each member, can also be a great start to bring the two functions together.

Have you been into meetings where people talked about leads, while they were only business cards from a conference or a trade show? Good to note that a lead isn't a company that is ready to sign the deal. Sometimes sales think that if a lead is not ready to sign the contract, it's just a waste of time.

Social media can really bring the two functions together by collaborating and working towards the same goals. Think of it as a community, where only members of the community can collaborate, share ideas and learn.

Employee advocacy programme

Nowadays there are several suppliers offering employee advocacy platforms that can be rolled out throughout the organizations. Most often brands see these platforms as a way to control what is being shared by employees and to push out as much content as possible. We've already mentioned that sharing company-approved branded content has some value, but without a structured programme in place this won't move the needle. A structured employee advocacy programme needs to cater for all types of employee personas and the function they work for. Leadership, sales, talent attraction, subject matter experts need different types of content (branded, third party and their own), they need slightly different training and enablement, and they would need to have their own internal community to share learning and best practices.

The employee advocacy platforms usually build on the trends that employees are more trusted than brands, governments and media. While this is true, just pushing out branded content without engaging and interacting on social media will have limited effects on your brand and pipeline. We see many companies' employees only sharing branded content with the same approved message. It's not unique, not personal. It still works as an advertisement.

Imagine social media as a networking event, where you are not mingling, asking questions, listening to others, just keep repeating corporate messages. It would be awkward, right? It is the same on social media.

Employees should always think about:

- What value does this add to my network?
- Why should they read it?
- Is there anything they can learn from it?

- How can I make it more relevant for my community?
- How can I start a discussion with my network?

Employee advocacy platforms and programmes are often rolled out when companies are in the 'controlled' or 'random acts of social' maturity stages. Employees have a follower count on Twitter and LinkedIn, mainly consisting of colleagues or ex-colleagues, sometimes competitors. When branded content is shared within these networks, it has a really limited impact, other than getting engagement in an echo-chamber and sharing branded materials with competitors. If a company stays at this stage, they won't see the full benefits of employee thought leadership, nor social selling.

Until you get to the 'structured programme' stage, when people understand how to grow their network, how to engage with external experts, influencers, peers, you'll not see results. Once networks are growing, trusted relationships are built on social media, then you'll see how it can be used for prospecting and nurturing.

Channel partner advocacy

If you have a channel partner or a value-add reseller programme, they are often too small to create their own content and would appreciate getting content from you. You can supply good, high-quality content and they can decide how and when to share it with their networks, through their channels. There are tools available to make this process more efficient by automation.

With this approach, you can get your content out through your employees and the employees of the channel partners, reaching wider audiences for amplification.

Now, you might think, let's push out as much content as we can and cross fingers some will stick. There are so many programmes like that in place today. Organizations are happy with the adoption rate and the amount of content shared. But when you look at the engagement rate for any shared content you often see that there is zero engagement. No likes, no hearts, no comments, re-tweets, nada. Just like with an employee advocacy programme – if you don't have a structured programme in place, you'll not see results. Training, enablement, coaching needs to be part of such programmes as well. Channel partners, just like employees, need to understand why they are doing it, how to grow their network, how to tweak content for their communities, etc. Take them on their own social media maturity journey.

Influencer marketing

Over the past few years, more and more suppliers offer influencer marketing platforms, where you can find influencers. Some vendors specialize in B2C or B2B influencer marketing.

The word 'influencer' is interpreted in many different ways and this can lead to confusion. There are online and offline influencers. journalists, analysts for example, are influencers who have an online presence, but their main influence is through their newspaper, periodical or publication. They are rather offline influencers. There are subject matter experts on certain topics, who over time, have built credibility and their network on social media platforms. They can be content creators or amplifiers, but their influence mainly comes from their social capital. We call them online influencers.

This is why it's important to always think about the big picture, cover online and offline all the time.

Influencer marketing programmes have no end, it's a continuous investment in building trust, and nurturing the relationships.

WHAT IS INFLUENCER MARKETING?

Marketing's main objective is not only to build awareness around products, services, but also to build trust, credibility and ultimately generate leads.

Building awareness is great, but not enough. How can you go beyond visibility to engage with customers, influence buying decisions and generate leads? Influencer marketing can be a great way to 'borrow' influence from others, who have built their own personal brand, trusted experts with capital on social media. They have the ability to influence others through their own authentic voice or through their content.

An effective and successful influencer marketing programme is not about pay-to-play advertisements. Many companies take this route to pay external experts and influencers just to amplify their corporate messages. Again, just like with employee advocacy, pushing out corporate content and messages has some value, but it's still seen as advertisement, hence less trusted. It doesn't matter if it's shared by an employee or an influencer. Advertisement is still advertisement.

People and buyers like to have independent, third-party views on products and services. Traditionally buyers turn to analyst agencies, like Gartner, Forrester for their analysis. Social media has brought in more independent, third parties, content creators, experts with social media influence.

To be successful, influencer marketing should be about building relationships with external experts and influencer communities. The ones who create content like blogs, videos, podcasts, articles, social audio and/or lives can take their own view on your topics, products and services. By partnering up with them for a longer term, they will understand your brand, values, products and services better. Ask them what they would value from your brand, besides payment. Access to your executives and/or subject matter experts? Access to your researchers and developers? Early access to white papers and reports? By providing the things they value, you can build better relationships with content creators.

We all make decisions based on trust, whether we admit it or not. From a marketing perspective control and trust are at the different ends of the scale. When we place trust in our salespersons, our employee advocates, employee thought leaders, we should also place trust in external experts, content creators and influencers. By allowing them to create their own content in the way they like and their community appreciates, they are able to tell your story, and advocate for your brand, products, services in an authentic and trusted way.

Again, letting loose of control and trusting your influencers will bring much more value and impact. It's really a win–win situation. Content creators, experts and influencer will feel more appreciated, and can help your marketing and sales team innovate and experiment to see what is working and what is not.

Content creators, experts, influencers can also bridge employee advocacy and customer advocacy. Customer comments and views are highly valuable in any buying process. In some cases, your customers are not ready or comfortable commenting or advocating for your brand, products or services. Influencer-created content, videos, articles, social media lives are a great way to talk about a topic from different angles – your company, external and customer. This type of content is great for all three parties and adds value to their network.

Customer advocates are a key component to any marketing mix. While most of the time customers are happy to share their experiences and advocate for you, they can also quickly turn against you. If this happens, how you manage the situation is key. These individuals and their feedback can provide valuable input for your product development. Never ignore any negative comment, they can be turned around and you can get the best customer advocates.

Influencer marketing, as we already mentioned, should be about trust and not control.

Marketing automation

There are tons of books on marketing automation, so we won't cover this subject in detail, but it's good to highlight how marketing automation can support the social selling process.

As with many topics between marketing and sales, marketing automation is seen differently by the two functions. Marketers look at it as a sales tool and when you ask sales who's responsible for marketing automation, usually they reply... it's in the name, marketing. Yet another example of why it's key that marketing and sales work together and collaborate.

You might ask as a salesperson, how can marketing automation help me spend more time with my customers?

If you are working on a key account where you need to understand each person, each persona in your buying committee, marketing automation can help you deliver personalized and relevant content to nurture or change perception, how they see your company, products or services compared to your competitors. This, combined with you listening and engaging with them through social media, frees up your time and provides you with actionable insights that you can use in your daily interactions. Intelligence and well-timed, smart content will set you apart from others. It will secure bigger deal sizes and faster deals.

If you are prospecting, not all of your contacts are ready to buy just yet, maybe in 3–6–9 months, or even in a year's time. This is where they can opt in and the marketing automation system takes them through a nurture process and in 3–6–9–12 months, in theory, the lead will pop up. These nurture programmes free up much time to focus on hot leads and take more customer meetings.

Just to note, a good nurture programme provides the right content at the right time, based on insights, listening, metrics. It's not about randomly pushing out all marketing content and hoping it will work.

Marketing automation is often introduced in a silo to marketing departments, without taking sales along the process. If it is introduced as part of a company-wide digital programme of transformation, and it is integrated with other social media programmes, it's a game-changer.

Summary

In this section we have shared the different maturity stages that companies usually go through as part of their digital transformation and as they implement different social media programmes and social selling.

Brands need to realize that digital and social transformation is mostly about culture and changing behaviour. Such change requires structured programmes, change management, a plan to embed new behaviour and actions into day-to-day routine. This won't happen overnight, and a company shouldn't expect that salespeople will become social sellers from one day to another. Change takes time and organizations should use the maturity model to assess where they are, and how to mature with their company-wide social maturity. They can accelerate the journey with a clear, holistic digital and social media strategy, a clear transformation and change programme.

THE EMPLOYEE ADVOCACY PRACTITIONER – DANIELLE GUZMAN

How do we get an employee advocacy programme that drives results? Build it for your people, not the brand. Identify that 5 per cent of your organization that is active on social media daily and wants to build their professional brand. Provide this community the tools and know-how to optimize their social profiles, to write effectively for their audiences and to define and refine their key focus areas. Next give them access to that company platform with brand-approved content, empower them and unleash them to cherry-pick brand content relevant to their focus areas and communicate it in their own words. Last, teach them how to build two-way relationships and a daily networking plan. Done successfully, employees will affect change or behaviour in their communities, attract target audiences, and drive the desired clicks, or registrations, etc. that the brand seeks. That's real influence. As a result you will see more leads, reduced deal cycle time, greater brand visibility, broader and more relevant networks, and a stronger sense of purpose for employees, and increased credibility in their space.

11

Five steps to getting started

This book so far has provided you with the theory as well as some practice to help you move from the world of analogue to digital selling. Before we talk about social selling and the future, here is a methodology to follow with the end point of you becoming a social seller.

The Changemaker Method

The Changemaker Method is our methodology that describes how social sales teams operate differently to traditional sales teams. This can be visualized as five steps along a path (as shown in Figure 11.1):

Step 1: Setting up shop – how to prepare the salespeople so that they can be discovered.

Step 2: Learning to listen – how to listen to what is happening in the wider network to scale up that discoverability.

Step 3: Building authority and influence – how to build up authority and influence so that the changemaker will select the salesperson to be part of their team.

Step 4: Optimizing – how to use technology to optimize the sales process.

Step 5: Enhancing collaboration – how to bring connected economy ideas into the organization so that it becomes more agile and flexible.

When taken together, the five steps define the path that needs to be taken to achieve the required organizational change to make social selling work. This is another very important point to understand early on. Successfully shifting to a social selling model relies on organizational change, specifically

FIGURE 11.1   Changemaker method steps

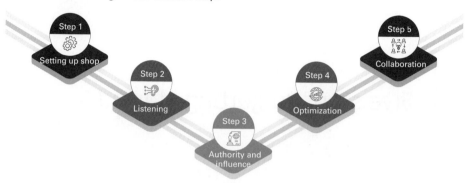

organizational change that is in tune with the shift in buyer behaviour as discussed at the start of this book.

A common mistake sales teams make is to regard social selling as something that can be 'spread' on top of how they currently work. Because we're talking about a sociological shift caused by the tipping point of mass adoption of the internet that has caused a change in buyer behaviour, the organization has to change its behaviour and culture. Staying the same isn't an option here, because if you stay the same you're essentially saying, 'The internet doesn't have an effect on how people work together', which self-evidently isn't true. We have seen so many people and organizations that have the mindset that 'I do these analogue tasks and then I do digital and it doesn't work.' People never find time for digital. Another concern you may have is that most people feel overloaded at work, and if you give your sales-people yet another thing to do they might rebel. You can, and in fact should, pilot these ideas on a smaller scale, but your final implementation must be couched as organizational change.

Getting started

We'll assume that at this point you are looking to run a pilot, and that you need to test and explore the ideas in this book. There are some initial pieces you will need to put into place. One change you will need to make straight away is to bring the marketing and sales teams closer together. Traditionally these teams tend to sit at opposite sides of the office and throw rocks at each other. You need to change that.

Social selling works by exposing individuals within the business on social networks. A common mistake people make is to assume that companies have any importance at all in social selling. They generally don't. Changemakers want to involve a person in their team, not a business. The fact they work for company XYZ is in some ways harmful because the changemaker is looking to manage out bias, and so the salesperson may be less attractive just because they work for such-and-such a company. The changemaker is very much in 'salesperson avoidance mode'.

(This changes at the point of implementation because the business then moves into a mode where capability overrides bias. The business will want to engage a supply partner with a proven brand, proven track record, etc. in order to manage out risk.)

Social salespeople therefore need to be adept at marketing because they are selling themselves and their own authority and credibility into the changemaker's social network, with some support from their employer's reputation and branding. A social salesperson must soften the market in the same way a marketing team would, preparing the ground with skilfully positioned messages that aid discoverability. A changemaker won't listen to 'Hi, I'm Bob from XYZ plc' because the changemaker doesn't 'see' the 'XYZ plc' part. A changemaker wants to hear 'Hi, I'm Bob, and hey did you see this reputation I personally have in the area of hosted telephony?'

Most salespeople will need help in improving this skill, and that help is more easily obtained if marketing and sales have a closer, more collegiate relationship. Some people use a neologisms to describe this new aggregated team: RevOps, or revenue operations, which represents the merger of sales and marketing.

Even in very large organizations, you are likely only to find one person who really gets this whole idea and can act as a champion (this might be you). You're looking for someone who is a white tiger or a black swan, in other words very rare. They need to understand the sociological changes that have created a change in buyer behaviour, they have to be able to work within the connected economy as if they were born into it, but they absolutely must have respect from the organization as being someone who is a changemaker and has over-delivered to the business time and time again. You need that person who will run with it, make the whole idea work, and have the trust of the organization, so that when it comes time to make this larger-scale permanent change, senior management will believe it will work.

A word of warning – in 10 years' time that person will almost certainly be the sales director of your business.

FIGURE 11.2   Sales and marketing working together for a common purpose

Step 1: Setting up shop

Salespeople have always known that the sales process centres around people. When we say, 'Go out there and find opportunities', we're not proposing
hunting around in the dirt in the way a pig might hunt for truffles.
Opportunities are always 'attached' to people, and generally speaking the
more people the salesperson deals with, the more conversations they have,
the more opportunities they will find.

Given that opportunities are attached to people, and given that changemakers don't see corporate allegiances, setting up shop is much more like
setting up multiple franchises as opposed to one huge, flagship, cornerstone-
of-the-mall type of shop. You will need exactly one franchise – exactly one
shop – per salesperson, and the first practical step on the path (Changemaker
Method Step 1) is to set up these shops. This is your social media profile.

Each shop needs to be branded as belonging to the individual salesperson, and this needs to be done in a way that aids discovery to the changemaker who is looking for a particular mix of skills and capability. 'Bob, the
expert in hosted telephony, who happens to work for company XYZ (the
leading supplier of hosted telephony services)' is the correct cadence here.
It's 'Bob' – it's personal. He's 'an expert' – he's attractive to the changemaker
who's trying to build an ad hoc team to ideate a solution. Finally, 'he works
for company XYZ' – however, this part comes into play more when it comes
to the 'beauty parade' part of the sales process when the supplier is chosen.

FIGURE 11.3   LinkedIn titles that create curiosity

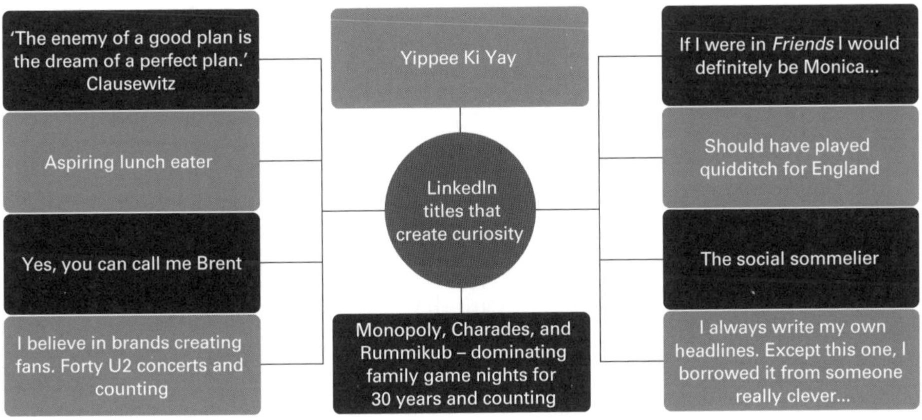

Social selling is 'bigger' than the social networks that we use today. At the moment, we have some services that we can use, but we have to assume that in the long term the presence and/or usefulness of those tools will change. Today, the tool you need to use in the first instance is LinkedIn. Remember, social selling is the result of sociological change, so in terms of strategy you need to be thinking in generational timescales. IT services pop into and out of existence very quickly over those timescales.

But back to LinkedIn for now. The most important thing to sort in the first instance is to get a picture up, and a summary. Your profile is about you, not your company and its products and services; as a buyer, I'm looking for a helper, a Sherpa, so this needs to tell a story about you. Let's not forget, you are unique and the thing that is attractive about you is all of your experiences.

Figure 11.3 shows some examples of LinkedIn summary titles – don't forget this is about getting somebody to be curious and come and read your profile. Of course, you can have your job title on your job details lower down on your profile. You may not like some of these titles, this is fine. In life, not everybody will buy from you and actually you are using this as a way of saving time. If somebody does not like your title, then great, you have qualified them out as they were never going to buy from you anyway. One of the many great efficiency savings of social selling.

Do not make the mistake of getting a profile writer in. This is fake and is spotted a mile away. It is also not 'change'. Rather than having a process where you end up with a team of social sellers, you will end up with a team of analogue salespeople who have had their profiles written by a profile writer. Each person's profile needs to be authentic and natural, and in the salesperson's own voice. But it needs to be done in a way that encourages discoverability and connection, and is in line with the organization's marketing strategy. This is why marketing needs to be closely involved.

The next stage is that you as a salesperson need to connect with people and to have conversations with these people. Who do you target? The people you are trying to sell to and influence. When you connect, don't pitch; we all hate being sold to. This is you building a network with the other person and engaging in conversation with them.

Conversations come from connecting, but also from posting content. This means they need to be posting content they find online (content curation), creating original content (content creation), prospecting for new people to talk to, and engaging with other people on the network (amplification – sharing, liking or direct conversations). If they don't do this, to keep stretching the shop metaphor, the doors are locked and the shutters are down. The shop is only open if the salesperson is engaging.

What does 'amplification' mean? A contact of mine has just tagged a leadership team in on one of my posts. This means my post is amplified, but it also means I have an 'excuse' to have a conversation with each of this leadership team. In the analogue world you had to make a number of calls, and in the digital world you also need to be connecting and having conversations. The difference is that in an analogue world you interrupted people and pitched, but in the digital world you will find that conversations will flow naturally. That is, as long as you don't pitch.

Most salespeople know if they make a certain number of calls, they'll get a certain number of meetings, then a certain number of opportunities, then a certain number of deals. For them, the phone calls are what keep the shop open. Tell them to stop making the calls and start spending that same time on LinkedIn. Social media is open 24 hours a day, 366 days a year and you can prospect whenever you want – the more time you spend on social, the more success you will get.

I also suggest that you take this approach over to Twitter. B2B social selling works extremely well on Twitter as this network evolved from the ground up to actually support the process of ideation – after all, Twitter is about conversations.

Step 2: Learning to listen – having conversations

At this point we have a group of salespeople all with their own 'shop', who keep that shop open by posting links to other people's content, posting their original content, and working to develop connection via conversations. The next step (Changemaker Method Step 2) is to start scaling the process out. In particular, you now need to solve the classic social selling problem of the salesperson, asking, 'How do I talk to someone I don't know?'

The approach that kills social selling stone dead is doing what you have always done in the analogue world but doing it on social. Turning up onto social and interrupting and pitching will be seen as spam and you will soon burn through your network. Remember our changemaker – they're trying to build a team, and you want to be part of it, but the changemaker a) doesn't know what they want yet as they're still ideating a solution, and b) doesn't want to hear 'biased' messages from suppliers at this point. If the changemaker says, 'Hey guys, can you help me understand why phone calls keep being dropped?', the social salesperson must *not* at this stage say, '10 Per Cent Off Hosted Telephony Solutions – Offer Must End Monday!'

Whilst the salesperson is working LinkedIn as per the above, they will naturally be having conversations. For example, if they share a post someone else has written on the benefits of hosted telephony, the original author may say, 'Hey, thanks for sharing my post.' The salesperson can then say, 'No problem – I thought it was interesting, especially the part about ABC, but I wasn't sure about the XYZ part?' From that point, a conversation can flow, and a relationship can be developed. This can seem strange to some salespeople, but think of the simple psychology – the modern buyer does not like being sold to, they want to be helped, so if you don't sell to the modern buyer and you help them, you get a great response. After all, that is what you want.

In our experience, what we have covered in this book will enable you to sell higher and faster than the traditional sales methods. We have also found that selling like this enables you to convert more senior-level calls.

In our work we see that there are three types of people out there:

- people you can sell to
- people that won't buy from you but may refer you
- people that are willing to amplify you through their networks

Social selling operates much more like networking, and the trick is to build up a good deal of high-quality connections, regardless of whether those people are likely to become your direct customers. We'll talk much more about trust, authority, and influence in a later section, but for now any relationship with someone who has authority and influence within their chosen space is valuable to a social salesperson, regardless of whether they have a burning desire to drop an opportunity into the sales funnel.

FIGURE 11.4   Example conversations on social media

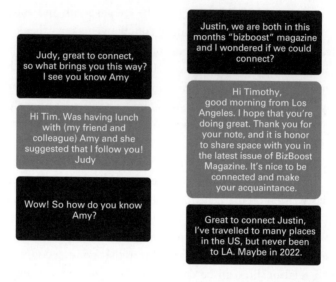

The second step is to start adding scale, and this means listening to what's happening on the social network and responding, as opposed to broadcasting a message to the market and listening and reacting to the response. This is an area that traditional salespeople typically do not understand. They are used to working through lists, trying interruptions typically crafted along the same proven message until someone bites. This is the classic sales mantra of 'If you ask enough boys/girls at a dance to dance, someone will dance with you.'

A traditional salesperson would approach all 50 people with the same broadcast message – 'Come Dance With Me! Offer Must End Midnight!' This is where the modern salesperson needs to grow their conversational skills. Of the 50 people you could ask to dance, find the one that looks a little nervous and go to them with a 'confidence' message: 'Come on, I'm really good at dancing, we'll have a good time!' To the second person who exudes confidence: 'I'm really good at dancing. Are you as good at dancing as I think you are?' The result is the same (you get to dance), the position is the same ('I'm good at dancing!'), but the message is different. In the digital world, personalization of message is key.

To an extent, the analogue method is a result of the traditional sales person having only a small amount of information available to them before they deliver the message. All they may have had is a name, a company name and a phone number. But with social media prospects are transmitting information all the time, and this information coming from the prospect allows the social salesperson to microcraft and retarget their positioning message. Plus, it stops them having to ask 50 people to dance on the off chance that two say yes. They can concentrate on the two they know they can craft a good message for and just approach them. This is one of the many efficiencies of social selling – you can easily qualify out people who are not going to buy.

I'll restate that as it's a particularly important point. Social selling is about carefully approaching the right people, slowly and in a considered fashion, one-to-one, with the correct message. It is not about plastering a 'good enough' message over a huge audience, hoping one will be interrupted in such a way that they bite. This is why traditional marketing is based on waste. You try to appeal to as many people as you can and at the same time appeal to nobody. As we talk about in this book, when you walk into a room of 100 people, using social networks you should have already worked out the 20 people useful to you.

One of the challenges to salespeople who are new to social media in general is that this can feel a little creepy. Those people tend to think of this as 'stalking'. It really isn't. People posting on social networks – even when that post is personal – want the audience; they want the attention in exactly the same way as a playwright wants people to go and see their plays. A playwright doesn't write a play in the hope no one will go and see the opening night! They write it in the hope every man, woman and dog in the country will go and see it. If I post an article, I want people to read it and to comment, they can agree or disagree, either way I am into a conversation with them.

Listening also applies to competitors. One of the dark secrets about social selling is that because your salespeople are operating out in public, everyone can see what they are doing, including your competitors. It's perfectly easy, especially on Twitter, to monitor conversations and map connections. As soon as you identify top social salespeople at your competitors, you can see who they are talking to and listen to the conversations. The information gleaned from that activity can only ever be useful. Then, if you're particularly Machiavellian, do feel free to find the top social salespeople at your competitors and poach them!

Step 3: Building authority and influence

At this point we have a collection of salespeople who have set up their own individual shops, they're active on their social networks and keeping the shop running, and they're learning how to turn their attention out from their immediate environment through social listening. At this point, they're starting to scale and have conversations.

The next thing that we need to do is to start building up influence and authority (Changemaker Method Step 3). Although this is midway through our five-step plan to change the organization, it is the final step in the maturation task the individual salesperson has to complete in order to become a social salesperson. Once they do this, the individual has completed their changes and can turn to optimizing their own social selling skills. The final two steps in the Changemaker Method look to change and optimize the organization.

Recall that the changemaker is ultimately trying to build an ad hoc team that is given the task of ideating a solution to a business problem. The changemaker chooses members of the team based on trust. The salesperson's job is to exude enough trust through the social network that the changemaker chooses them to be part of the team. The first two steps – setting up shop and listening – go towards making the salesperson discoverable. This third step is about making them trustable. The changemaker says, 'You seem to know what you're doing – can you help us with this problem about dropping calls?' The 'you' can only happen if they have been discovered; the 'seem to know what you're doing' comes from trust, and that comes from influence and authority.

You have to have set up your shop window on social, to be connected to the right people you want to influence and to be posting engaging content if you want to be found. If you don't do these three things you are invisible to the people you want to sell to and influence.

Building authority and influence is actually very easy. You need to be putting messages out into the network that deliver insight. This is done through content curation and content creation. Content curation is where you find information that might be of use to people who you want to have relation-ships with and put it out into your social network. The idea is that if you say to your contacts, 'Hey everyone, here's a great piece on the risks around hosted telephony implementation', you're offering something up on the understanding that it might be helpful. It also makes you not look like just another salesperson, but an expert who can help. Social networks exist within the connected economy, and the currency of the connected economy is appreciation. If you deliver insight to someone by pointing them at some interesting content, that person will 'pay' for that value by increasing your authority.

Think about it – if somebody retweets your content, you are going to feel inwardly pleased about that and pleased with the person. If they make a comment about how good your content is and amplify that through your network then (hopefully) you will make a mental note that the person is 'good'. Which is why your shop window needs to be 'memorable' and stand out. The mechanism by which this happens is they (at a baseline level) amplify your message by sharing or retweeting, or they will 'pay more' by actually going out into their network and advocating you. 'Hey everyone, Bob/Brenda shared this great piece on XYZ – you should follow them.'

Content curation is by far the easiest thing to do when it comes to build-ing authority and influence, and this should be happening on a daily basis. The nature of these networks is that posting a lot of curated content is per-fectly OK – if it's on message. If you have 1,000 people in your network, and you curate 10 links a day on Twitter, they are not getting 'spammed' each with 10 links a day. It'll appear on their timeline and if they happen to look at their timeline when you post something they'll see it. Timelines and news streams on social networks are something that people dip in and out of, so don't fear posting a lot.

However, content curation only gets you so far. Effectiveness of content curation can be measured by how much you are being amplified, and from there you can use amplification to gauge authority and influence. Those measures tell you that you are delivering value, which is obviously good. If you share a Forbes article, the influence sits with Forbes. People may recog-nize you for sharing that article, but we know you didn't write it. We love what you wrote in terms of the context, as it saves me reading the article, but it does not make you an expert. I'm not saying don't share articles, I'm just saying sharing other people's insight only gets you so far.

If you want to deliver more value, you have to deliver unique ideas into the network, and this means you need to create content. You can create whatever content you like – blogging is very easy. Video blogging is also easy, and is sufficiently 'new and shiny' that, in comparison to blogging, the same ideas should get amplified more through video channels. (We believe the future of content is video (and live streaming) so if you have an appetite to get into this, you should.) You can also create content on Pinterest, Snapchat or Instagram. The channel or packaging is not important – what's important is that ideas are novel and original, and create curiosity in the reader to find out more about you. And you end up in a conversation with them.

(Also, don't be worried about using the 'wrong' sort of channel for B2B. If you run a network cabling business and want to put (with permission) photos of particularly good cabling jobs on Instagram, go right ahead. The changemaker doesn't care where this stuff is. All you want is for the change-maker to look at it and go, 'That's a neat cabling job – I should get to know that person!')

It is likely that, in a team of salespeople, not everyone will want to do this or indeed be able to do it. Creating content is a skill in itself, and creating good content is difficult. We'd recommend managers find the one or two people who can actually make a decent job of it, and a) encourage them and b) give them the freedom to do it. We are aware of a sales guy whose dog has 2,000 followers on Twitter. Embrace this.

This will seem like a lot of work, but the reality is that this aspect is essential to reaching a broad audience. You ultimately want each salesperson and the greater sales team to be 'attractors' to the changemakers out there in your chosen space. They are looking for initial value by way of information as an indicator of trustability. If you provide that, and you have salespeople who are able to have meaningful conversations with those people they meet on social networks, you're home and dry.

A final piece of advice on content creation – while you need to give your team guidelines, you should also empower them to be authentic and let them talk in their own voice. Why? Because your ideal client may not like you and your tone, but they may like one of your team. After all, this is about winning a sale and letting the buyer find the person they work with best. As a business, you should have wide and varied content and tone of content across your business.

FIGURE 11.5   Build authority and influence

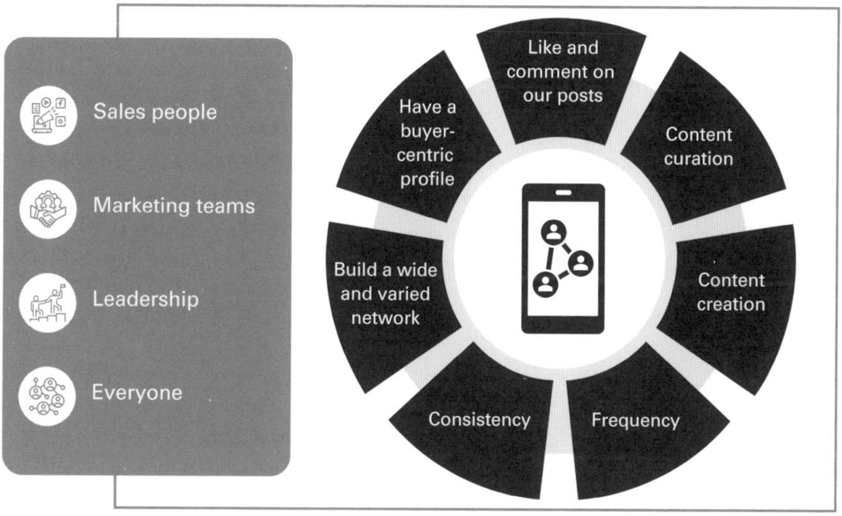

Step 4: Optimizing

At this point, the individual salesperson's job is complete and, as mentioned, they will be in a place of optimizing what they do. They have a shop, they have a network that they are developing relationships in, they are scaling out that network by using listening and having conversations, and they are building authority and influence through content curation and possibly through content creation. At this point, they are social selling.

The next steps look at improving the organization's capability at executing social selling. This step (Changemaker Method Step 4) is about starting to fill in support to the sales team and giving them the tools to optimize around this new way of working.

Generally in social sales, the process of nurturing a lead to close doesn't change from how it worked in traditional sales. You still need to qualify the lead into an opportunity. You still need to have meetings and conversations, develop the solution into an implementation plan, and then look attractive enough so that the customer chooses you to deliver the final product. Using social selling, you use the same techniques I talked about in terms of prospecting to nurture the sales along. In the old days of sales, to nurture a sale you had to call or email the prospect and annoy them with an interruption. Now, with your amazing content, help and wisdom you are waving at them every day. As they want to be on social this isn't seen as an interruption, in fact it's seen as helpful. If the whole of your business is doing this, this is where you can be digitally dominant and the client sees you and your business as the only answer to their business issue.

A particular point of caution here is that if you do this badly, the 'voice' that comes through will be inauthentic. An inauthentic voice – an overly robotic, obviously automated voice – is anathema on social media. An inauthentic voice indicates that messages are not being individually 'micro-crafted', as we discussed before, and it will cause a decrease in authority, and a knock-on decrease in influence.

Step 5: Enhancing collaboration

At this point, individual salespeople are acting as social salespeople, and the sales organization is starting to discover and deploy tools and procedures to support this new way of working.

The final step on the path (Changemaker Method Step 5) represents scaling out of the collaboration that you have created between the sales and marketing teams and starting to take it out to other departments and channel partner organizations. It represents the digital transformation of the entire business to one that 'plays nicely' with the connected economy.

Organizations have traditionally been set up in a way that predates the connected economy – i.e. they are mostly hierarchical (top-down management), and mostly siloed off into separate departments. Those departments tend to be operated in a reasonably procedural fashion. All of this makes sense – businesses are like sausage machines; all you have to do is crank the handle, the machinery turns and raw meat goes in at one side and sausages come out at the other. That process of transformation is how value gets delivered, and profit is given as a reward for that value.

The idea of the connected economy is to allow people to work together in a more natural and fluid way. At the end of the day, we're all people who are looking to work together and do a good job. Take two businesses that want to work together as customer and supplier. In reality, it's not and never has been the two businesses that want to work together; it's human beings who happen to be employed by one side or the other that want to work together.

FIGURE 11.6   Social media is an enabler across the whole of your business

This is the first principle of the connected economy – stripping away organizational boundaries and allowing people to do the job they need to do in the best way they can. Those boundaries can be internal (as we have said before about needing to bring sales and marketing together), or they can be external (as in the example above, of two business).

Businesses that are very rigid, partitioned and siloed, with lots of boundaries, are very inflexible. Connected economy ideas 'plasticize' inflexible businesses, making them more able to react and adapt. In our opinion, all businesses should operate internally, with suppliers, partners and customers, as connected economy entities, which is why we say that enhancing this capability to collaborate completes the organization's journey from traditional selling to social selling.

Summary

In this chapter we took you through a thorough grounding in the 'how' of social selling. We started by looking at the five steps of the Changemaker Method – setting up shop, learning to listen, building authority and influence, having conversations, optimizing the process and enhancing collaboration. Importantly, we discussed how social selling had to be introduced as complete organizational change, as opposed to something just to be 'spread' on top of the sales process. We then drilled into a detail of each one, looking at practical ideas that you can use to start delivering results from social selling.

This methodology enables teams to get social selling, to break through the mantra of personal branding and really start building their own communities and influence. Yes, this requires us to change the way we work, but it is our belief that we need to disrupt ourselves in the connected economy.

Conclusion

We hope this book has convinced you that analogue selling has changed, along with social selling and personal branding, and that you can recognize the emergence of Social Selling 2.0. Digital selling is no longer about a LinkedIn profile giving you the competitive edge. An amazing LinkedIn profile won't pay the rent. A sale, after all, is about leads, conversation, sales pursuits and winning deals to create revenue and profit.

As the digital landscape has changed buyer habits, it is increasingly difficult to reach them early enough in their decision-making process using traditional sales methods. Developing relationships with decision makers through social networks has become an increasingly critical skill – enabling sales professionals to engage early on and 'hack' the buying process.

Social Selling provides a practical, step-by-step blueprint for harnessing these specifics, and we hope you have enjoyed these proven techniques, including:

- how to use networks purposefully to build social trust and create a high-quality community
- how to develop real influence and authority in your subject area, and connect and have conversations with the buying team, which may include changemakers
- how to scale the social selling strategy across an organization, including maturity and investment models, risk and governance, and technology platforms

In addition, we have outlined what we think is essential reading for sales professionals, digital sales directors and subject matter experts who want to embrace the power of social selling in their organization. Regardless of whether your company is big or small, B2B or B2C, you now have:

- a 'how to' guide, providing a clear, step-by-step blueprint for social selling success based on building authority and influence in target communities

- practical and proven advice borne of hard-won experience rolling out these techniques across large sales forces
- an outline of how to roll this strategy out across an organization, including investment, risk and governance, and working across teams and technology platforms

The day when Matt Reynolds and I sat in a coffee shop in London and came up with the idea for the first edition of this book is still etched in our memories. We both felt that the arguments for social selling hadn't moved forward in years. Since I set up DLA Ignite we have proven the arguments and turned social selling from a niche into selling. There is no need to call it social selling anymore, as it's the way high-performance companies sell.

Many people saw social selling being all about starting a sale, often called prospecting, the start of the sales process and demand generation; there was nobody writing about how to use social and digital during the sales pursuit. In fact, the whole subject had been (and we don't mean to offend any marketers reading) hijacked by the marketing department, because people see them as demand generators and therefore surely social selling all sits with them?

Our other observation of social selling was that it was all about creating a personal brand, which we felt was all very 'So what?' Or people were talking about social selling as being about a tool such as LinkedIn. As a business, we are all about selling things and generating cash, and this book has connected being on social with revenue and EBITDA.

When we pitched the idea to our publisher Kogan Page, they went away and did a review of social selling books. We breathed a sigh of relief when they came back and said, 'We don't want a book on personal branding; there are already too many books on this subject.' The fact that we were going to completely change the narrative about the use of social and digital selling was what got us the book deal. Since writing the first edition of social selling, we have seen many books on how to use LinkedIn, or books on templates, in other words how to spam on social, but no books on the process of being social, on social.

If there is one thing we can predict with certainty, it is that there will always be change taking place in the world of social and digital. Social or digital selling is very much in its infancy, and people will think up more and more ways for how social can help find influencers, change agents and buyers within accounts and how social media will continue to help us sell products and services.

That said, there are some things that won't change. We have always said that selling has not changed with the introduction of digital. Yes, maybe there are new methods, but we are still looking for people in our accounts and then trying to build rapport with them. It is now just easier to do this using online techniques.

Since writing the first edition of this book, we now foresee a complete switch to social. People who tell you that cold calling is dead are right – there is no place for any form of interruption and broadcast (including email marketing and advertising) in the world today. By reading this book, you are gaining significant competitive advantage through being able to implement this strategy ahead of the competition. I'm sure your competitors will be sitting in a meeting one day with their sales figures gradually going downwards and ask, 'Where did that come from?'

One of my team told a story the other day about one of our customers. They posted a humanized post on LinkedIn, got into a conversation and were immediately asked to bid for $100,000 of business. He was in the right place at the right time, but isn't that often the case in sales? The other two companies on the shortlist had been out-sold by social.

With the evolvement in social and digital, so, too, do you need to evolve the ideas we have written about in this book. If everybody is creating an online community, then what moves the needle any more? We therefore see an 'arms race' in online techniques, and in fact companies will start seeing the strategies, behaviours and techniques they employ as core to their identity. Online will become part of a company's DNA.

We are not aware (yet) of any company that has built social and digital into the terms and conditions of an employment contract. People have rules about contacting customers and using physical assets, but not digital assets. For example, say you work for company A and they pay for your LinkedIn profile, and during your time working for them in sales you build a strong community and network. If you leave company A and go to their competitor, who now owns that asset? In the United States people already have separate personal and work LinkedIn and Twitter accounts. Will this just become seen as 'noise' as we move from role to role and company to company? In the old days, people took their Rolodex or 'black book' of contacts with them, and companies didn't do anything then.

The future of personal branding

Personal branding is great, but it has key limitations. Yes, people will look you up before a meeting and make a judgement on what you are like and how that meeting will go; interesting, boring… They will do that by looking at the blogs you have written, the industry knowledge you can demonstrate, and most of all whether it looks like you can help them.

While a few 'corporate articles' will be OK, being the echo chamber of your company PR department is going to look pretty boring. In fact, because it will look like you obviously cannot have your own opinions or an open view, I doubt the person in that meeting will trust what you say, or want to meet you. The expectation is that you will just be talking the company line. But people want help, they need to be educated.

Over the next few years, people will realize that we cannot all be a thought leader, and therefore to expect everybody to strive to be so is a waste of time. That said, there does seem to be a rise in the 'corporate nominee thought leader'. As corporations move up the social maturity model, they suddenly realize they have 'social champions' and 'change agents'. But what they won't have done is nurture this talent. So they do one of three things, using what are known as black hat techniques (the baddies in cowboy movies always wore black hats, and the good guys wore white hats).

The first would be for a corporation to socially promote a vice president or senior person, but with somebody else running their social for them. My advice to anybody reading this is, if you suspect any person of having their social run for them, ask them questions. Ask them online and when you see them about the material they have posted. You can soon see the charlatans.

The second thing corporations do is promote people who have little or no social footprint; usually they are cajoled into writing corporate articles under the pretence they are writing for themselves. This often works for a short while and is done as part of a project to increase 'share of voice'. Let's not forget that 'share of voice' is a measure of how much mud you can throw at a wall, the aim being to throw more than the competition. This is great, but we're not sure how many leads it creates. Buyers today are not fools, they can all smell when somebody is having content written for them and they know it's false. Sometimes, good does come out of this, though, as often just forcing people to blog means they gain confidence and then find their voice. The Rolling Stones started as a covers band until their manager locked Mick Jagger and Keith Richards in a room and told them he wouldn't let them out until they had written a song.

The third thing that companies do is bring in outside talent, in the belief that they don't have social talent within the company. Companies have to get better at finding and nurturing talent internally. This is something you cannot force. People are believable thought leaders or they are not. People either want to be and have a passion to be a thought leader or they don't. Somebody once asked us in a meeting, 'So how do I find these people in my company?' The answer is very simple – you will find them online.

For us, personal branding has a 'high watermark' (apart from being likeable online) that people need to be looking to achieve: gaining inbound traffic. What do we mean by that? This is where people are approaching you, the ultimate being a request about your products and services. But then again it could be a speaker request.

One sales guy we trained was almost a blank canvas, as the company he had previously worked for didn't do social. We helped him rewrite his LinkedIn profile from scratch, and explained how to use LinkedIn to build a community and nurture a platform. He rang me up one day when a prospect of his liked a graphic he had posted. It was a great example of cause and effect, and this was the start for him of a journey in social, personal branding and the aim of inbound and influence. Since starting DLA Ignite we have trained and coached thousands of businesses to lead with social, and the transformation has changed business.

Talking with strangers

In Chapter 3 on talking to strangers we discussed how social, in a way, goes against everything our parents told us, which was never to talk to strangers. Social and networking requires us to work in teams and collaborate, but it also requires us to talk to people we don't know.

As we discussed, networking for networking's sake has a very low return, as we can end up talking to people who are of little or no use to us. We have to get better at finding the right people and having the right conversations with people. There are no excuses not to have found out about somebody before you meet him or her.

The clever bit is still about finding and focusing on who the right people are to talk to. Influence has many guises. In the previous chapters we talked about how influence in your territory can come from outside your territory. A person might have left one of your accounts, but prospects may still call up for his or her advice and guidance.

There is a view that the territories of the future will be allocated based on who you know and the community you have built rather than the usual postal/zip codes, etc. If you could measure a salesperson's network, influence and community based on amplification, engagement and interaction then that would be useful. Better still would be if you could do this across multiple social graphs and see it visualized. This would certainly help (along with a sales track record and excellent references) recruit the 'A-players' of the future. I'm sure companies would pay for this as there would be a great business case for reducing the number of failed recruits and enabling salespeople to get selling quicker.

Growing your network

People often ask us, how do we measure progress? Here you can use leading indicators, such as the number of connections a salesperson has, the growth of that network, the amount of engagement a salesperson gets on their content, the number of online conversations they have, the number of offline meetings they have, the number of proposals, etc.

The difficulty is that influence crosses many social networks and extends, whether you like it or not, into Facebook, Instagram, etc. Wouldn't it be great, as a recruiting company (and also as a salesperson) to have a way to measure a salesperson's influence, network and community?

At the time of writing, I understand that LinkedIn is looking to map connections and networks (we use the term network and not community). This is more about helping sales teams or companies where they have multiple salespeople selling into the one account. When we played football (soccer) at school, the whole group of us ran round the ball hoping to get a kick. Then somebody introduced us to passing and marking, and suddenly the game changed. This is the objective we have always wanted to achieve through team selling, and maybe through LinkedIn we will.

But that still does not allow us to see the influence on our accounts from externals.

Changemakers

Changemakers are people in accounts who have influence but probably have little authority.

In our experience, organizations are becoming more reliant on them for decisions. Many boards of directors have realized that they don't 'get' social and that they need people they can rely on to help them make the move to a digital business. As we covered in the chapter on risk, just getting your intern to do the social may be low cost but could have a negative impact on your brand.

Changemakers, therefore, are seen as being social but also having the business acumen to know what makes a good social media post and which post will see the world come crashing down around your ears. As they further enhance this role, and become mentors to sales, marketing and management, we see them becoming the leaders of the future.

As suppliers, you need to be seeking out changemakers and nurturing their talent so they can lead the social projects that will implement the strategies in this book, which will create leads, revenue and competitive advantage. In sales pursuits, you need to be looking out for them and bringing them onside to your campaign. In fact, we think that without access to a changemaker you won't make a sale.

LinkedIn figures say that on average 10 stakeholders in any organization are needed within the company to make a sale. Companies such as this have a requirement for multiple people to make a decision. Internally for a company this works as it lessens (by spreading) the risk of a wrong decision being made. Most people understand that nowadays you need consensus in any decision. But any decision for your product or service will most likely require a level of change, be it a change in supplier or a change in the way people will work. Naturally people don't like change, and you may well therefore come across people who will block or stop your proposal. They may even tell you they like your proposal but still try to block it. That is why we see changemakers as people who can see a tangible benefit to your product and service. You still need to follow the same routes, build a business case and talk to and influence the usual stakeholders. At some stage in the selling process the changemaker will be asked, 'What do you think of solutions A, B and C? What's your advice?'

Changemakers are often involved in the buying process, but sometimes they are not. Don't forget their natural habitat is online. So, just as we will make a decision to stay at a hotel by looking on Tripadvisor, they are likely to be making decisions based on what they see online.

Influence marketing

We can see that influence marketing will grow in its use by brands and suppliers. Television has limited reach as people watch more YouTube videos and stream more content. It is now easier for some brands and marketers to pay a blogger/vlogger money to promote a product, or to give their product to an English Premier League footballer, than it is to create an ad and buy ad space.

As we mention in this book, influence comes in many forms, and the large companies such as Gartner, Accenture, etc., will always provide influence. But we will see a further rise of the online influencer and 'micro' online influencer. Influence can be very 'David and Goliath', and the Goliath influencers will still be out there: the social media celebrities – we all know who they are. In addition, there will also be the social media 'Davids' who may be relevant for your niche, target market or the message you want to get across. Sometimes the influence may extend to a particular social network platform. You may be targeting people and a Snapchat influencer will fit the market and age group you are looking at.

Brands still cling to the belief that the employee brand advocacy programme is great as you can control the message by telling people what to tweet. But if you want more reach and influence you need to let go of the leash on the employees and open up to influencers. You may not be able to control the message, but you will get more reach and amplification for your dollar.

Brands and suppliers do have to become more sophisticated about influence marketing. Currently sophistication levels are pretty low, with it not being very different from old-school advertising, sales events or product placement. Often this is because people don't understand how to harness influence, or they use old world/analogue techniques in a digital world. Brands also have to understand that sometimes it doesn't work. A brand once gave us free phones, and when we used them we didn't like them. Obviously, the actual cost to the supplier of the phone was relatively low, but it did mean there was a major impact for that supplier.

How the marketing mix changes

We are not saying you should move everything into one area. Marketing has been and always will be about a mix of activities. We are saying that you need to move your marketing budget to where your customers are, and that's online. At this point, you need to experiment and find what works for you. In this age of disruption, all the old assumptions we made about business are up for re-evaluation.

Creating content is just about sitting down and finding the time to write that content. But is anybody listening? That is why we wrote about the need for community and not just followers so early in the book. This is such an important investment and asset for a company. As we said, community is *not* an email list, it is an active network of people sharing and amplifying ideas and content. They will be your prospects, customers, advocates and influencers, all working together to drive your brand's success. Note I've said prospects, as there is no reason why people who haven't purchased won't be ready to buy from you when their time is right.

Social maturity – ramping up quicker

In Chapter 9 on social maturity, we went through the steps that a company needs to take to move from being an analogue business to a digital one. We argued that there are no short cuts; there needs to be an organic growth of social in an organization, and you cannot just decide to be social by command and control. That said, many companies need to accelerate their way through the steps and the only way you can manage any change programme that needs different processes and behaviours is by training. We see so many companies 'doing' social, when really they are just 'spinning their wheels' and wasting their time while their competitors overtake them. Training must be top-down and this means that the senior management must lead by example.

We see so many opportunities for CEOs of organizations to explain to the world their company's story and brand. You only have to look at the number of Richard Branson quotes that are shared online. We wonder sometimes, did he actually ever say them? But it doesn't matter; we have inspirational quotes posted by people who have nothing to do with his brands, and this is free advertising. There are many more inspirational CEOs out there than the few we see quoted. Getting the message across is pretty simple. Just think of the (revenue) impact it would make if your CEO's leadership and inspiration was visible and being shared.

We agree that you run the risk of producing navel-gazing management consulting speak that is full of jargon. But isn't that the point of employing

SOCIAL SELLING

and nurturing people that understand social, have the relevant business acumen and are able to stand up to the internal forces that don't actually 'get' social but think they do?

One of the reasons we came up with the maturity model was so that companies can benchmark themselves as to where they are. Senior executives who might not really 'get' social can spot the symptoms or effects of what is being played back in their organization. We have seen people in organizations get prizes for posting the most corporate content. As I've said before, people are not on social to read your brochures.

There used to be a health and safety video in the UK about the dangers of swimming in the sea. The video explained to the layperson why they needed to be careful about being swept out to sea, but it also explained what a person should do – firstly to recognize that somebody was drowning, and secondly what to do to save them. These random acts of social are like watching a drowning person thrash around in the sea. Organizations need to understand that random acts of social don't help you. In the health and safety video, a passer-by thinks the drowning person is waving at them and just waves back. Random acts of social are not about how you are progressing – you are drowning. You need to recognize this and throw somebody a lifeline.

Taking the organization together for all disciplines and skill sets is critical. Random acts of social just put people off and they just mentally 'pull up the drawbridge' and switch off.

Future technology

Since writing the first edition of this book, there has been an explosion in the world of marketing technology, often shortened to martech. There are many tools that offer the buyer a claim that they will do social. In the tools I have seen, and I tend to have somebody pitch me a 'new' tool on a weekly basis, none actually do social selling. They may do an element of it, but not the whole process. But there again, how will a tool replicate your humanity? I mentioned before that social networks are based on the fact that buyers and sellers turn up. If one person sends a robot, this is a signal to the team that you cannot be bothered and then they will not turn up. This is when social media collapses.

Changes in terminology

Digital has provided businesses with a step change in terminology and language. Terms such as MQLs (marketing qualified leads), BQLs (business qualified leads), and SQLs (sales qualified leads) do increase the amount of terminology, which isn't good. But they help to define what a lead is, and provide a common framework for sales and marketing. For us salespeople we can define how a lead is qualified, and so how likely it is to turn into revenue. This is a major step forward.

But what about qualifying these leads? There is a qualification acronym called BANT – budget, authority, need and timescales. There are others, but what is their relevance in this digital world?

Lack of relevance of BANT

A note on BANT: we are seeing in the sales world that qualification mechanisms like BANT are becoming redundant as a lead qualification methodology. In the past, sales teams would qualify an account based on the fact that you were talking to somebody with a 'need' who had 'authority'. Sales managers and sales training would always insist that a salesperson ask the customer or prospect, 'What is the budget?' The customer would say yes, they had a budget, whether they did or they didn't. They knew that if they said they didn't have a budget the salesperson would get in their car and drive away. The salesperson was always taught to ask when the customer would buy. That is, what month or week, etc., enabling the salesperson to fill in the fields in the CRM systems.

We are now seeing – especially in the world of digital selling – that the buyer is doing most of the buying process online. Combine that with a digitally dominant sales force and your business will often be seen as the only answer to a client's business problem, and that means you get business via a single tender.

Salespeople now, using digital as well as their own selling skills, can create content that walks the buyer through the buying process. You can use content to create desire as well as create content that provides the customer or prospect with a business case. Any vendor that has been through the last few recessions will have created an ROI tool in some shape or format. Now while a customer won't always believe a vendor's ROI figures – sometimes they can read a bit like the Immaculate Conception – they will want to work with a partner. The content you create will demonstrate your expertise and give the prospect a head start.

Any B2B purchase will require some change to go with it, and customers will want to understand how it will impact their organization; the people, the process, the technology and the risks. Customers will want to know how you implemented it elsewhere, where it went wrong and where it went right. Again, you can help buyers with content that will support all of this. Buyers also, as you have demonstrated your expertise online, invite you in to sit on the 'top table' to advise them in terms of their challenges. After all, the prospect can see online that you are an expert.

Customers are far too wise for suppliers to hide where things went wrong. Everybody knows that any programme of change will hit 'turbulence', but what customers want to know is how you managed it and what they can do to mitigate those risks. Buyers are not stupid, they are not interested in corporate content, but they are interested in content that will genuinely help them. So when you read that the modern salesperson needs to 'add value' and provide insight to the customer, this is what is meant. You should be able to articulate the steps the customers need to go through to gain the benefits they are planning for. Part of this may be teaching them new concepts, for example, in cloud the lack of reliance on the internal IT department. That is why BANT is no longer relevant. You must be working with the customer on the budget and business case and you must work with the client on the timescales.

Close plans are dead

We are seeing, in the organizations that understand customer experience, that they have killed off the close plan. The close plan was always of the making of the salesperson. I don't ever remember a customer coming to us and saying, 'Let's put together a close plan.'

The close plan was always about what steps the customer organization needed to put together to help the salesperson close the deal. If the customer had come across this before they might build into it the first kick-off meeting in which there was a handover to the delivery team. Or, better still, the customer would ask for a meeting with the delivery team before signing so they could see if there was a meeting of minds. The close plan was how sales would get the relevant paperwork, purchase order and signed contract, and then once that paperwork was in the salesperson's hand, you never saw them again. Or you only saw them when it was time for a renewal or they wanted a reference for the next sale.

Customers are now more demanding, and salespeople need to wake up to this and offer a go-live plan proactively. That is, customer and salesperson work back from the go-live date, through the requirements for the project over the various project stages. Social and digital means that, based on the amount of research a buyer has undertaken, you should need to 'close' the buyer; it is really more about empowering the buyer to buy. Again, this isn't anti-sales. The buyer will know so much about the business issues, the solutions, the competition; part of your added value as a salesperson is to help them through the final stages of the purchase. A purchase buddy.

One of our clients is a car manufacturer. In a recent meeting with the managing director of that firm he said that there is no way any of his salespeople can know everything about every car. Most buyers have read the websites, spoken to their friends and been on all the forums, so the job of the salesperson was to guide the buyer, maybe to look at the right finance deal or often to help make the choice of the final car model. He gave the example of one model, which has a fast saloon and a sporty model. The fast saloon was only a few bhp less than the sporty model and had a higher resell value. If resell value was important to the client they would guide the buyer to the fast saloon, rather than the sporty version. It's expertise that couldn't be found on the internet in the forums. It does bond salespersons closer to the clients and means that closing is more about empowerment to buy and is more customer-friendly, providing an ongoing supportive partnership.

Social selling as a software suite

We are being contacted all the time about influencer solutions, LinkedIn solutions, social selling apps, etc. In the future we are looking for companies to create a go-to-market around social selling – a set of software solutions that are sold to salespeople to support social selling: selling in a digital world. We are not talking about a CRM system that just holds names and addresses, but a solution that will support a company's internal digital sales initiative.

Of course, this may not cover everything – there will be a requirement for links to other mobile apps or companies such as LinkedIn – but it would be a 'stake in the ground' and show the major IT companies that, if they do this, they understand digital. Without it, we think it shows they don't. It would also mean that the social selling industry would have research and development dollars going into looking at how to use digital technologies to sell, rather than the investment dollars that currently go into how we market.

So many times I sit in meetings and people ask me, 'Can you tell me which tool I can use so I can come in on a Monday and create my tweets so I can hit my KPI for the week?' Hopefully, having read this book you will understand that social is now part of our daily lives and processes. This isn't about doing a bit of digital, 'ticking the box' with our KPI and going back to working as we did before.

Digital selling requires a different mindset, an online mindset, and this means tweeting, informing and teaching. As we always did, but online. Random acts of social just confuse everybody and often let senior management off the hook. This really is about a change in working as we move from the industrial age to the digital age.

Summary

We wish you luck, but with this book, you shouldn't need it! I'm always keen to connect and hear about your journeys – what is working, what isn't working. Please share with us your best practice; we'd be happy to keep this confidential or maybe even write a blog or interview you on a webcast.

I know authors say these sorts of things at the end of books, but I am genuinely interested in hearing about what you have found works and also what does not work. This market continues to evolve as people change, as social networks come and go, as legislation, algorithms and people's usage of social alter. One final world of advice – experiment and keep experimenting.

If you'd prefer to get in touch directly, please do come over and say hello on Twitter: @timothy_hughes or come and contact me on LinkedIn. I also encourage you to connect with the wider DLA Ignite global team – they will be more than happy to hear from you.

Good luck and happy selling!

Epilogue

The future of sales and marketing

I want to share with you some of my predictions for the future of sales and marketing. I would love to hear your views on this on social media, as well as your suggestions.

Boards must develop digital strategies

My background is in selling accounting systems, or enterprise resource planning (ERP) software as suppliers of these solutions like to call them. If you think about a project like this, it would be seen as strategic and the board would have been involved. A strategy will have been developed and the whole board, if not the business, would know why the business was making this investment. Most likely a project team from finance will have been assigned and they will have been given a budget.

Social media for business is also strategic, but it seems to have been left in a cupboard in marketing. Not that this is marketing's fault. They were given this as it seems like it was a good idea, but things have moved on. Boards now need a strategy. We are already seeing this in companies, and over time it will become the norm.

Digital transformation is about the people and the process

When companies think about digital today, they seem to think it's about a tool or computer software change. Whereas being digital actually means embracing digital process from the CEO right through the organization, not as technology but as people and process.

In his *Harvard Business Review* article (2003), Nicholas G. Carr, famously said, 'IT doesn't matter', and he's right. If you think about a road, it gets you from A to B, and if you dig up that road and lay new tarmac, nothing changes – the road still gets you from A to B. The same with any technology system. An accounting system is still an accounting system, regardless if you moved from on-premise to cloud. The same with any change of computer system. However, social media has changed the world. It's changed society and it's changed the way we do business. I hope I've demonstrated in this book, that social media can generate revenue for your business and I hope you've been motivated into action that this is right for your company. But this isn't about systems and tools – this is about activating and investing in your team.

RevOps will grow in dominance

The pandemic has shown that we have to find every deal we can win, and then win every deal we find. We have to be out there in the world of digital and working together as a team. Revenue operations (RevOps) is a business framework for putting all revenue generating departments under one strategy and leadership. Marketing, business development, lead generation, sales development representatives, business development representatives, account executives, salespeople, account managers, renewals, customer success, etc.

Moving forward, salespeople need to work as a team. It can be likened to the difference between the Ford motor car production line and Formula One (F1). Ford have a production line, everybody has a role and responsibility, somebody fits the engine and somebody else fitted the gearbox, everybody worked in their own silo, and a car comes out the end. Whereas in F1 the people all work in a team. They all work for the good of the team, with their own roles and responsibilities, but they all work in synchronization on the car. No silos – it's about teamwork. Both have an outcome, but F1 is a high-performance outcome. This is RevOps.

RevOps is interlinked with the board of a digital business and that board's insistence to inspect the revenue generation from process. From initial desire building to revenue. For many companies, a sale is often a start as they 'land and expand', have an account-based marketing policy and have contract renewals.

Continual improvement – people and process

Sales is very different from other departments. Anybody can be a sales-person. They don't need a qualification and there is no training to update people with new skills. If we look at accountancy, you need to have a degree to be an accountant, you need to have passed additional qualifications, then once you are qualified you have to keep up with regular training to keep that qualification.

In the section above I talked about RevOps. This is the time that sales need to come alongside other parts of the business and realize that contin-ued learning is a benefit to the revenue part of the business. I would expect other departments within the business to also challenge sales as to what they are doing in keeping up with changes.

At my last corporate role, we had seven salespeople that always did 200 per cent of their number. I was asked to do some analysis on what these A-players did versus the B-players. One of those attributes was that all of the over-achieving salespeople always did a training course every quarter. All the B-players said they didn't have time.

In all high-performance companies, they all have a culture of continually improving as a business. How can we as a business improve our efficiency and effectiveness? How can we make sure that we are leading in our vertical and markets? Is there a way we can increase margins? Can we do more for less? Can we increase the customer experience by reducing our costs? By asking these questions, boards will be driving social media for sales. It stands to reason; you have to run a pilot.

Marketing will be front and centre to the business again

In the past, the place to work was the marketing department. It was cool and it was sexy. Over the last 10 years, marketing seems to have been demoted to the 'colouring-in' department. We have seen over the last five years a reduction in the output from the traditional marketing campaigns, such as events, advertising, cold calling and email marketing, as covered at the start of this book. Many businesses during the Covid-19 pandemic have cut this budget as they just don't see the return.

Once there was a time when, if you spent $10,000 on advertising or an event, you knew what return you would get. Now nobody is sure, and in fact nobody is sure whether you actually get a return. Marketing, need to embrace digital, and I don't mean digital marketing as in sending out emails, as I covered before in this book. Marketing needs to embrace the power that social media provides to them. This means that marketing needs to change the way they work. But how?

Brands are commodities

We have seen how, over the last few years, brands have become commodities. People don't listen to what a brand says and nobody believes it. Of course, you might have a 'star' brand that you have an affinity with, but this is the vast majority of brands and companies.

Your buyers and customers are interested in people and experiences.

Marketing needs to understand that their role now is to build a digital bridge between the people in the company and their prospect and customers. They also need to be empowering people. It could be salespeople, or in a digital organization it could be empowering a wide variety of people, teams and disciplines to build those digital bridges. Empower people, from the day they join the company, activating new starters to be authentic and be able to build these digital bridges and have conversations on social.

Understand what needs to happen so the business is found. For example, they will be responsible for the website, also the keywords they want to be famous for. This will have a Google SEO objective as well as a search from a social media perspective. Now more people search on social than they do Google.

Digital will mean new measures and new governance

With digital comes new measures, no longer do marketing need to chase MQLs or SQLs – digital is 'on' or 'off'. Marketing can now measure the new digital lead generation flow.

Let's think about the new sales process. Salespeople will connect with people they want to influence on social, they will try and get conversations with them, and this will lead to meetings and proposals. All of this can be measured by marketing. Salespeople will be sharing content; it is the way they harvest this content that will enable them to get conversations and meetings, and again marketing can measure all of this.

All of these are leading indicators as to how a business is going to make its number or not. The business can also see which of the salespeople are contributing and which are not. This will put them front and centre with the CFO and CEO. By providing a new set of data, that can give the business visibility exactly how the company is trading, by leading the quarterly business review process. This will place marketing back front and centre and make it the place to be, and marketing will be sexy again.

The terminology of business will change

As digital and social media usage accelerates, some people say that social selling at some point will be called 'selling', as that will be the way we sell. These changes mean there will be a change in the lexicon of business.

The C-suite will become influencers

The first thing you think about when you hear the word 'influencer' is the Kardashian family, and I can imagine any leader reading this will be whispering, there is no way I'm going to do that. But let's take a step back. If you think about what a business wants, they want their prospects and customers to know them for something. It could be technical expertise, it could be operational, it could be commercial, but you want to be known as experts in your market or vertical and wouldn't it great if your clients knew this too?

This is what I mean by being an influencer.

Most business are rubbish at social. Sorry to say that, but it's true. That does mean that for your business there is an opportunity to take that digital space and be recognized by your clients, future clients, employees and future employees. This is how you become an influencer and in fact digitally dominate the market your business is in. As we have talked about before, the modern buyer is not interested in brands, they want relationships with people. That means a company can activate its employees to rise up and take control of the digital chat and digital share of voice.

Business leaders now need to want their people to be the lead digital influencer in your market or sector and getting the commercial credit for that. But why would I want to be an influencer? As a managing director or a CEO of a business, in a digital world not only do you have responsibility for driving the bottom line, you are also the CEO of a media company (see my next point) and you are the chief influencer. While you don't want to be famous for the same things as Kim Kardashian, if you had the same media reach as her in the areas you wanted to be famous for, this would be transformational for your business.

In February 2018, Kylie Jenner tweeted, after Snapchat's redesign 'Sooo does anyone else not open Snapchat anymore? Or is it just me... ugh this is so sad.' Snapchat's stock lost 6 per cent of its market capitalization, which equated to $1.3 billion. Now if that opinion was by you, in your industry and it had that much sway, the last thing you would be worrying about would be where your next deal is coming from. But, like Kylie Jenner, you only get that place and that influence by working it.

Every company is a media company

I talked earlier in the book about how each business is now a media company. We know that the modern buyer is looking for insight, to be helped and entertained. It is our job as leaders and salespeople to give our prospects and clients this content. Not in the shape of brochures and brochureware, which nobody is interested, but in the shape of authentic content. This will mean that our buyers will see us as the obvious choice to solve their business issues.

Each business needs to strive for digital dominance

What does digital dominance mean?

Picture this – it's the night before a big conference and there is a cocktail party, and you walk into the party and look around. The room is filled with your customers and prospects (my ideal customers). But then you take a second look and realize that these prospects and customers are all drinking, laughing and pals with somebody next to them. The person that these customers and prospects are talking to will either be one of your team mates or one of your competitors. And whoever it is, your team mates or your competitors, these are the people that dominate the airways. With digital dominance, we are talking about bringing this into the 21st century.

Video will become the mainstay of content

Any article looking forward will tell you that video is important. Often video is positioned (by people who supply video solutions of course) as something that will take over the world. The trouble with these predictions is that the assumption is that 'interruption' and 'broadcast' is the way that video will be delivered.

Consider this. I sent you an email, which you deleted and created a rule so from then onwards the email will always go into the email wastepaper basket. Somehow, if I send you an email with a video, does some sort of magic change everything and you say 'Wow, an email with a video – I must open that'? Of course not, nothing changes and if an email with a video actually gets through the firewall, you will delete it with all the other junk that tries to steal your time. Nobody wants to be interrupted.

One of our clients ran a campaign, not sponsored by us, I should say. They hired a video company, wrote a script and got the senior VP to make 100 videos, where he 'introduced the company'. Along the lines of 'Hi, I'm Robert and I work for X company and we do this...' All professionally made. They had a target list of clients and these emails were sent all with a video attached. And the result? Of the 100 that were sent, two were opened. Apart from that, nothing. Zilch.

Video works where you are giving the viewer insight or educating them or even entertaining them. Nobody is interested in being interrupted and pitched at – it doesn't work like that anymore. Video is a great platform to offer insight. It does not take long, or great expense, to use a iPhone and Apple clips and post short, two-minute videos on your social profiles. The same rules as for any content – help people, give them advice, explain how to solve their business issues.

Video streaming will become business-as-usual

I want to break out of the video section and place streaming as a separate section. Steaming is available on most platforms today, and products like Restream.io and StreamYard enable you to stream to multiple platforms.

I run a podcast and look for interesting people to interview and I stream these interviews live to LinkedIn, Facebook, Twitter, YouTube and Twitch. The platform is excellent at getting audience participation as watchers can interact with comments on the platform they watch. This provides performer and watcher with instant feedback and allows the audience to ask questions. As part of my podcast, I interviewed Kathy Klotz-Guest about improv-comedy and we ended up doing a complete improv session live with the audience participation.

If you are looking for examples, you can find all my videos on my YouTube channel www.youtube.com/c/TimothyHughes1. While my live streams will go out live, I will always put the recording on YouTube.

If you are looking for innovation in video then look no further than Eric Doyle's *The Big Live Breakfast Burrito...!* on YouTube at www.youtube.com/channel/UC2SZeQDMLp4nzhFRJIHORqw. This is a morning show, every, Thursday at 07:45 to 09:00 UK time and it's like a 'zoo radio' format. It provides the team with reach and visibility, it creates communities amongst the listeners, more importantly it generates leads, conversations and closed business. Eric calls it 'networking for the 21st century'.

While the above is a B2B example, there are also B2C examples. In B2C, live streaming has become big business; you might tune into a television station like QVC to watch people selling products now, and you can tune into live streams on, for example, Amazon or (in China) Alibaba. Li Jiaqi is a top live stream salesman in China, widely known as the 'lipstick brother'. He sold $1.9 billion in goods in 2021 on the first day of Alibaba Group's annual shopping festival. Li, who earned his nickname by trying out various makeup products on his show, pre-sold 12 billion Yuan in products ranging from Shiseido lotions to Apple AirPods, according to preliminary data compiled by ecommerce data specialist Taosj.com. Li's sales are a record for any show live streamed on Alibaba's Taobao online marketplace, according to data.

Buyers and consumers want instant access to people, not brands, and will buy from people they, know like and trust. Whether B2B or B2C, by creating influence your leadership team and salespeople can create conversations and commercial interactions with live streaming.

Cookies and their use will force us to think differently about advertising

You will already have read that I don't like advertising and don't think it fits into a modern business. It is after all 1930s technology. Apple's iOS 14 update, which is allowing people to decide whether they are targeted by ads, is shaking up the world of advertising. It comes as a shock to nobody, apart from people who work in advertising, that nobody likes being targeted by ads, and given a choice people always choose not to see advertising.

Brian Bowman, CEO of Consumer Acquisition, told VentureBeat (2021) that advertisers had seen revenue fall 15 per cent to 20 per cent, with some experiencing losses of up to 40 per cent. Brian said 'We believe technology should protect users' fundamental right to privacy, and that means giving users tools to understand which apps and websites may be sharing their data with other companies for advertising or advertising measurement purposes, as well as the tools to revoke permission for this tracking.' Putting it like that, it just proves that advertisers are using tracking data and as a brand we should not want to be part of that. You probably saw the reports that Snap, Snapchat's parent, lost 22 per cent of its market cap in October 2021 after the publication of its Q3 earnings for this very reason.

While I'm talking about advertising, it would be wrong not to mention ad fraud. This is where people are placing money for digital ads in good faith, and the success of these ads are measured based on 'views' and 'clicks'. The trouble is that these clicks and views are undertaken by robots or click farms. A study by PwC/ISBA (Barker, 2020) found that only 50 per cent of the dollars spent by advertisers makes it through to websites for showing ads. The rest of the dollars are absorbed by adtech (advertising technology) companies in the supply chain as their own profits. More concerning, though, is that about a third of these dollars (15 per cent of overall) simply 'went missing'.

People often pass on this with a shrug of the shoulders. What they miss is that ad fraud is often being used to fund terrorism, porn, cyber crime, drugs etc. As we talk about in the next section, buyers are making decisions based on a company's culture and what they stand for.

Your company must stand for something

Twenty years ago, the advice in business was not to be disruptive. People would suggest that you don't 'rock the boat' as it might lose you a customer. That has been turned on its head, and the modern buyer wants to know where you stand on data privacy, diversity, sustainability, inclusion, Black Lives Matter, etc.

Talk to any parent and they will tell you that societal matters, such as sustainability, diversity, inclusion, etc. are all high on the agenda of their children. We are also seeing a number of books being issued on the subject. I have just read Michelle Carvill et al's book *Sustainable Marketing: How to drive profits with purpose* (2021). It's clear to me that people are going to take 'green' into account when they are selling or marketing. Green will also be a competitive advantage.

In 2021, James Watt the CEO of Brewdog posted on LinkedIn how an agency had got a meeting with him. James posted:

> I always get bombarded with pitches. But this one from Norris Media is worth sharing because it is exceptional.
>
> They sent me 23 grams of charcoal (which is almost 100 per cent pure carbon) and this 23 grams represent the amount of carbon a Facebook advert generates for every 500 impressions it receives.
>
> What an incredibly thought-provoking thing to send: absolutely everything we do has a carbon impact – even digital advertising.
>
> Norris Media also mentioned that they are the first agency to measure and reduce the carbon impact of digital advertising and we will of course be in touch about working together.
>
> And bonus points for the handwritten letter too!

While you have to admire the entrepreneurial marketing message, societal issues are now front of mind for the buyer, and if you don't say you are *for* something it is assumed you are against it.

The metaverse will become a thing

On the 28 October 2021, Facebook changed its name to Meta and all of a sudden the metaverse became interesting.

What is the metaverse?

The metaverse is a 3D place on the internet. It's a virtual environment – think of being able to get inside a computer game. There have been technology environments in the past, for example Minecraft and Second Life. The difference is that the technology has moved on.

What does that mean for business?

You are already having virtual meetings. At the moment you are able to have virtual meetings via Zoom or Teams with anybody around the world. We are able to talk to people in real time and the Covid-19 pandemic has accelerated our acceptance of this. Even my 83-year-old mother runs her wine club on Zoom. She was told by one of the members, an ex-computers studies teacher, ironically. that the club could *never* be run virtually. Now, of course, we see Zoom as natural.

The metaverse means that we can build virtual meeting places and sit down with people and have real conversations. This could be in a virtual office or a virtual meetings place. This means we can have a conversation on LinkedIn and, rather than take it to a phone call or a Zoom call, we can sit down with that person in a virtual world.

At the end of the day, this is all about you and your business doing what you and your business are all about. Selling more. While none of my clients are doing this right now, and clients don't have a virtual reality headset, I remember when all my clients didn't have email addresses, I remember when all my clients were not on social media. We've seen so many things change.

I remember being told recently there is no way people will buy shoes online. Now I buy five pairs online, try them on at home and send four pairs back. Things change, and as a business you need to be aware of what is possible.

Wow, I got through that section without mentioning crypto, web 3.0, blockchain, NFTs and Ethereum.

Marketers can no longer deny the existence of TikTok

TikTok has taken the world by storm, and surprised by many of us, as there have been video sharing sites before that never took off. The problem that brands (and often marketers) have with TikTok is that it places a disingenuous world of social media marketing front and centre. Why?

You go to TikTok because you want to. No longer can marketers interrupt us with adverts. TikTok videos are all about the people and not the brand. Yes, there are some brands on there, but it's the exception not the rule.

Anybody can be a content creator – you don't have to be a creative in a design agency, marketing agency or a marketing department. It's punk. When the punk music started, it was people with ideas and talent that became famous – you didn't need to study music for years. We've talked a lot in this book about creating authentic content, content that provides insight, that engages your audience and provides buyers with entertainment. For brands to ace TikTok they must empower their employees.

Artificial intelligence won't save us

There has been a lot of talk about artificial intelligence and how it is going to save us. At the moment I have been underwhelmed with the response. As I write this, most AI developed and for sale is nothing more than automation. There is nothing wrong with getting a machine to do a job we find boring, but automation will only take you so far.

The week I am writing this, an Australian company asked me to submit a proposal to transform their salespeople and said could I supply some typical results from a customer that we could expect to make by using social selling. I supplied the results and the person asking for the proposal came back and said, what automation tool are you using?

I pointed out we didn't use any form of automation; we have a methodology and if you follow that you will get this level of results. He still does not believe me. There seems to be the assumption that to get stellar results requires a tool or automation. In fact, doing the right thing and following a process will get you great results.

The problem with automation on social media is that social media is based on reciprocity. There are millions of people on LinkedIn. Some of those are buyers and some are sellers. We turn up and play our roles, the sellers will try and sell and the buyers will be there to buy. If I decide to not turn up and send a robot, then the buyer will do the same. At that point there is no reciprocity and the whole thing falls down. Buyers want their sellers to be human – they don't want to deal with robots.

The future of sales and marketing is human

In a 2021 interview Bryan Kramer said:

> The future of digital marketing is a combination of digital *and* human. Brands should be present everywhere and relevant while consumers are looking for information or interacting online (at their time, in the form they prefer). It's also about patience: it will take longer to build relationships. But we'll better understand customers and have better results over time.

When people say things to you, so often you hear something else. That is why many jobs end in one of those situations where the employee says 'But you promised if I did this, you would give me this pay rise or promotion.' What the employee heard and what the employer said may be two different things. For example, a boss may say, 'If you work hard, you will get a promotion', the difference being in what the boss means by working hard and what the employee means. The same goes for personalization. When we hear that word, we think of somebody treating me as an individual, but actually personalization is treating me like I'm a group of 10, 100 or 100 people. That's the difference between personalization and being human. Personalization could mean I am an email in a group of thousands, where as social media allows you to build a one-to-one relationship with a person. That's what it takes to be human today.

Final words

What I hope you understand from this book is that while there are many advancements in the world of technology, there are some fundamentals that never change:

- People want to be treated as human.
- People are looking for insight, they want to be helped, they want to be entertained.
- People will buy from people they know, like and trust.
- People don't want to have their time wasted with irrelevance, such as brochures and brochureware.
- People are not interested in your company or its products, but they are interested in you.
- People are just like us.

If you have liked this book, please connect with me. I love to hear feedback and suggestions. It would be great if you posted a selfie of yourself with the book – don't forget to tag me.

My contact details:

Company website: DLAIgnite.com

LinkedIn: www.linkedin.com/in/timothyhughessocialselling/

Twitter: https://twitter.com/Timothy_Hughes

You Tube: www.youtube.com/c/TimothyHughes1

Facebook: www.facebook.com/TimHughesSocialSelling/

Instagram: www.instagram.com/tim_hughes1/

Clubhouse: @timothy_hughes

TikTok: www.tiktok.com/@timothy_hughes

Please also, leave a review on Amazon and Goodreads – reviews always help with sales.

References

Barker, A (2020) Half of online ad spending goes to industry middlemen, *Financial Times*. www.ft.com/content/9ee0ebd3-346f-45b1-8b92-aa5c597d4389 (archived at https://perma.cc/KUF6-XPMZ)

Bowman, B (2021) Apple's IDFA change has triggered 15% to 20% revenue drops for IOS developers, VentureBeat. https://venturebeat.com/2021/07/13/brian-bowman-apples-idfa-change-has-triggered-15-to-20-revenue-drops-for-ios-developers/ (archived at https://perma.cc/YM6A-9J4U)

Carr, N G (2003) IT doesn't matter, *Harvard Business Review*. https://hbr.org/2003/05/it-doesnt-matter (archived at https://perma.cc/3T5P-ZX9V)

Carvill, M, Butler, G and Evans, G (2021) *Sustainable Marketing: How to drive profits with purpose*. Bloomsbury.

Kramer, B (2021) VIP Q&A: Bryan Kramer on humanizing marketing, personalizing CX and more, Jivox. https://jivox.com/thought-leadership/vip-qa-bryan-kramer-on-humanizing-marketing-personalizing-cx-more/ (archived at https://perma.cc/KM4B-KAY3)

Rodriguez, S (2021) Snap plummets 22% after missing on revenue expectations, CNBC. www.cnbc.com/2021/10/21/snap-earnings-q3-2021.html (archived at https://perma.cc/WEC6-MVS3)

Watt, J (2021) James Watt's post, LinkedIn. www.linkedin.com/posts/james-watt-21a5a912b_i-always-get-bombarded-with-pitches-but-activity-6860912110218567680-Sfcf (archived at https://perma.cc/K3FQ-RKNN)

INDEX